FREUD AND FUNDAMENTALISM

Freud and Fundamentalism

THE PSYCHICAL POLITICS OF KNOWLEDGE

Edited by

STATHIS GOURGOURIS

FORDHAM UNIVERSITY PRESS

New York 2010

Fordham University Press has no responsibility for the
persistence or accuracy of URLs for external or third-party
Internet websites referred to in this publication and does not
guarantee that any content on such websites is, or will
remain, accurate or appropriate.

Fordham University Press also publishes its books in a
variety of electronic formats. Some content that appears in
print may not be available in electronic books.

Library of Congress Cataloging-in-Publication Data

Freud and fundamentalism : the psychical politics of
knowledge / edited by Stathis Gourgouris.—1st ed.
        p. ; cm.
Includes bibliographical references and index.
ISBN 978-0-8232-3223-9 (cloth : alk. paper)
ISBN 978-0-8232-3224-6 (pbk. : alk. paper)
    ISBN 978-0-8232-3225-3 (ebook)
1. Psychoanalysis.   2. Freud, Sigmund, 1856–1939.
3. Fundamentalism.   I. Gourgouris, Stathis, 1958–
[DNLM: 1. Freud, Sigmund, 1856–1939.   2. Freudian
Theory.   3. Homicide—psychology.   4. Religion and
Psychology.   5. Social Dominance.
    WM 460.5.F9 F8893   2010]
        BF175.F76 2010
        150.19′52—dc22
        2010016253

Printed in the United States of America
12 11 10   5 4 3 2 1
First edition

CONTENTS

FREUD AND FUNDAMENTALISM

Introduction

Stathis Gourgouris

The idea for this volume began some years ago after the affirmative response I received from audiences for two panels I had organized for the Modern Language Association meetings in New York, with the title "Freud and Fundamentalism." The initial point was to raise some questions about the psychic components of certain modes of thinking that we call, somewhat abusively, "fundamentalist," in reference to thought that disavows multiplicities of meaning, abhors allegorical elements, and strives toward an exclusionary orthodoxy. In retrospect, I realized that the impetus for the initial project and the whole framework of inquiry derived from my own interest in reconfiguring and enhancing the task of secular criticism, a task in which psychosocial parameters are epistemologically crucial. Though most people, in seeing or hearing this, would think that it entails some sort of secularist or antireligious enterprise, the fact is that underlying this impetus is an express concern with combating transcendentalist orthodoxies of all kinds (secularist or religious) in the hope that a new appreciation for dialectical thinking could be fostered on the way to reconfiguring a new humanist politics of social autonomy.

Having said that, I do acknowledge that the most common interpretive framework of the term "fundamentalism" is theological. The historical legacy of fundamentalism is established as a crucial component in the development of the American Evangelical movement. We could arguably place a starting point for the emergence of this sort of ideas around 1870, but the term itself does not arise until the Baptist Convention in 1920, which inaugurates what was termed the "fundamentalist-modernist debate" in American Protestant theology and may be said to extend, in various guises and with broad shifts in reference and meaning, as far as what nowadays signifies the virtual collapse of the name "fundamentalism" with the tenets and practices of evangelical and moral-conservative Christianity as a whole. Though this collapse of terms and practices is primarily rhetorical and perhaps inaccurate, the specifically American history of fundamentalism, in its many permutations, should not be forgotten, even if this volume, aside from David Adams's incisive essay, does not engage this aspect extensively.

I insist on highlighting this American history precisely because it demonstrates that the recent attachment of the term "fundamentalism" to the Islamic world is yet another instance of naming the other, of imperiously exporting definitions and terminologies, and thus derivative of the proliferation and imposition of American "culture"—more precisely, of an American framework of meaning—onto the provenances of the other. Note that "Islamic fundamentalism" attains popular usage in the American vocabulary during the Iranian Revolution, and specifically as an outcome of the takeover of the U.S. Embassy in Tehran and the ensuing hostage crisis. In other words, this is a case of American categories of signification being imposed abroad as a reaction to the experience of American political interests being forcibly redefined by an adversarial other. What cannot be missed, however, is how the response to this redefinition of political interests is not configured in political terms, but with a term borrowed from the history of (American) religion. The slippage in signification from a framework of international state politics to a culturalist framework of religion marks, to my mind, a domain of psychical investment: repression of the overt political signifiers and, at the same time, mobilization of primary narcissistic defenses that produce a specific site of collective sublimation, more proximate to the wounded social-imaginary than the straightforward sociopolitical sphere, which is why the ultimate battleground is drawn from and within the sphere of culture. How a political conflict, otherwise conducted along overt imperialist lines of conquest and resistance, comes to be codified in less than a decade as "a clash of civilizations" seems to me to bear precisely this web of psychosocial elements in politics that this volume addresses in many different ways.

But despite the dominant resonance of the term "fundamentalism" in the discourse of and about religion, my intention was not—and is not—to make this project a mere dialogue between psychoanalysis and religion (though obviously this does remain a decisive dimension). The range of the conjunction that names the framework and object of inquiry was deliberately expanded from the outset, so that the particular relation between psychoanalysis and religion—after all, of great concern to Freud himself— would be given a sharper focus as a relation internal to psychoanalysis: that is, a relation between a therapeutic practice that expands the horizon of knowledge and a mode of interpretation with presumed sets of claims that often prefer to remain strict and restricted. Surely, fundamentalist elements in psychoanalysis itself would also have to placed in the equation as objects in question, and indeed the simplest assessment of the texts in this volume would discover a much more rigorous interrogation as to those problematic elements than not.

I acknowledge some risks here. Fundamentalism is a polemical term and, given that nowadays it has assumed a facile fashion, it runs the danger of becoming even less useful conceptually. One might argue that a term riveted with such confusion should not be given the position of title for an inquiry that aspires to raise questions against confusion. Yet, there is a discursive power to this term that is altogether real and bears tangible, material consequences. The decision to use it is drawn from the urgency of these consequences. Though the meaning of fundamentalism may be altogether confused and confusing, the force of fundamentalism in the real world registers with real clarity. And though it would be an error to streamline the affinities between the various fundamentalisms in the world (religious or otherwise)—for it would enact the abusive deployment of language I just mentioned—it would be fair nonetheless to bring attention to the fact that every fundamentalism, in some way or other, mobilizes an accession to universalist claims, if we take seriously the etymological significance of the matrix term: *uni-verse*, all becomes one, or one turns into all, into the whole. In other words, fundamentalism pertains to a structure of meaning that explains the world *totally* and *univocally*, and not just its own world but the world of its adversaries, its others.

It is this self-ascribed universalist clarity of the force of fundamentalist thinking (religious or otherwise) that poses the biggest challenge to the "ambiguous universality"—to use a term famously championed by Etienne Balibar—that a mind focused on the nontranscendable worldliness of things can recognize, articulate, and contemplate. Because the claim to brutal clarity wields an oppressive force that multiple and nuanced understanding cannot combat on the same terms, it becomes important that whoever wishes to resist such clarity attempts to elucidate, as much as possible, the psychic parameters that produce, defend, and fortify it to begin with. There is an internally deconstructive impetus here, in other words. Fundamentalist thinking fashions itself as a repudiation of the excesses of modernity, if nothing else in its desire to return to the foundation. However, in this desire for foundation, fundamentalist thinking denies that it emerges precisely out of conditions of modernity (indeed as one of its excesses), since modernity, by definition, remains open to its own undoing and fosters conditions of creation/destruction without guarantee. Fundamentalism's intrinsic relation to modernity should not be ignored in the broader task of elucidating the unfinished project of modernity as an open-ended and self-interrogative project of autonomy.

The overall aspiration of this collection of texts is thus to interrogate discourses of orthodoxy, literalism, exclusion, and dogma, or discourses obsessed with monolithic (monolingual, monological, monolateral, monomythical—and by all means, monotheistic) encounters with the world, which certainly include discourses of universalism or catholicity that remain unconscious of the trap of (their) singularity. The epistemological field on that end of the equation is actually wide open. But I do want to hold on to the Freudian element, not only by engaging with discourses on Freud himself, but also by accounting for the broader psychic dimensions in the production of knowledge and in political practice, dimensions that rest on the wager that knowledge and politics have a *corporeal* significance. I understand this corporeality in a twofold intertwining sense: on the one hand, configuring the epistemological dimensions of psychoanalysis as a problem of not merely theory but of worldly action, and on the other hand, tracing the material force of this problem in its actual social-historical dimension—that is, not merely as it pertains to mentalities, but to actual bodies that are, at once, both subjects and objects of history. This crossroads marks my own sense of the encounter between Freud and fundamentalism from a standpoint where fundamentalism indeed does not set the terms.

This standpoint is, in many ways, unyielding—if nothing else, precisely because it is multilateral and multifaceted. The collection of essays here bears this out. I am not invoking some cliché notion of inconclusiveness, inordinate variability, or lack of totality. Every collection of essays by different authors, even if the product of a specialized workshop, would ultimately resist totalization, if the authors remained steadfast in their particular approach to a collective research project. Here, however, we have a collection of really different idioms, evident sometimes in wide-ranging aspects of style, and, more important, inherent in each author's particular dedication to his or her own self-fashioning in relation to the two terms *Freud* and *fundamentalism*, whether in conjunction or disjunction, apposition or entwinement, presupposition or consequence. The idiomatic character of these essays cannot be reduced to a single-minded purpose, regardless if this seems to be de facto the outcome of any collection. In any case, my own wager, as an editor—and for this I bear sole responsibility—is to invest in a multiple intersection of arguments, framings, and viewpoints, without minimizing the risk that the flow among them might produce contradictions, derailments, or even collisions.

Though the book is structured like a mosaic, there is nonetheless a logic of sequential passage from piece to piece. Contrary to what is conventionally demanded of an editor's introduction, I would rather not anticipate the reader's response by summarizing each author's argument, for all the risks this entails. But I do owe the reader an explication of the sequence, and in this vein I will provide an interpretive sketch of the essays according to my own conception of what trajectory is forged by their juxtaposition. In overarching terms, I conceived an itinerary that moves from work pertaining specifically to Freud toward work that addresses the broader forces of psychoanalysis as epistemology in its own right. Hence the decision to open with Andrew Parker's succinct stage-setting of the entire problematic. The precise economy of this essay serves as sort of a manifesto, with the crucial exception, however, that it does not advocate the terrain it manifests, perhaps because this terrain is expressly multivalent and problematic. Much of what follows—from critiques of Freud's own reflections, or lack thereof, to the epistemological discussion of psychoanalysis as a science beyond Freud's own conceptualization—returns to Parker's ruminations, though obviously on different terms; the questions he raises are sites of interpretation, not ends of passage.

If Parker sets the sites of a precarious journey, David Adams's historical account of how the fundamentalist-modernist controversy in American Protestantism resonates with the historical pressures that led to certain of Freud's metapsychological queries in the same era provides the historical ground by which the two domains—Freud and fundamentalism—might be said to initiate their heterogeneous intersections. Adams's astute handling of this historical *co-incidence* within the broader zeitgeist suggests that, despite Freud's own recoil from further pursuit (lest it disrupt the status of psychoanalysis as a science), his mythical configurations of the Eros-Thanatos dialectic leave nowadays a most fertile trace against the surge of a deeper—*fundamental*—orthodoxy. I should add that Adams's understanding of myth is extremely nuanced, very much against the conventional notion, and, if I may say, very close to my own configuration of it in *Does Literature Think?* For Adams—and I agree—myth is quintessentially configured to be contrary to dogma.

Branka Arsić's essay on Freud's inability to encounter the full magnitude of masochism as a source of psychoanalytic knowledge may be deemed as the conceptual countermirror to Adams's configuration of the myth of the death drive. Arsić too seeks grounding in a certain historical *co-incidence*, here between Freud, Nietzsche, and Jung, which produces a terrain of conceptual paradox, perhaps because it is mediated by a woman, Sabina Spielrein, who is, moreover—all at once and *unmediatedly*—lover, patient, pupil, and psychoanalytic theorist. However, while for Adams the configuration of the death drive is mythical ground for psychoanalysis, for Arsić masochism might be deemed the performative ungrounding of this myth. As central concept, masochism entails the undoing of the conceptual framework; it is thereby antiphilosophical, inasmuch as it derails the "ontological" autonomy of the death-drive concept. By Freud's own admission, masochism is unanalyzable; its real existence in human life ultimately bears no psychoanalytic logic, yet pertains (as it undoes them) to central psychoanalytic principles. The implication of Arsić's essay is that, perceived through the conceptual framework of masochism, the myth of Thanatos is differentially reentwined into the dialectic with Eros. However differently from Adams's standpoint, this reconfiguration of Thanatos also reiterates the work of myth against dogma, even though the purveyor of this myth (Freud) remains ineluctable—one might even say dogmatic—sovereign over it.

In her multifaceted passage through Freud's sovereign conceptual terrain, Arsić opens an array of paths that elucidate how the psychic molding of identity proceeds around cleavages and cracks, which psychoanalysis cannot efface even if it purports to cure them. Of course, most important is the psychic mark of an ultimately unmasterable sexual difference, but also—and they go together—what Arsić calls "micropolitical" or minoritarian intransigence to the psychoanalytic project at the outer "ethnic" edges of the Hapsburg Empire: Jewish and Slavic. The next three essays in the sequence may be considered explorations of precisely these untamable edges of intransigence in respect to mechanisms of identity production. Though all three wrestle in different ways with certain fundamentalisms—or at the very least, dogmatic facets—of psychoanalysis, the very work they set themselves upon demonstrates just as well the self-interrogative capacities that make psychoanalytic thinking corrosive in relation to any sort of fundamentalism.

Like masochism for Arsić, anti-Semitism figures as a problematic element in the fashioning of psychoanalytic knowledge in Gil Anidjar's reflection on one of the classics of Freudian case histories, the Rat Man. Anidjar sees a fundamentalist framework of thinking in anti-Semitism—but, importantly, in the reverse as well: the monological correction of anti-Semitism as strict (and restricted) identity principle. In addition, he alerts us to an altogether untheorized matter in discussions of fundamentalism: interpellation. His central queries—what is fundamentalism's interpellation, how does it form the addressee, how does it name, and so forth—are trenchant to the relation between fundamentalist thinking and subjectivity or subject-formation. Anti-Semitism exists because of, or insofar as it enacts, an interpellation, Anidjar argues. It produces the subject, even when it misses the purported addressee; it operates just as well by misrecognition. The interpellated subject does not exist prior to interpellation. Anidjar reminds us that many Jews in the Nazi era came to know themselves as Jews by virtue of anti-Semitic violence against them. By this he underlines an identity-producing mechanism of subjection (in both senses: subjugation and subjectification), which, in this case, is literally deadly. The outcome of injurious speech turns the singularity of interpellation to a totalizing gesture that swallows individual subjects into a depersonalized (and depersonalizing) identity vacuum that leaves no possibility of response. Such identity is unambiguous because it is entirely conferred by an external force over which one has no authority; not only is this identity monological but perfectly heteronomous. In this sense too, it is fundamentalist. What distinguishes fundamentalist interpellation, whether of text or person, is that it aims at both totalization and unambiguity: all in one and one in all.

Concluding her reflections on masochism, Branka Arsić evokes a Slavic allegory of destabilization, echoing Freud's curious notion that Slavs (like masochism) are unanalyzable since they don't respond to therapy based on a rubric of Oedipal sexuality. Dušan Bjelić picks up this specific strand (with reference both to the Rat Man case history and the explosive significance of Sabina Spielrein) and spins around it a pervasive texture that entwines the institutional armory of psychoanalytic categories with the institutional panoply of nationalist excess. Though the essay initially pertains to Freud specifically, it also signals the shift in our trajectory toward the broader paths of psychoanalysis itself and its implication with fundamentalist attitudes and practices of its own, which destroy its emancipatory rubric.

Bjelić's essay is animated by a bold gesture that configures, on one hand, fundamentalist attitudes and practices implicated in the social production of madness, and on the other hand, the geopolitical restrictions of the psychoanalytic imaginary which can be mined for ethno-genocidal violence. The two sides are implicated in each other's authority. Bjelić demonstrates the self-Orientalization of Balkan identities to be "the geopolitical supplement" to the psychoanalytic canon, which becomes in turn both animating source and psycho-ideological justification of genocidal nationalism. This enables him to draw an epistemological complicity between, on the one hand, the psychoanalytic self-theorizations of Slavoj Žižek and Julia Kristeva (who might be said to epitomize a "Westernized Balkan" analytic subject) and, on the other, the bona fide homicidal insanity of Serbian psychiatrists Jovan Rašković (mastermind of Yugoslav microcharacterology and the notion of madness as a political category) and his pupil Radovan Karadžić (executor of the Srebrenica massacre in 1985). Even though it would be false to extend a causal straight line between the two sides, Bjelić makes a daring argument that leaves no presumption about the political neutrality of psychoanalytic categories intact. The implication is that to speak of the fundamentalism of psychoanalysis at all is to engage with its explicitly affirmed geopolitical (thereby, symptomatically, ethno-nationalist) restrictions. By the same token, to embark on an interrogation of fundamentalist attitudes and practices from a psychoanalytic standpoint means to conduct simultaneously a self-interrogation.

The lack of such self-interrogation in the psychoanalytic categories of Slavoj Žižek, especially as they pertain to his analyses of film, is precisely the thesis of Kriss Ravetto-Biagioli in the essay that follows Bjelić's. Insofar as both writers engage with Žižek's theory of enjoyment specifically, there is a direct thread linking their essays together. There is, as well, an additional parallel between Ravetto-Biagioli's theorization of misogyny (or "phallic fundamentalism," as she calls it) and Bjelić's theorization of *ethnocidal* fundamentalism. But in Ravetto-Biagioli's essay, the reflection on certain fundamentalist elements of psychoanalytic thinking takes up a different path, first insofar as it pertains specifically to film analysis (Žižek's interpretations of David Lynch films), and second insofar as it echoes Arsić's account of how sexual difference destabilizes the conceptual categories of psychoanalysis. The specific focus here is Žižek's own sort of fundamentalism, a charge that Žižek himself would not necessarily deny, though certainly not consider in terms of this argument. Most important is Ravetto-Biagioli's insight that Žižek's psychoanalytic interpretations abolish the immanent psychoanalytic logic of the films themselves. Much like Arsić's argument about Freud's recoil before Spielrein's theorization of masochism (or, by analogy, the arguments of both Anidjar and Bjelić), Ravetto-Biagioli's critique of Žižek's misogynous film criticism points to a fundamental incapacity, symptomatic of a certain failure of psychoanalytic logic to deal with the challenge of a radically different epistemology that emerges from within it.

Ravetto-Biagioli's essay completes a cluster of texts that come together precisely on the issue of the symptomatic incapacity of psychoanalysis to absorb internal epistemological disruptions from its margins. In the essays that follow, the epistemological status of psychoanalysis itself comes explicitly into focus. We might say there is yet another shift in trajectory toward an affirmative consideration of the uncertain cognitive framework of psychoanalysis, the impetus being to contemplate in what sense this provides an alternative (and adversarial) imaginary to fundamentalist thinking.

Lecia Rosenthal's elegant reflections on how psychoanalysis encounters questions of the occult stand in many ways as a bridge text. Rosenthal returns us to Freud himself as object of inquiry, by contemplating the many contours of his own struggle to draw a genuine metapsychology from the encounter of psychoanalysis with occult domains. At the same time, she continues to pursue the larger metapsychological questions, pertaining to the nature of psychoanalytic epistemology, which the previous essays have already raised, but she does it by opening rather than foreclosing the emancipatory potential of psychoanalysis. Her demonstration of how Freud understands and mines the potential of telepathic elements in transference, which he conducts in acrobatic fashion (for he must guard against any tendencies in psychoanalysis toward occultation), is an exemplary exercise in psychoanalytic thinking—but also, in the sense that it involves an astute way of reading texts, in literary criticism.

Crucial for our inquiry is Rosenthal's reminder that the metapsychological Freud is always wrestling with the problem of psychoanalysis' ultimate unverifiability (in scientific terms), the very thing on which the legitimacy of psychoanalytic epistemology hinges. The lesson here is that the epistemological uncertainty of psychoanalysis is precisely the ground for the subversive communication that enhances the liberating potential of the unconscious. In this light, the psychoanalytic encounter with alterity (both external and internal to the psyche) exemplifies a resistant cognitive framework to the fundamentalist encounter with alterity.

I have opted to follow Rosenthal's contribution with a somewhat unorthodox editorial gesture. Even though my current research adheres to some of the questions this collection raises, I decided to withdraw my own initially planned authorial contribution. Instead, I thought I would add to the explicit self-reflections on *Freud and Fundamentalism* as such two older essays by two major thinkers, who are no longer living but whose work addresses presently the broad implications of psychoanalysis as an epistemological framework for understanding the social-historical realm. My rationale is that these two meditations would not merely contribute extra dimensions to how psychoanalytic knowledge deactivates the certainty of fundamentalist thinking, but in fact open even further an already cleft horizon of inquiry at the outer edges of the issue, as we move from Freud's own thinking to the broader cognitive parameters of the legacy of his thinking.

Both these texts, which are otherwise very different and perhaps even opposed in sensibility and orientation, share one crucial fact: they bring the rigorous interrogative mode of psychoanalysis back onto itself, as a self-reflexive, self-critical practice, whether it pertains to the epistemic operations of religion or anthropology (the latter understood not in terms of cultural variants but insofar as it concerns the constitution of *anthropos*, the very measures of accounting for what is human). Without being programmatic, both texts also share an investment in the future of psychoanalysis as mode of both knowledge and action, as it intersects with other modes that still remain resistant to the epistemic conquests of psychoanalytic thinking.

Jacob Taubes (1923–87) wrote his brief but sinuous essay "Religion and the Future of Psychoanalysis" in 1957 for a special issue on "Psychoanalysis and the Future" in the American journal *Psychoanalysis*. He was at that time resident in the United States, as professor of religion at Columbia University. The date of publication is particularly evocative in the context of the impetus of the essay (and the entire issue of the journal) to contemplate the future of psychoanalysis. This future is now our present—and to the degree that the essay considers the future of psychoanalysis in relation to (the future of) religion, this present may be deemed to be, in a very precise sense, the present framework of this particular collection of inquiries. In many ways, though Taubes was an exemplary archivist of thought in relation to things past, he was always concerned with the most radical sense of the present, and thereby—by virtue of his rigorous understanding

of the dialectics of modernity—with the most radical sense of the imminent (even if imminently deferred) future. This mode of thinking characterizes Taubes's own specific messianic sensibility, eminently laid out in
his celebrated lectures on *The Political Theology of Paul*, to which this short
piece might be said to serve as initial prelude.

Indeed, here Taubes proposes an idiosyncratic consideration of Paul
as Freud's precursor. This makes Freud a theologian—and Paul a social
theorist—but a paradoxical theologian of atheist persuasion, who nonetheless recognizes (like Paul) the religious imaginary to be linked immanently
to humanity's negotiation with the primordial experience of guilt: in
Taubes's words, "the dialectic of guilt and atonement." But the affinity
ends there. Whereas Paul invents a religion that claims to overcome guilt
through eschatological redemption, Freud opts for a humanist discipline
that claims to reconcile the impossible overcoming of guilt with the emancipation of self-critical consciousness. In this specific sense, Taubes reads
Freud as a bona fide Nietzschean thinker. Unlike the later lectures on
Paul, this short prelude seems to linger further on the side of tragic humanism and against political theology. However we may debate possible
shifts (or not) in Taubes's lifelong meditation on Pauline theology, this
early essay provides us with a rigorous assessment of the power of Freudian thinking to resist theological transcendentalisms of all kinds and, of
course, religious fundamentalisms of all kinds.

This is all the more refreshing in light of the current secularism debates
and the tendency—whose most illustrious proponent is arguably Charles
Taylor—to discredit Freud (not to mention Nietzsche) as so much out-
dated Enlightenment. It is especially important—and surely worth serious
theoretical reflection—that a theologian and professor of religion underscores the importance of Freud's view of religion as a matter, not of tradition (in the classic academic secularist sociology of religion), but of
collective memory: of social imaginary transmission, institution, and reins-
titution, in which the atheist perspective is not reducible to scientism or
technological rationalism, but rather to psychosocial human(ist) energies,
the very same energies that animate religion.

Following Taubes is the second of the two added essays: my translation
of a lecture that Cornelius Castoriadis (1922–97) gave in Greek in 1993,
which elaborates on his long-term meditations on psychoanalysis since the
publication of *The Imaginary Institution of Society* (1975). Woven practically
throughout his published work subsequent to this book—sometimes concerning theoretical or technical aspects of the practice (Castoriadis being

an analyst himself), other times addressing the big picture of societal institution and humanization, especially in terms of his own theory of sublimation—Castoriadis's contribution to psychoanalytic thinking proper is vast
and yet to be fully accounted for and appreciated. Part of the rationale for
publishing this piece is that it gives us a cohesive sense of how Castoriadis
conceptualized precisely this big picture. For readers well versed in the
details of Castoriadis's psychoanalytic thinking (his theory of the subject,
the monadic core of the psyche, the radical imaginary, or the political-
anthropological dimension of sublimation), this text will provide an overarching inventory, with the added dimension—somewhat unusual in most
of Castoriadis's psychoanalytic writings—of showing the shortcomings of
psychoanalysis in respect to its own anthropological or sociological theoretical claims.

Castoriadis's essay proposes to investigate precisely what it announces
in the title. The notion of contribution should be understood dialectically.
That is, psychoanalysis contributes a certain mode of inquiry about society, but this inquiry does not produce an explanation of society's emergence; or rather, the explanation psychoanalysis produces about how
human society emerges is inadequate, even though its mode of inquiry is
precisely what enables us to elucidate this inadequacy. In this, Castoriadis's thinking is exemplary. Let us not forget that he raises questions about
what psychoanalysis can or cannot do as a psychoanalyst as well as a philosopher and political thinker. Going through this set of questions one by
one—though the answers vary in length and depth—he determines the
common denominator to be that psychoanalysis cannot produce a theory
of how society is generated because society must already have been generated for human beings to live as human, which is also to say, for human
beings to have a human psyche. But it is also the reverse, in a certain
fashion. The human psyche, of which psychoanalysis speaks so profoundly, is human insofar as it extends itself into—which also means, enables, makes possible—a self-altering process of socialization: a process
that fulfills it as human psyche (gives it meaning) by going precisely against
its psychic constitution.

This paradoxical humanization of the human animal takes place, as it
were, in a mutual and dialectical complicity between psyche and society
that, in the large expanse of mythical time, might be said to take place
simultaneously. In other words, there is neither ontological nor ontoge-
netic primacy, despite Freud's mythical-anthropological claims. This cleft
plane of emergence carries over to all levels of social-imaginary institution,

but also human psychical operation. Hence the decisive importance of affective ambivalence, which, for Castoriadis, is the exclusive psychic characteristic of human animals. This is especially important for the terms of our discussion. If ambivalence is the expression of "a biologically anomalous development of the human psyche," as Castoriadis puts it, then the abolition of ambivalence—the elemental desire in every sort of fundamentalist thinking—signifies a second-order anomaly: the institution of a specific social-imaginary that nullifies the interrogative and creative potential of ambivalence in respect to knowledge. In psychoanalytic terms, this signifies an instance when the meaning that society grants to the psyche reinforces, rather than tempers or transforms, the psychical phantasm of narcissistic omnipotence.

For Castoriadis, psychoanalysis is a mode of creative/interrogative knowledge that preserves and even enhances the emancipatory potential of this ambivalence. Despite its inadequacy as anthropological theory of societal emergence (which is one way to conceive the problem of its own dogmatic—perhaps even fundamentalist—tendencies), psychoanalysis resists the self-ascribed transparency and stability of fundamentalist thinking. The ultimate point of Castoriadis's argument about how politically crucial psychoanalysis is to the project of autonomy hinges on his understanding that the lucid transformation of individuals that psychoanalysis proposes is—and can only be—tantamount to the transformation of society. In light of the discussion in the previous essays in our inquiry, I would add that this might be another way to consider that Freud's Eros myth extends, as it were, beyond merely the pleasure principle.

Joel Whitebook, who might be arguably the only American psychoanalyst to have substantially incorporated Castoriadis's ideas into his own thinking, provides us with yet another perspective through which we might (re)consider the creative/interrogative elements of a psychoanalytic mode of knowledge. His chief gesture is to bring back to the forefront what Paul Ricoeur famously called "the hermeneutics of suspicion" by dialectically reversing the classic postmodernist argument of "suspicion about the masters of suspicion" (Marx, Nietzsche, Freud). Throughout this essay, Whitebook provides a concise overview of the shift in frameworks and discourses that characterizes our current predicament—the curious, nebulous, and certainly as yet untheorized "post" of postmodernism's all-around critique of the human sciences, a "post" deriving from the entwinement of both the achievements and the dead ends of postmodernist epistemology. It is precisely these conditions, Whitebook correctly suggests, that enabled contemporary antisecularist thought to take advantage of the postmodernist demolition of privileged Reason in order to hail—in a context indicatively named postsecular and posthumanist—the so-called reemergence of religion (no longer considered psychosocial investment or cultural tradition but form of thought or lifestyle) to a new political and epistemological privilege.

In response to these conditions, Whitebook argues, psychoanalysis produces a radical postmetaphysical move that does not celebrate the death of the Absolute but contests the very ground of its demands. Whitebook conducts himself through the vicissitudes of this move by way of Adorno's negative dialectical understanding of the subject-society equation, pointing out the possibility and desirability of critique of the transcendental subject without the trappings of reductive objectivism or dogmatic immanentism. Psychoanalysis is a mode of practical and speculative knowledge focused on the epistemological problem of humanity's passage into an emergent second nature (society/culture) out of a residual first nature (the mortal field of bio-nature). The psychical world belongs to—indeed, traverses—both domains, and the continuous process of negotiating their *coincidence* is elucidated by a theory of sublimation. This theory, however, cannot be of the order of scientific neutrality, precisely because sublimation, though always involving the most internal elements of the psyche, is not a mechanical but a social-imaginary process; in other words, it always has a politics. In this respect, we might consider that the specific hermeneutics of suspicion that psychoanalysis mobilizes is especially trenchant in the interrogation of what sort of sublimation enables, for example, fundamentalist imaginaries to flourish, or conversely, what sort of sublimation enables imaginaries that pursue, in Castoriadis's sense, the project of autonomy.

Whitebook's discussion of the radical epistemological capacities of psychoanalysis, especially in relation to arguments in analytic philosophy and philosophy of science as to what constitutes "proper" science and "proper" philosophy, anticipates keenly the closing text in our circuitous trajectory: an interview with Aristides Baltas about precisely this problem of the epistemology of psychoanalysis. Baltas is an internationally recognized philosopher of science and is the premier contemporary Greek philosopher, equally deft in physics, psychoanalysis, and political theory. In the European reference frame, he would be characterized as an epistemologist in the tradition of Bachelard or Canguilhem. We find him here in an encounter with two Lacanian analysts, conducting an erudite and illuminating conversation that restages many of the queries already performed in the volume. Yet, this conversation also serves as a profound reflection on Baltas's entire range of thinking: a backward glance over the multifaceted work of many years and an unfolding of a precise philosophical vision into the future.

Engaging the question of whether psychoanalysis is a science, Baltas refuses to settle for easy dismissal of the categorical determinations of the "hard sciences" established and represented by physics since the seventeenth century. He argues that you can sustain the rigorous demands of physics toward experimental method, object, and conceptual universe of inquiry without, however, conforming to its specific model of internal (or inter-constitutive) relations between these three elements. Psychoanalysis cannot be tested by the terms of verifiability and falsifiability that pertain to physics, for the simple reason that its experimental method, object, and conceptual universe of inquiry is not—and cannot be—identical to that of physics or any other science. That the cognitive universe of physics does not recognize the validity of such terms in another science is irrelevant—one might even say, contrary to the demand on the part of physics (and all so-called hard sciences) for internal coherence.

Like Whitebook, Baltas determines psychoanalysis to be the "science of human subjectivity." The issue of whether human subjectivity is a "proper" scientific object is irrelevant. What matters is whether, as object of psychoanalysis, human subjectivity meets rigorous and internally coherent criteria within the domains of theory and practice (that is, the methodological and experimental field) of psychoanalysis. Baltas develops this argument on his basic epistemological thesis that human thought is characterized by different forms of rationality, so that the incommensurability in the categorical content of physics or psychoanalysis (or historical materialism, if one were to take into account Baltas's Althusserian writings or his provocative argument about physics as a mode of production) is really not the proper problem to behold. The singularity of the scientific object of psychoanalysis—each and every psychoanalytic encounter, each and every theater of transference and countertransference, as well as the evident unrepeatability of each and every psychoanalytic experiment—makes psychoanalysis an altogether different epistemological framework. Precisely, because all the elements of the experimental field are interventional elements—nothing is ever neutral or inert—this epistemological framework is especially conducive to the transformation of any preconceived notions or conditions or established orders of things. Baltas's rigorously scientific conceptualization of the psychoanalytic epistemology shows it also to be intrinsically political—not in the sense of being vulnerable or conducive to ideologies, but in the deeper sense of enabling and fostering conditions for social transformation.

In the end, this intrinsic politics of psychoanalysis—a politics of psychosocial transformation inherent in the idiomatic conditions of its practice, not constructed as some sort of ideological project—is what this collection of essays addresses, even if not always so explicitly. Indeed, to the degree that psychoanalysis assumes an ideological content, it thwarts its transformational capacity. On such occasions—admittedly plenty since Freud's own time—a certain dogmatic desire to control internally the theoretical sphere of psychoanalysis has produced what can be called its fundamentalist tendencies. These tendencies, however, always seem somehow to get broken, again from within, as the process of psychoanalytic thought emerging from within the experimental field—analysis itself as a practical experience of fostering self-alteration—interrogates its own theoretical categories and produces new and open epistemological terrains. Sometimes these terrains too coagulate in turn into equally dogmatic splinter groups or schools of thought, according to whatever vicissitudes of neo-Freudian or post-Freudian fractionalism. However, as nowadays we have passed through the era of the Freud wars and the overt polemics against psychoanalysis—sometimes deserved, other times merely serving an ideology and an industry of normalizing therapeutics—the gesture of gathering together a nonpartisan and heterodox collection of texts that put into practice the best tenets of Freud's self-interrogatory tendencies, even against the authority that animates them, is itself an explicit gesture against the dead ends of fundamentalist thinking.

Modeling Freud and Fundamentalism

Andrew Parker

Stretching to the limit all that psychoanalysis can know and say about itself, *Freud and Fundamentalism* enjoins its contributors to survey anew some sector of the hotly contested borderland between "psyche" and "society." My own contribution surveys, typologically, three of the forms that this surveying may take. To think Freud together with fundamentalism will be, in the first place, to construe fundamentalism as an *object of psychoanalysis* that may then be diagnosed as the noxious expression of a collective unconscious foreign to Freud's therapeutic ethos. From a second perspective, psychoanalysis will itself be considered a *subject of fundamentalism*, acting out within its own discourse and institutional history just what it deems noxious in the psychic lives of other groups. In the last of the framings (the most inchoate and statistically the rarest of the three), psychoanalysis and fundamentalism will form each other's condition of geopolitical possibility, thereby permitting a return in conclusion to the discourse of territory broached here.

The first approach is the most straightforward, since it follows in the familiar tracks of other forms of "applied psychoanalysis," more specifically Freud's critique of religious illusion: "Religion would thus be the universal obsessional neurosis of humanity; like the obsessional neurosis of children, it arose out of the Oedipus complex, out of the relation to the father."[1] What Freud said generally about religion would apply all the more in the particular case of fundamentalism, which indeed is the argument pursued by Robert Jay Lifton and others who view fundamentalism as a symptom of pathology writ large.[2] We are not surprised, of course, to find the Father lurking here; the Freudian reading of culture (re)discovers its own truth everywhere it looks, and fundamentalism would seem to offer no exception. But what, perhaps, *is* surprising is that we can find traces of this truth even in contexts that are not particularly Freudian. Here, for example, are Michael Hardt and Antonio Negri on the nature of fundamentalism:

> Another symptom of the historical passage [to Empire] already in process in the final decades of the twentieth century is the rise of the so-called fundamentalisms. Since the collapse of the Soviet Union, the great ideologues of geopolitics and the theoreticians of the end of history have consistently posed fundamentalisms as the primary danger facing global order and stability. Fundamentalism, however, is a poor and confused category that groups together widely disparate phenomena. In general, one might say that fundamentalisms, diverse though they may be, are linked by their being understood both from within and outside as anti-modernist movements, resurgences of primordial identities and values; they are conceived as a kind of historical backflow, a de-modernization. It is more accurate and more useful, however, to understand the various fundamentalisms not as the re-creation of a pre-modern world, but rather as a powerful refusal of the contemporary historical passage in course. In this sense, too, like postmodernist and postcolonialist theories, fundamentalisms are a symptom of the passage to Empire.[3]

Though it may be difficult to tell the authors' views apart from those with whom they take issue, what stands out nonetheless in this passage is its rhetoric of resurgences, primordial identities, backflows, and refusals—as if the only language it had at its disposal is one that comes from Freud. Fundamentalism is thus not only, as Hardt and Negri contend, a symptom of the passage to empire; a blockage in the hydraulics of "normal" historical development, it is also and preeminently the name of a formal diagnosis, a symptom of a symptomatic reading.

This practice of treating fundamentalism as a symptom is much more explicit in several recent works by Slavoj Žižek, who distinguishes between "authentic," tolerant fundamentalisms (such as that of the Amish or the Tibetans) and the "inauthentic" fundamentalism of the Moral Majority, which is intolerant because it bitterly envies the excessive *jouissance* of the

Other.[4] In his post-9/11 book *Welcome to the Desert of the Real*, Žižek switches at moments to a Marxist lexicon—"the Muslim fundamentalists are not true fundamentalists, they are already 'modernists,' a product and a phenomenon of modern global capitalism"—though even in these instances fundamentalism retains its heuristic value as a symptom.[5] Žižek generally invokes Lacan in framing these diagnoses, but it might be fairer to regard this impulse as a revitalization of a properly Freudian tradition of *Massenpsychologie*, since, unlike Lacan, Žižek puts enormous weight on the analogy of the individual to the social.[6] A recent commentator gets this relation precisely right: "Just as an individual subject's discursive universe will only ever be unified through the recourse to a fantasy (mis)representing the *jouissance* of the Other; so too the public-ideological frame wherein political subjects take their bearings can only ever function by the positing of what Žižek calls 'ideological fantasies.' "[7] "Just as/so too": this practice of viewing social psychology on the model of individual psychology is not only basic to Freud's critique of religion, but it also underlies all attempts to treat fundamentalism as a symptom understood classically as the mark of collective repression.

Freud relies on this analogy to underwrite his analysis of culture even as the terms he uses vary enormously in qualification and coherence.[8] The *locus classicus* is the opening of *Group Psychology and the Analysis of the Ego* (1921), where the analogy is no sooner introduced than undone. Preparing to make the case that the Leader is the Father writ large, Freud downplays the presumptive difference between individual and group psychologies in suggesting that everyone's psychic experience has been social from the outset:

> The contrast between individual psychology and social or group psychology, which at a first glance may seem to be full of significance, loses a great deal of its sharpness when it is examined more closely. It is true that individual psychology is concerned with the individual man and explores the paths by which he seeks to find satisfaction for his instinctual impulses; but only rarely and under certain exceptional conditions is individual psychology in a position to disregard the relations of this individual to others. In the individual's mental life someone else is invariably involved, as a model, as an object, as a helper, as an opponent; and so from the very first individual psychology, in this extended but entirely justifiable sense of the words, is at the same time social psychology as well.[9]

Individual and social psychologies are thus the same "in this extended but entirely justified sense." Freud is seeking here to counter any imputation

that psychoanalysis is a theory of psychic immanence; the individual is a
social subject from the moment that he/she has become a subject: "The
relations of an individual to his parents and to his brothers and sisters, to
the object of his love, and to his physician—in fact all the relations which
have hitherto been the chief subject of psycho-analytic research—may
claim to be considered as social phenomena."[10] Curiously, however, Freud
derails this train of thought in completing it:

> and in this respect they may be contrasted with certain other processes,
> described by us as "narcissistic," in which the satisfaction of the instincts is
> partially or totally withdrawn from the influence of other people. The con-
> trast between social and narcissistic—Bleuler would perhaps call them "au-
> tistic"—mental acts therefore falls wholly within the domain of individual
> psychology [*seelischen Akten fällt also durchaus innerhalb des Bereichs der Indi-
> vidualpsychologie*], and is not well calculated to differentiate it from a social
> or group psychology [*und eignet sich nicht dazu, sie von einer Sozial- oder
> Massenpsychologie abzutrennen*].[11]

Having just refused to distinguish individual from social psychologies,
Freud reintroduces that same distinction, now as a contrast between narcissistic and social acts, but wholly *within* "the domain of individual psychology." It would be difficult, indeed, to calculate the difference between
individual and social psychology when one term of the analogy seems to
have swallowed the analogy itself.

Eight years later, in *Civilization and Its Discontents*, Freud's analogy
seems to have swallowed the world:

> If the development of civilization has such a far-reaching similarity to the
> development of the individual and if it employs the same methods, may we
> not be justified in reaching the diagnosis that, under the influence of cul-
> tural urges, some civilizations, or some epochs of civilization—possibly the
> whole of mankind—have become "neurotic"? An analytic dissection of
> such neuroses might lead to therapeutic recommendations which could lay
> claim to great practical interest. I would not say that an attempt of this kind
> to carry psycho-analysis over to the cultural community [*Kulturgemein-
> schaft*] was absurd or doomed to be fruitless. But we should have to be very
> cautious and not forget that, after all, we are only dealing with analogies
> and that it is dangerous, not only with men but also with concepts, to tear
> them from the sphere in which they have originated and been evolved.
> Moreover, the diagnosis of communal neurosis [*Gemeinschaftensneurosen*] is
> faced with a special difficulty. In an individual neurosis we take as our start-
> ing-point the contrast that distinguishes the patient from his environment,

which is assumed to be "normal." For a group all of whose members are affected by one and the same disorder no such background could exist; it would have to be found elsewhere. And as regards the therapeutic application of our knowledge, what would be the use of the most correct analysis of social neuroses, since no one possesses authority to impose such a therapy upon the group? But in spite of all these difficulties we may expect that one day someone will venture to embark upon a pathology of cultural communities.[12]

Despite Freud's intermittent warnings concerning "the diagnosis of communal neurosis," it remains an open question whether the limits that beset the use of this analogy are simply political—a matter of authorization and collective will—rather than epistemological. All subsequent psychoanalytically oriented discussions of fundamentalism inherit this question. For example, in her recent *For the Love of the Father: A Psychoanalytic Study of Religious Terrorism*, Ruth Stein claims not to be diagnosing the psyches of particular Islamic terrorists, since to do so would have led to her to judge whether their acts "are pathological or not." Her "psychodynamic" model would refrain as a matter of principle from such judgment:

> Whereas the psychopathological refers to *specific* categories of psychic sickness in *individuals* (and is to a considerable extent relative to culture), the psychodynamic deals with a reality that, in being formed by unconscious fantasies and perduring in mindsets, constitutes a general order of psychic life. . . . In brief, when we speak psychodynamically, we deal with the unconscious operations that regulate and shape psychic life *in general*.[13]

Stein would appear here to have assumed as self-evident and stable the relationship between an individual psyche and "life in general" that Freud continued to find both attractive and troubling even in a text as late as *Moses and Monotheism*. In seeking one last time to save the analogy by uncovering its scientific basis, he finds he cannot avoid adducing yet again the phylogenetic explanation—the Primal Horde and the originary murder of the Father—that he knew few would find persuasive:

> It is not easy for us to translate the concepts of individual psychology into group psychology; and I do not think we gain anything by introducing the concept of a "collective" unconscious. The content of the unconscious, indeed, is in any case a collective, universal property of mankind. For the moment, then, we will make shift with the use of analogies. The processes in the life of peoples which we are studying here are very similar to those familiar to us in psychopathology, but nevertheless not quite the same. We

must finally make up our minds to adopt the hypothesis that the psychical precipitates of the primaeval period became inherited property which, in each fresh generation, called not for acquisition but only for awakening. In this we have in mind the example of what is certainly the "innate" symbolism which derives from the period of the development of speech, which is familiar to all children without their being instructed, and which is the same among all peoples despite their different languages. What we may perhaps still lack in certainty here is made good by other products of psycho-analytic research. We find that in a number of important relations our children react, not in a manner corresponding to their own experience, but instinctively, like the animals, in a manner that is only explicable as phylogenetic acquisition.[14]

If psychoanalytic practice unearths memories of an archaic parricide that persist in every modern person's psyche, Freud then can lay claim to "have bridged the gulf between individual and group psychology: we can deal with peoples as we do with an individual neurotic."[15] Few have been ready to follow Freud over this bridge; indeed, many have wondered whether psychoanalysis can ever admit that there's more to the social than Oedipal identifications.[16] Even some of Freud's sympathetic readers have suggested that his analogical bridge should be closed for structural repairs:

> Society-as-individual: here the "analogy" meets with a major difficulty which, for me is quite simple: in order for a message to be repressed, a repressing ego must be constituted. A repression is effected in the first person. The constitution of the ego is a correlate of repression. But then the idea of collective neurosis immediately—when used in the *proper* sense, and not as a sum of individual neuroses—comes up against the impossibility of conceiving of a repressing ego in the group, and of a locus and status of the repressed.[17]

Whether or not one finds this objection decisive, the Freudian approach to fundamentalism—and the analogy on which it stands—stakes itself on the exteriority of (its own) science to the beliefs that it considers unreasoned and dogmatic. Fundamentalism, *c'est l'autre*. This is just what is called into question in our second model. For if fundamentalism couples an appeal to the letter of scriptural authority with a disavowal of the necessity of reading, such a description is at least as applicable to psychoanalysis as to any religious fundamentalism. This point is made unintentionally by Robert M. Young, a British psychotherapist whose essay "Psychoanalysis, Terrorism and Fundamentalism" has been circulating online since 9/11: "To be a fundamentalist is . . . to cling to certainties drawn from sacred texts or the pronouncements of charismatic leaders."[18] Indeed, the more one reads recent writing purporting to explain fundamentalism, the more one is led to recall the embattled history of the psychoanalytic institution. As an experiment, try substituting "psychoanalysts" for "fundamentalists" in the following passage from Ruth Stein's *For the Love of the Father* and you might hear, say, echoes of Freud's falling out with Jung and Adler, the history of Lacan's institutional dissolutions, bitter disputes at congresses over the smallest matters of doctrinal difference, and other squabbles against enemies inside and outside the circle of believers:

> It has been said that fundamentalists do not want understanding, negotia-
> tion, compromise, or even dialogue. . . . For the fundamentalist lens, noth-
> ing is opaque and truly puzzling, nothing needs further interpretation
> beyond the preestablished frame of reference. Within this narrowed mind-
> set, there is nothing genuinely new under the sun: everything is self-evident
> and self-identical. Such a mode of thinking finds order and certainty, and
> creates a patterned, predictable worldview that offers feelings of safety and
> freedom from potentially self-eroding doubt.[19]

To identify psychoanalysis as itself a kind of religious fundamentalism is not necessarily a disqualification (as it would be, say, for a Frederick Crews or a François Roustang). Eric L. Santner, for example, argues that religion may be what psychoanalysis has aspired to all along: "Freud's mostly negative assessments of religion are in some way undermined or at least challenged by what I can't help but characterize as the 'spiritual' dimension of the new science he founded. . . . Freudian thought resonates with forms of thinking, feeling, and imagining that he sought to 'disen-chant.'"[20] Irrepressible as always, Žižek proclaims that Lacan stands to Freud (and Lenin to Marx) as Paul stands to Jesus—and that all of this is a good thing, which it could hardly have been for Freud, already horrified that psychoanalysis might be regarded as a Jewish science.[21] Indeed, where Santner and Žižek try to blur productively the lines separating psychoanal-ysis from religious belief, Freud sought to keep the two distinct at least on the level of principle, for on this division rests the very possibility of sci-ence. Religions are delusory, Freud says, for they are (as Popper and others have said of psychoanalysis) "insusceptible of proof": "No one can be compelled to think them true, to believe in them." While "a believer is bound to the teachings of religion by certain ties of affection," science is by definition independent of such ties, even if the science in question is one that studies inner life: "scientific work is the only road which can lead us to a knowledge of reality outside ourselves." Of course, Freud wouldn't be Freud if he failed to hesitate over this distinction, but his conclusion that "in the long run nothing can withstand reason and experience" is never much in doubt, for while "our god *Logos* is perhaps not a very almighty one . . . science has given us evidence by its numerous and important successes that it is no illusion."[22] In pursuing this argument, of course, Freud would be seeking (in Joel Whitebook's memorable phrase) "to justify his faith in reason," a paradox that may prove finally irreducible for psychoanalysis.[23] J.-B. Pontalis therefore counsels us: "Do not believe in psychoanalysis; have faith in it."[24] Fundamentally, as it were.

Suggesting that a common ethics lies "at the core of both psychoanalysis and the Judeo-Christian tradition," Santner brings us finally into the territory of our last approach to "Freud and Fundamentalism," which may indeed be called the territory of territory.[25] In this model—certainly the least familiar, and thus perhaps the most intriguing of the three—the very term "fundamentalism" turns out to be coextensive with the institutional geography of psychoanalysis. According to the *Oxford English Dictionary*, "fundamentalism" was coined by Protestant denominations in the United States following World War I to describe "strict adherence to certain tenets (e.g. the literal inerrancy of Scripture) held to be fundamental to Christian faith." In the *OED*'s second definition, fundamentalism "in other religions, especially Islam" is "a similarly strict adherence to ancient or fundamental doctrines, with no concessions to modern developments in thought or customs." This second definition is, obviously, an argument by extension from the Anglo-Saxon norm. The phrase "Islamic fundamentalism" dates only from 1961, "Hindu fundamentalism" from 1957, with each usage implying that these phenomena are in some way comparable to the Protestant original. Revealingly, however, there are no equivalents in Arabic and Persian ("fundamentalism" is rendered *usuli* in both languages, which sounds highly contrived), nor are there equivalents in Tamil, Sinha, or Hindi (most commentators in the latter would use instead the term *sampradayitka*, "communalism"). No equivalents, at least not yet, though one may imagine the kinds of global pressure that will be brought to bear on these languages to produce equivalents—the same kinds of global pressure that have made Christianity the model to which other religions must conform.[26] On the other hand, equivalents abound already in almost all the modern European languages. A few examples:

French: *fondamentalisme*
German: *Fundamentalismus*
Italian: *fondamentalismo*

Spanish: *fundamentalismo*
Greek: *fondamentalismós*

This survey is not, of course, intended to be exhaustive, but rather to suggest that the limits of the word "fundamentalism" *are* the geographical limits of psychoanalysis; the places where the word has come to translate itself are the very places Jacques Derrida has called *terra psychoanalytica*. He reminds us that there are

> areas of human settlement where psychoanalysis has made no inroads what-soever—sometimes not even with the help of all the paraphernalia of colo-nization: almost all China, a good portion of Africa, the entire non-Judeo-Christian world. . . . These are among those parts of "the rest of the world" where psychoanalysis has never set foot, or in any case where it has never taken off its European shoes.[27]

In this third modeling of "Freud and Fundamentalism," the shoes psycho-analysis never takes off appear to be, today, more American than Euro-pean. Which makes them, perhaps, much less stylish. But with more potential for market penetration.

These three foregoing ways of linking psychoanalysis with fundamen-talism are not intended to be exhaustive, of course. Each, however, finds itself reflected in "the psychoanalysis of fundamentalism," where the "of" signals an instability in the genitive. For if, as a symptom, fundamentalism can become an object of psychoanalytic science, that science—coextensive with a certain West—is also and to the same extent subjected to what it analyzes. To suggest as much is perhaps to explain why thinking about "Freud and Fundamentalism" remains so compelling to us.[28]

Myth and Dogma in 1920:
The Fundamentalist-Modernist Controversy
and Freud's "Death Drive"

David Adams

"God's not interested in other people—He's interested in *His* people," bellows televangelist John Hagee in a sermon series titled "Bible Positions on Political Issues."[1] Hagee's declaration embodies the spirit of fundamentalism, if we take seriously Jerry Falwell's definition of the fundamentalist as an evangelical who is angry about something.[2] The anger, reflected in the wrath of the fundamentalist's God, is always about *someone* as well as something, resulting in a Manichaean opposition between good and evil, the saved and the damned, us and them. Given their eagerness to see God finally and violently resolve this opposition, many fundamentalists have welcomed the violence of 9/11 or the prospect of the "war on terror" spiraling out of control. Note, for example, the initial reaction of Falwell and Pat Robertson to the events of 9/11, which was to blame the ACLU for having made God mad. And Hagee welcomes the war in Iraq as "the gateway to the apocalypse," certain, on the authority of Ezekiel, that it will "destabilize the Middle East," "lead to World War III," and provoke a "furious" God to "kill 85% of that Islamic horde . . . so the whole world will know that He is the Lord of Israel." This is cause for celebration because God's people "will be raptured before this battle happens!"[3] Such views are not marginal in the United States: according to recent surveys, more than one-third of all Americans believe that the state of Israel is a fulfillment of the biblical prophecy of the Second Coming, and such apocalyptic thought shaped the rhetoric and policy of the Bush administration.[4]

Fundamentalist fury has animated America's culture wars for over eighty years. Liberals and moderns, both religious and secular, have often failed to understand the depth and tenacity of this anger. It has seemed at times to retreat—most notably for several decades after the 1925 Scopes monkey trial, but also, less dramatically, after the televangelist scandals of the 1980s and after the overreaching of the Newt Gingrich congress in the 1990s—only to return each time with greater energy, organization, and success. The inclination of liberals to underestimate the anger stems from a failure to perceive the depth of the discontent with modernity, a discontent that fundamentalism expresses and addresses. Nothing better demonstrates how radical this discontent is—and thus how great the obstacle to any rapprochement with liberals—than the premillennialism that contributed to the emergence of fundamentalism during the First World War. Based on a literal reading of the book of Revelation, premillennialists believe that Christ will return at the beginning rather than at the culmination of Christianity's promised thousand-year reign on earth. Thus, they view modernity as the latest stage in an irreversible historical disintegration, and they interpret present crises as welcome signs that Christ's return is imminent. Such interest in the End Times represents a powerful death drive, an impatience for this world to suffer the vengeance of the Father. Dispensationalism intensifies this death drive with the notion of the rapture, a vision of salvation for elect believers whom the Father will transport suddenly aloft, sparing them the tribulation suffered by those left behind. If religion is, as Freud says, a regressive longing for the father, then fundamentalists are the most religious of the religious, the most infantile of the infantile.

The "fundamentalist" and the "death drive" are twins: they came into being simultaneously, in 1920. Curtis Lee Laws, a Baptist pastor, coined the former term in connection with the Buffalo meeting of the Northern Baptist Convention; Freud introduced the concept of the death drive in *Beyond the Pleasure Principle*.[5] At first glance, the coincidence of timing highlights the distance between the two events, between Buffalo and Vienna, between American Protestants and a European Jew, between militant faith and resolute iconoclasm. The distance certainly leaves open the possibility of fruitfully applying one term to the other. For example, fundamentalism calls for a psychoanalytic reading, given that anger is its distinguishing characteristic; conversely, Freud himself, like Jacques Lacan after him, calls the drive a fundamental concept (*Grundbegriff*), inviting reflection on the orthodoxies of psychoanalysis. These perspectives come into play but remain secondary here, for I incorporate another approach suggested by the origin of the concepts. Their simultaneity is not merely an accident. Both of these concepts are responding to the profound cultural and psychological crisis resulting from the First World War. The developments of 1920 show us that fundamentalism and psychoanalysis, for all their differences, share critical functions and characteristics. Both constitute comprehensive theories of interpretation, offering frameworks for reading authoritative texts and signs of the times, and both deal with anger and aggression. Both respond to the collective trauma of the war by turning to myth, and in particular by developing or strengthening their eschatological or teleological elements. Juxtaposing these two patterns of thought will demonstrate the extent to which Freud's metapsychology was shaped by the same pressures that produced fundamentalism, but with radically contradictory results. Unlike Freud's writings on religion, *Beyond the Pleasure Principle* offers a comprehensive alternative to religion: a myth that precludes dogma, a fundamental phenomenon distinguished by its silence rather than by a sacred text, and the liberating conviction that the only normal person is a dead person.

From World War to Culture War

All of the theological and social elements of fundamentalism were present in American religion before the Great War, but the war served as a catalyst, binding them together in a particular configuration with a new militancy. Thus, the fundamentalist as a clearly defined social being did not exist until around the time the new word was introduced. Laws, editor of *The Watchman-Examiner*, had helped organize a faction of conservatives at the Northern Baptist Convention, and his report on the Convention made the following proposal: "We here and now move that a new word be adopted to describe the men among us who insist that the landmarks shall not be removed. . . . We suggest that those who still cling to the great fundamentals and who mean to do battle royal for the fundamentals shall be called 'Fundamentalists.' "[6] Militant rhetoric has been an integral part of fundamentalism from the beginning.

Laws's familiar reference to "the fundamentals" indicates he did not need to reach far for this neologism and the related dogma. A series of twelve volumes titled *The Fundamentals* had been published between 1910 and 1915, consisting of ninety articles by conservative theologians and preachers. Brothers Lyman and Milton Stewart, Los Angeles oilmen, sponsored the pamphlets with instructions that free copies be sent to "every pastor, evangelist, missionary, theological professor, theological student, Sunday school superintendent, Y.M.C.A. and Y.W.C.A. secretary in the English speaking world."[7] Three million copies were distributed. While neither the militancy nor the premillennialism characteristic of fundamentalism are pronounced in *The Fundamentals*, the series nevertheless became associated eventually with five fundamentalist tenets:

The literal inerrancy of the Bible
The virgin birth of Christ
Christ's substitutionary atonement
Christ's bodily resurrection
The imminent Second Coming

The first of these is arguably the most important, laying the groundwork for the others, and it shows that fundamentalism has its roots in the Reformation. The most recent commentary on this lineage is in David Katz's history of the English Bible, which concludes with a chapter on fundamentalism as a return to Luther's precepts of *sola fide* and *sola scriptura*.[8] The democratic insistence that the Bible is accessible to all became, in America of the late nineteenth and early twentieth centuries, the conservatives' response to the growing influence among liberal theologians and church leaders of German Higher Criticism, which reconciled the teachings of the Bible to historical and scientific knowledge.

If the intellectual roots of fundamentalism reach back at least to the Reformation, the social roots extend to American evangelicalism of the nineteenth century. Conservative Protestants were responding during this time to a number of cultural and social developments: corruption and exploitation in the Gilded Age, following on the apocalyptic expectations surrounding the Civil War; the acceleration of industrialization and urbanization and their related social ills; the growth of immigration from countries not predominantly Protestant, perceived as a threat to the religious and cultural homogeneity of the United States; the influence of Darwin's theories; and the spread of Higher Criticism. In reaction to such developments, prophecy and revival meetings flourished, providing a hospitable environment for dispensational premillennialism, which was introduced by Irish minister John Nelson Darby and codified in the annotated Bible published by Cyrus Scofield in 1909. Various conservative gatherings and organizations also attempted to enumerate the tenets of the faith.

Most notably, the Niagara Bible Conference, which met annually in the late nineteenth century, produced a fourteen-point creed in 1878,[9] and in 1910 the General Assembly of the Presbyterian Church endorsed the famous Five Points.[10]

The five Presbyterian points differ in one significant way from the five tenets associated with fundamentalism after the war. The last of the Five Points declares the reality of miracles, and in place of this the fundamentalists substitute the premillennial Second Coming. George Marsden has shown that before the war some premillennialists were pacifists or were politically uncommitted, in keeping with a certain logic to premillenarian thought.[11] In contrast to the liberal Social Gospel, which worked for social progress to prepare the world for the Second Coming, premillennialists believed that the Second Coming was both imminent and a necessary prerequisite to establish the millennium, making political activity unnecessary. But this changed with the war and intense anti-German sentiment, which exacerbated many of the fears to which the evangelical movement had been responding. Germany, perceived as a Christian country that had sunk into barbarism, was linked to Higher Criticism and Darwinism. More generally, the war and the secular Russian Revolution made it more difficult to believe in progress and thus undermined the liberal Social Gospel. Speaking at the World Conference on Christian Fundamentals shortly after the war, William Riley declared that "the reasons for His return are manifest in a world wild with confusion, reeking with anarchy, writhing with pain," and then proceeded to quote his contemporary, Augustus Strong: "this war is God's proof that science and philosophy, literature and commerce, are not sufficient for man's needs, and that Christ must again come, if our modern world is ever to be saved."[12] The conference took place only six months after the end of the war, yet its resolutions and reports as well as the speeches make clear that much of the overheated war rhetoric had transferred quickly from Germany to a new enemy, to the liberals at home who had gained increasing control of the churches and seminaries. The war in fact coincided with a heightened separatist impulse among premillennialists following their failure to integrate successfully with the established denominations.

The postwar configuration of conservative concerns gave greater emphasis to social issues, including resistance to the teaching of evolution, support for prohibition, and, in a less clear but unmistakable way, tolerance for the racism that contributed to the rapid rise of the Ku Klux Klan. In short, a theological debate grew into a culture war, with some participants feeling that the fate of civilization was at stake. The central concerns remained theological, however, and prominent among these now was an activist premillennialism. Karen Armstrong has declared dispensational premillennialism, with its belief that those raptured would observe from above the tribulation of those left behind, "a fantasy of revenge."[13] Armstrong's apt phrase suggests the possibility of refining Freud's description of religion as a childhood neurosis to apply specifically to fundamentalism. The dual vision of fundamentalism, split between celebration of the gift of grace and glee over the eternal suffering of the damned, involves a defusing of two classes of drives, of love and hate. One of the conditions Freud associates with such defusing is a regression from the genital to the sadistic-anal phase of development, encouraging us to remember, in the spirit of Freudian punning, that one meaning of "fundament" is "anus." The fundamentalists, those preoccupied with the dispensations of the fundament, could not have chosen a more appropriate name. The anal-sadistic phase also exhibits a division between active and passive roles, and beneath fundamentalist fantasies of revenge, accordingly, lies a desperate helplessness. The premillenarian conviction that the end is imminent corresponds to the perceived urgency of the need for salvation; prophecy seems to gain in timeliness as history becomes increasingly unbearable. Such desperation helps explain why people continue to believe that the apocalypse is imminent despite the contradiction continually provided by experience.

The influential theory of myth proposed by Hans Blumenberg credits myths—stories that cannot be contradicted by reality—with helping to move humankind away from extreme helplessness, in which the reality principle is absolute, along a continuum toward the opposite extreme, where wishes and images are absolute. In particular, he has shown myth and dogma, associated respectively with the Hellenic and Hebraic roots of Western culture, to be distinct methods for responding to the insufferable indifference that time and space possess for the human subject. Myth negates such indifference by creating significance (*Bedeutsamkeit*), by filling up time and space with stories that generally lack authoritative versions or sacred texts.[14] Fundamentalism and Freud's "death drive" both provide such significance, presenting stories of origin and end that position the subject in relation to ultimate questions and answers. Blumenberg observes that by providing established patterns, myth lessens the expectation for human freedom—and with a decrease in freedom comes a decrease in responsibility. In this sense myth provides excuses, and this partially explains its appeal in 1920, when it could serve as a disavowal of human responsibility for the nightmare of history, whether by invoking an over-due deity (the fundamentalists' God) or a cosmic force affecting all organisms (the death drive). One contemporary critic pointed to this consequence of myth when he wrote that conservative Christianity is "a means of getting off rather cheaply by the simple device of being sorry and believing something."

In contrast to myth's creation of significance to mask the indifference of time and space, dogma adapts itself to such indifference by making the events of salvation temporally and spatially transportable. This transportability comes in part from the fact that the terms of this salvation are fixed in writing. Blumenberg observes that a sacred text allows for the development of an abstract system of dogma, and Christianity's embrace of this possibility to distance itself from its own mythic elements helps explain its success in becoming a world religion. Part of Blumenberg's contribution to the study of intellectual history has been to show how this system of dogma, with its distancing of myth, its use of precise formulas, and its rigorous claim to truth, was a precondition for the modern age's idea of science and theoretical exactitude. Given the tension between myth and dogma in early Christianity, the ability of fundamentalism to combine and strengthen the two simultaneously is striking. Fundamentalism is self-evidently dogmatic, with its insistence on the literal inerrancy of the Bible and codification of faith in a few brief tenets. However, some of the other fundamentals growing out of the claim of biblical inerrancy do not increase the abstraction of Christian doctrine; rather, they push in the opposite direction by making miracles less metaphorical, by insisting on the material reality of events in Christ's life, resurrection, and imminent return. They restore mythic significance to Christian dogma by insisting on the narrative specificity of the Bible—by insisting specifically on the return of Christ within the lifetime of the current generation. The grand delusion of fundamentalism might be said, in short, to reside in the combination of the first fundamental (biblical inerrancy) and the fifth (premillennialism), in the yoking together of dogmatic literalism and mythic eschatology. The insistence on the absolute congruity of narrative and doctrine in the Bible constitutes a radical reconciliation of myth and dogma, and in the process it claims to remove any room for interpretation.

Fundamental Death

Freud was clearly the victim of his own misplaced hope when he wrote, in *The Future of an Illusion* (1927), that "nothing can withstand reason and experience, and the contradiction which religion offers to both is all too palpable,"[15] a hope proved untenable in part by the ability of Christian prophecy to survive the repeated contradiction of experience. Such confident endorsements of reason seem out of place in Freud's work since he was acutely aware that reason is of minimal assistance to the subject confronted by the indifference of time and space; having studied so thoroughly the experience of helplessness in childhood and trauma, Freud knew the power of the compensatory fantasies with which reason must contend. "Our god Λόγος [Logos] is perhaps not a very almighty one, and he may only be able to fulfill a small part of what his predecessors have promised," he acknowledged, also in *Future of an Illusion*, with the telling deification of reason failing to counterbalance the apology for what reason cannot accomplish. Another statement of this god's limitations appears in the last lecture of the *New Introductory Lectures on Psycho-Analysis* (1933), where Freud defines *Weltanschauung* as "an intellectual construction which solves all the problems of our existence" and which "leaves no question unanswered and in which everything that interests us finds its fixed place."[16] Psychoanalysis, he asserts, belongs to science, with its incomplete worldview. According to his definition, however, an incomplete worldview is no worldview at all.

Freud adopted varying attitudes toward the awkward gap between the present needs of the individual and the unfulfilled promise of psychoanalysis as a branch of science. He concludes *New Introductory Lectures on Psycho-Analysis* by distancing himself from "any of our fellow-men" seeking the "momentary consolation" of a *Weltanschauung*: "We shall not grudge it him, we cannot help him, but nor can we on his account think differently."[17] Yet in *Future of an Illusion*, where he acknowledges that religion arises from "the difficulty of finding one's bearings in the world," he momentarily counts himself among those who remain unconsoled by the god *logos*: "Our God, Λόγος, will fulfill whichever of these wishes [for "the love of man and the decrease of suffering"] nature outside us allows, but he will do it very gradually, only in the unforeseeable future, and for a new generation of men. He promises no compensation for us, who suffer grievously from life."[18] Despite such moments of understanding for the individual in need of more than *logos* can presently offer, *The Future of an Illusion* is Freud's least satisfying work on religion and civilization precisely because of its strong faith in the inexorable progress of reason. This Enlightenment view that history progresses from *mythos* to *logos* was not in evidence in 1920, when he entertained precisely the opposite position: all drives are inherently conservative, he speculated, and any evidence of a drive toward change and progress (*Fortschritt*) is deceptive.

Beyond the Pleasure Principle remains a more compelling document than *The Future of an Illusion* by not commenting on religion so much as mirroring it. It provides the sort of myth Freud elsewhere claims psychoanalysis must forgo, connecting the subject to stories of origin and end, filling time and space with significance. Reading in the repetition compulsion a desire to return to earlier states of being, Freud arrives at the notion of a drive in all living substance to return to nonexistence, to our original, inorganic state:

> It would be in contradiction to the conservative nature of the drives [*Triebe*] if the goal of life were a state of things which had never yet been attained. On the contrary, it must be an *old* state of things, an initial state from which the living entity has at one time or other departed and to which it is striving to return by the circuitous paths along which its development leads. If we are to take it as a truth that knows no exception that everything living dies for *internal* reasons—becomes inorganic once again—then we shall be compelled to say that "*the aim of all life is death*" and, looking backwards, that "*inanimate things existed before living ones.*"[19]

Life, then is a circuitous path, a process of "ever more complicated *détours*" on the return home to nonexistence. Freud's speculation essentially transforms the odyssey myth into a "universal endeavor" of all living substance. Partly a response to the war, this turn to myth opened a new phase in psychoanalytic thought. Certainly the "death drive," like the "fundamentalist," had a prehistory extending back to before the war: Freud's own theory had long emphasized aggression and the desire to return to earlier states of being, two important aspects of the death drive; the Russian analyst Sabina Spielrein anticipated the concept of the death drive with a similar concept of her own as early as 1911; and Freud opened the way for *Beyond the Pleasure Principle* with "On Narcissism" (1914), which made his earlier dualism of sexual and ego drives problematic. Unlike the neologism "fundamentalist," however, the concept of the death drive represented a dramatic shift within the tradition to which it belongs. Freud maintained his dualism in a radically different form by now opposing Eros to Thanatos rather than to the ego drives.

Freud's newly discovered Thanatos is "the first drive [*Trieb*]," prior to and in a sense more fundamental than Eros. At the same time, the drive "to return to the quiescence of the inorganic world" is itself quiescent, working "unobtrusively," revealing itself only in contaminated form, producing no unequivocal signs. As Freud writes in *The Ego and the Id* (1923), "We are driven to conclude that the death drives [*Todestriebe*] are by their nature mute and that the clamour of life proceeds for the most part from Eros."[20] Hence the avowedly—and necessarily—speculative character of *Beyond the Pleasure Principle* and the fact that Freud's story of the conflict between Eros and Thanatos is, like all myth, subject to reception and revision, as he readily admits. The quiescence of both death and the death drive ensures that Freud's metapsychology can have no sacred text. Therefore, no "literal" or dogmatic reading of the death drive is possible; Freud's myth is antidogmatic. When death is understood as the fundament of life, fundamentalism is dead.

In precluding literalism and dogmatism, the notion of the death drive has a number of salutary effects. For example, it weakens the inclination toward exclusionist thought and behavior found in fundamentalism and to a lesser degree in psychoanalysis itself.[21] Any conception of what is normal loses the deepest level of its justification when all living organisms are perceived to be fundamentally abnormal. Critics as different as Harold Bloom and Lacan have observed that Freud's notion of Eros is inherently metaphorical, belated, and pathological in opposition to the mute, antecedent death drive. In other words, Eros, like Thanatos, resists literalism and dogmatism and notions of inerrancy; life consists of nothing but error. Freud uses verbs like disturb, divert, and diverge to describe the emergence of life from inorganic quiescence, our natural state. Ideas central to his thought during this time—concerning the function of Eros in binding people together into groups and the function of the ego-ideal, or superego, in enforcing group norms—suggest ways in which social and sexual roles are constructed and perpetuated. Yet in the concept of the death drive he provides a tool (even if he never made full use of it) to question these roles, to undermine the view that the heterosexual male is the psychological and sexual norm. When he is discussing the death drive, his language associates Eros with multiplicity rather than conformity and exclusion: he speaks of the "colorful variety of life's phenomena" as well as the "clamour of life."

Freud did not himself fully exploit the various implications of the new concept—the myth—he presented in 1920. In part this is because he continued to see psychoanalysis as a science limping toward its goal, a science unwilling and unable to provide what religious belief provides. The penultimate sentence in *Beyond the Pleasure Principle* attempts to deflect the pressure to match or replace religion: "only believers, who demand that science shall be a substitute for the catechism they have given up, will blame an investigator for developing or even transforming his views."[22] Yet it is precisely as a response to such pressure that the concept of the death drive gains its interest and effectiveness. Shortly before this conclusion, Freud mischievously and defensively raises the question of his own belief (*Glaube*) and stops just short of inviting the reader to associate him with the devil:

> It may be asked whether and how far I am myself convinced of the truth of the hypotheses that have been set out in these pages. My answer would be that I am not convinced myself and that I do not seek to persuade other people to believe in them. There is no reason, as it seems to me, why the emotional factor of conviction should enter into this question at all. It is surely possible to throw oneself into a line of thought and to follow it wherever it leads out of simple scientific curiosity, or, if the reader prefers, as an *advocatus diaboli*, who is not on that account himself sold to the devil.[23]

Throughout his subsequent work, Freud would attempt to preserve this distinction between conviction and scientific inquiry. He pretends, as in this passage, to suspend the question of belief in relation to the death drive, and yet all of his subsequent work may be seen as devil's advocacy because this new theory of drives is never overturned or superseded. He acknowledges that deep-rooted prejudices make impartiality elusive when ultimate things are concerned, and *Beyond the Pleasure Principle* gains its power by shedding scientific impartiality, not by preserving it. Precisely because it responds to "daemonic" forces with the "emotional factor of conviction," Freud's metapsychology rises to the level of myth, and it remains perpetually open to development and transformation for this reason, not because it is incomplete.

As a myth, Freud's metapsychology is tempered by the reality principle to a far greater extent than fundamentalism and many other mythical constructs. In its respect for reality, it may risk at times providing too little or no consolation, allowing its adherents to succumb to the sort of pessimism found in *Civilization and Its Discontents* (1925). Even in the best of circumstances, it cannot provide the same satisfactions for the individual as fundamentalism: the certainty of dogma, the fantasy of revenge, the privilege of election, the conquest of death. But these fundamentalist delusions carry with them the frustration of never quite being realized, of always waiting just around the corner. A metapsychology grounded on the death drive offers the satisfaction of addressing our relation to ultimate things at the present moment, inviting us to embrace the heresy of momentary presence under the reign of ultimate absence. Its substitute god is not *logos* but Death, a god ubiquitous and fearsome enough to send us into the arms of his adversary, life. If Freud's discovery of the conservative nature of the drives, like premillennialism, announces the end of all hope for progress, the divergence of premillennialism and psychoanalysis on teleological questions can be summed up best in the observation that for the premillennialists the end cannot come soon enough, for Freud it must be deferred as long as possible. What he says of the individual might apply to the group: "the organism wishes to die only in its own fashion,"[24] as part of an internal process, and thus the drive for self-preservation works to prevent any shortcuts on the circuitous path to death. To those able to embrace a life contaminated by Thanatos, a clamor always weighted with silence—to those relinquishing hope in a reversal of fortune as dramatic as the rapture—Freud's myth can also lend a certain significance to the life of the individual. The proposition that quiescence is all that awaits us—and that we in fact desire an eventual return to quiescence—can have an invigorating effect, throwing life into sharper relief, quickening Eros.

Trees, Pain, and Beyond: Freud on Masochism

Branka Arsić

Freud was fundamentally opposed to many things: letting himself be analyzed, quitting smoking, Reik's theory of acoustic personality, allowing a prostitute any sexuality other than the polymorphously perverse, tolerating use of cocaine for any reason other than pain management. The list is too long. But if there is one thing on it that assumes a privileged position, if there is one thing, that is, to which he was opposed in a fundamentalist way—by which I mean that he interpreted it almost in bad faith and for doctrinaire reasons—it is, I will propose, masochism.

As will become progressively clearer in what follows, the question of masochism is not just one among many. For Freud, it is the question upon which the status of psychoanalytic discourse (the sustainability of its principles, its coherence) depends. For masochism falls back on another programmatic fundamentalist claim of psychoanalysis, namely that "what decides the purpose of life is simply the programme of the pleasure principle."[1] The program imposed by this principle is, however, rather vague. Strictly speaking, it says only that life wants to enjoy itself, but it does not specify what kind of enjoyment is pleasurable. Everything else: that enjoyment excludes pain; that pleasure is wanted by the ego; that whenever the ego welcomes suffering it has to be called perverted; and, quite simply, the whole idea of the psychic economy of pain and pleasure is less in the program of pleasure than in the doctrine of psychoanalysis of the Freudian type.

According to that doctrine—which Freud announces by calling it "simply the program"—pain and suffering come from the outside (bad reality), for neither the id nor the ego wants them. Understanding that pain is unavoidable the personal life (which is another name for the ego) "calculates" that it is better to sustain it; or else it endures it thanks to cocaine; or finds its way to live with it by developing various more or less pathological symptoms. Those "calculations" aim at warding off pain to the point of disguising it as something else (a symptom) so that the ego gets the idea that no matter what kind of trade is going on between it and reality it always obtains pleasure. Masochism—a certain noneconomical attitude toward pleasure—disturbs this calculus and unpleasingly complicates things.

If one remembers that psychoanalysis is used to ambivalences and that various threats to the "stability" of thinking are its exclusive interest, then to advance the thesis that psychoanalysis is threatened by masochism is to propose that the openness of psychoanalysis toward uncertainties presumes that something like masochism is not possible. For if it is possible, the whole economy of our psyche crumbles under the force of a phenomenon that puts the very existence of commerce into question. That is the paradox Freud encounters time and again: masochism does exist, and yet no matter how he tried to analyze it, it always appeared as a psychic phenomenon without economy, hence, unanalyzable.

If, however, a psychic phenomenon exists that cannot be read because it contradicts the very idea of (psychic) life, then it is possible—and that is a disturbing consequence that Freud had to face—that everything we know about the economy of psychic life is affected by what we cannot know. Everything then swims and risks drowning in the oceanic confusion of terms and promiscuity of meanings.

Definitions Full of Wonder

Freud's discontent with masochism is already visible in *Three Essays on the Theory of Sexuality* (1905). There it is placed in a class to which it does not belong. Masochism is classified as a perversion but perversions are then shown to be perversely economical and as such based on a logic that cannot account for it.

Sadism seems to be a nice clean perversion, hence, not a problem (for thinking and for analyzing). A sadist is, basically, a control freak in the business of protecting his own Ego. He thus exaggerates only what we all want: to subjugate another and to crush her resistance: "The sexuality of most male human beings contains an element of *aggressiveness*—a desire to subjugate; the biological significance of it seems to lie in the need for overcoming the resistance of the sexual object by means other than the process of wooing. Thus sadism would correspond to an aggressive component of the sexual instinct which has become independent and exaggerated and, by displacement, has usurped this leading position."[2]

This genealogy of sadism, which understands it to be a perversion that grows on the tree of normalcy, suggests that a certain ideological a priori guides the classification of perversions. For they are classified on the basis of their closeness to normalcy understood as the practice of "enlarging" one's Ego at the expense of another. In other words, maintaining "normalcy" is understood to be an aggressive activity, a cruelty that can "normally" lead to the infliction of pain. By extending the tendency to master the other, the sadist would merely embody a "normal" fantasy of the master who never fails (absolute lordship outside of the dialectic that turns him into an inane character). As an exaggeration of the common desire to subjugate, sadism would be something like a rhetorical embellishment, a litotes of the literal desire to overcome the resistance of others, the poetics of prosaic subjection.

Freud insists that things are far more obscure when it comes to masochism. One of the reasons for such vagueness is the confusion of "life" instincts with psychic interests, which were in conformity in the case of sadism, where the psychic economy follows the interest of life itself. Here, however, the confusion of the two brings about a confusion of the body with the mind. Freud is aware of this blurred distinction and blames it on Krafft-Ebing; for Krafft-Ebing seems to suggest that masochism is not only "the pleasure in *pain*," but also "the pleasure in any form of humiliation or subjection." In other words, Krafft-Ebing refers to masochism both as "passive flagellation" and as enjoyment of symbolic scenes of punishment and subjection (his terms are "symbolic" masochism and "ideal" masochism, and they are similar to what Freud will later come to call "moral" or "secondary" masochism), thus suggesting that the masochist does not have to enjoy the pain inflicted on the body but can suffer the ideal or the symbolic.[3]

The fact that such a possibility disorients Freud's argument suggests at least two things:

1. As early as 1905 Freud was convinced that pain has to be physical and that, in the final analysis all suffering is or has to be reducible to bodily sensation; hence, that there is no difference between suffering and pain. The thesis will be clearly formulated much later, in *Civilization and Its Discontents* where Freud discusses three sources of suffering or unhappiness: from our own body; from the external world; from our relations to other men. The fact that the "suffering which comes from this last source is perhaps more painful to us than any other,"[4] signals that psychic suffering can be more painful than physical. The suggestion is, however, negated by the argument advanced in the very next paragraph where Freud claims that "in the last analysis, all suffering is nothing else than sensation; it only exists in so far as we feel it, and we only feel it in consequence of certain ways in which our organism is regulated."[5] Thus, pain is the same thing as suffering; it is always physical and related to our organs. By extension, all psychic pain—if there is such a thing—would have to be tied to the body and its organs (for example, thoughts would be the pain of the brain).

The insight is dangerous, inasmuch as it subverts the very power of psychoanalysis insofar as the most effective way to deal with such a pain is not through the language of analysis but with "chemicals": "the crude, but also the most effective among these methods of influence is the chemical one—intoxication. I do not think that anyone completely understands its mechanism, but it is a fact that there are foreign substances which, when present in the blood or tissues, directly cause us pleasurable sensations."[6] If pain, including psychological pain, is always physical, then completely understood, cocaine is the best way to deal with it: psychoanalysis has to go pharmaceutical (unless it is to become something like yoga, the second effective palliative strategy listed by Freud).[7]

2. If, all pain is thought to be physical and organic then, to come back to the argument of the *Three Essays*, not only will enjoyment in "humiliation" not be (or should not be) called enjoyment of pain but also, more important, no such thing as pleasure in pain should be possible because it would negate the difference between organs and thoughts. What is more, and to the extent that our psychic life has a fundamental interest in staying alive, it should not enjoy a physical pain that negates the organs, sublates forms, and so contradicts life.

As an "attitude" in contradiction to life, masochism already points to its crucial difference from sadism. If sadism is the exaggerated aggressivity of the "normal" sexual instincts (which is how Freud accounts for its "biological significance"), then masochism would not just be a question of the way psychic life deviates from instinctual life but would be a deviation of life from itself. A perversion somehow performed by life.

For Freud the term masochism "comprises any passive attitude towards sexual life and the sexual object."[8] Thus, whereas sadism is said to be an attitude of sexual life, masochism is defined as an attitude toward sexual life. But the attitude of whom or of what? The attitude of the masochistic ego withdrawn from its sexuality (hence asexual), or the attitude of life itself acquired by its self-reflexive doubling? In both cases it would require a gesture of mirroring (or self-splitting), which, since it is by definition an "act," would have to end up in an active relation to itself. Freud doesn't seem to be proposing any of these possibilities. The passive attitude he has in mind is less an active attitude insisting on its passivity than a certain passivity regarding attitudes as well as events.

For the curious thing about the masochist is that he doesn't in fact appear to be involved in the economy of pain; he does not develop the strategy of being exposed to it looking for the pleasure in it, seeking its "best value." Rather, he is simply exposed (and exposed to the absence of pain too); his attitude is therefore one of come what may, "whatever." In what Freud calls the "extreme instance" of masochistic perversion (which is only the logical consequence of its passive attitude toward sexual life) "satisfaction is conditional upon suffering physical or mental pain at the hands of the sexual object," which is why, as he immediately clarifies, "masochism, in the form of a perversion, seems to be further removed from the normal sexual aim than its counterpart."[9]

What makes masochism more perverse than any other perversion is that in not doing anything to satisfy its desire, it posits a perversion that does not act, whereas the acting of a perverse desire toward its satisfaction is precisely what, according to Freud, differentiates perversion from neurosis. One cannot even employ here the (otherwise always helpful) Hegelian way of thinking and propose that it is in not acting that the masochists acts, being exposed to the pain of waiting because that is precisely what Freud denies: the satisfaction of the masochistic desire is conditional upon the other. It is not that the masochist finds its pleasure in the strategies of self-mediation; to the contrary, his satisfaction is conditioned by the other, and for that reason it may not arrive. Thus, masochism is passivity toward its own perversity, too. It is a perversion that does not have to be, which makes it far more abnormal than sadism.

This stance toward its own standing signals another important difference between sadism and masochism. The gesture of sadism is territorial and topological, which is why Freud describes it by means of spatial tropes:

"thus sadism would correspond to an aggressive component of the sexual instinct which has become independent and exaggerated and, by displacement, has usurped the leading position."[10] Aggressivity is as if extracted from the sexual instinct where it can get confused with the other ingredients, relocated, encircled and enlarged in order to now "lead." Sadism is the work of separation and thus is in love with boundaries. It is perversely identitarian.

Masochism is not much into identities at all (for it is not even into the labor of identifying itself as perversion). It blurs genres (is oblivious of genders, being interested in the deformation of organs), substitutes time for space (waiting, suspension, failure is preferred to the dislocation of the sadist), chance or event for the safety of territory, and arrival or surprise for the standing still of a sadist. It is elusive, slippery, unidentifiable. It is a mixing of genres that pains both psychoanalysis and literary criticism.

In disturbing the very logic of perversion, masochism troubles the whole distribution of psychopathological genres established by psychoanalysis, for example the distinction between perversion and neurosis. In order to avoid action, the neurotic turns himself into a ceaseless labor of writing for his symptoms are "substitutes—transcriptions as it were—for a number of emotionally cathected mental processes, wishes, and desires, which, by the operation of a special psychical procedure (repression), have been prevented from obtaining discharge in psychical activity."[11] In contrast to the neurotic who finds a "substitute" for reality to be a good enough reality, the pervert transgresses the distinction between text and act. He wants the real thing, which is to say that the difference between the neurotic and the pervert thus amounts to a difference between two ontologies (the reality of the symptom as opposed to the reality of the act). Neurotics are "saved" perverts because they remain in the domain of textuality, whereas perverts sink into its referentiality. In other words, neurotics do things with words whereas perverts do things with things. That is why Freud defines the distinction as the difference between "positive" and "negative:" "neuroses are, so to say, the negative of perversions."[12]

But no sooner is that classification established than masochism subverts it. For in reading neurotic textuality psychoanalysis discovers that the sexual instinct of psychoneurotics is in fact driven by "the perversion:" "An especially prominent part is played as factors in the formation of symptoms in psychoneuroses by the component instincts, which emerge for the most part as pairs of opposites and which we have met with as introducing new sexual aims—the scopophilic instinct and exhibitionism and the active and passive forms of the instinct for cruelty."[13] The thesis is confused for being based on the term "component instinct," which (as the editor notes) appears here for the first time and precedes its own definition. It seems, then, that the neuroses would be an assemblage of instincts (from which perversions are formed). In that case, instead of being a symptomatic transcription of "instincts," or desires, neuroses would, somehow manifest the "literal" itself, the instinct, which would negate their specificity and come close to the perverse claim that there is no such thing as neurosis. In order to save neuroses Freud introduces a curious definition for instincts, and as a result Freudian reading shows its own deeply neurotic symptomatology: it has to save the possibility of neuroses after almost collapsing into perversion.

According to this new determination, instincts are both mental and physical. They cannot be purely physical, for that would turn neuroses and perversions also into something purely physical, something like tissue degeneration or an ulcer. On the other hand, a purely psychic instinct is a contradiction in terms, and, more importantly, in that case neither perversion nor neuroses would have anything to do with instinctual life. A confusion arises: "The simplest and likeliest assumption as to the nature of instincts would seem to be that in itself an instinct is without quality. . . . What distinguishes the instincts from one another and endows them with specific qualities is their relation to their somatic sources and their aims."[14] Instincts are close to Musil's understanding of a petty middle-class man (they are without qualities); their qualities come, however, not from the psyche but from the body and its aims. A body with differentiated aims (but how the aims are differentiated without instincts remains obscure) establishes the difference between instincts that are otherwise perversely confused and formless. Formed and separated instincts would thus function as somatic representations of the body's goals.

But that is not what Freud says. He claims the opposite. Instincts are differentiated by the body but are "provisionally to be understood" as the "psychical representative of an endosomatic . . . source of stimulation."[15] Obviously this solution does not solve the problem, for it is unclear how psychic representations (called instincts) can be reconciled with somatic aim (called instincts). The dualism is still there. And because it is far from clear (even to Freud himself) what instincts are, where they come from, and what they represent, he proposes a curious definition which is supposed to miraculously link our minds to our bodies. The proposal is a kind of "emergency" solution to the Cartesian dualism that obviously haunts psychoanalysis, but the solution is so strange that it faces psychoanalysis with its own psychoses for—psychotically enough—it forces it to substitute words for things. The instincts are now defined as concepts and the concepts are turned into things inhabiting the space between psyche and body: "The concept of instinct is thus one of those lying on the frontier between the mental and the physical."[16] It is as if Louis Wolfson rather than Freud were providing the definition of instincts, for the concept of instinct is said not to reside in the psyche at all; concepts are not mental, but somehow "lie on the frontier" between mental and the physical. Between our bodies and our minds lie those strange bodies called concepts.

How does this definition of instincts affect Freud's understanding of neuroses and perversions? Neuroses are said to be assemblages of those strange thing-word instincts, which, in Freud, for some reason always emerge in couples: scopophilic instinct with exhibitionism, and the "active and passive forms of the instinct for cruelty."[17] But even though all perversions are perverse, masochism assumes a privileged position in the formation of neuroses. For it is the contribution made by the last of these [passive forms of the instinct for cruelty]," one that "is essential to the understanding of the fact that symptoms involve *suffering*, and it almost invariably dominates a part of the patient's social behavior."[18]

Masochism—now determined as the passive instinct for suffering cruelty without the existence of such an instinct ever being identified— "almost invariably dominates" the social behavior of neurotics. To say that neurotics both suffer and enjoy their suffering in their social behavior is, however, to suggest that they suffer while acting the suffering; their enjoyment would be based on the actions of suffering and would thus have to be counted as a form of a masochistic perversion. Neurotics would be transgressors.

Short Steps to Humble Subjection

Psychoanalytical classifications are further threatened—and psychoanalysis exposed to a strange ethical dilemma—once hypnosis shows that the technique of analysis capitalizes on the masochism of neurotics: "In this connection I cannot help recalling the credulous submissiveness shown by a hypnotized subject toward his hypnotist. This leads me to suspect that the essence of hypnosis lies in an unconscious fixation of the subject's libido on the figure of the hypnotist, through the medium of the masochistic components of the sexual instinct."[19] The very phenomenon that opposes the idea of the psychic economy is now shown to be necessary for the economy of hypnosis used by the analyst to enact the transfer; what escapes the economy is what makes the economy of psychoanalytic exchange possible. This is also to say that in order for the analyst to be able to hypnotize the subject, the subject has to be hypnotized already; before hypnosis there has to be hypnosis, the mystical writing inscribing its text into the unconsciousness of the patient, seducing him. When his libido is so fixated, the patient can translate the libidinal investment (the "literal") into the figural (into the "figure of the hypnotist" as Freud puts it). In so doing, the patient substitutes the word (the figure or the symptom) for his body (for example, desire and its satisfaction) and from then on he will submissively suffer this uneconomical substitution. Thanks to the masochistic components of the sexual instinct the figure of the analyst can perform the role of the symptom necessary for treatment of the symptoms. Psychoanalysis depends on the successful inducing of neurotic suffering in order to treat it, or more precisely, it finds its condition of possibility in the masochistic components of the sexual instinct.

The hypnotized person (here playing the role of the masochist in love with the analyst) will reappear later in *Group Psychology and the Analysis of the Ego*, only this time as an ordinary person in love. In *Group Psychology* Freud will determine that "from being in love to hypnosis is evidently only a short step. The respects in which the two agree are obvious. There is the same humble subjection, the same compliance, the same absence of criticism toward the hypnotist as toward the loved object. There is the same sapping of the subject's own initiative; no one can doubt that the hypnotist has stepped into the place of the ego ideal."[20] Love is the experience of humble subjection and the enjoyment of that subjection (just like being hypnotized is or being analyzed). And if (as psychoanalysis teaches) one falls in love because one loves love itself, then it follows that what one actually loves about it is submission, pain and suffering. One is in love with a peculiar type of passivity that borders on self-negation ("the sapping of one's own initiative"); one is in love with masochism. It is at this point that psychoanalysis faces the disaster of its classifications; for not only are neurotics perverts, but also everybody is a pervert, at least to the extent that everybody can fall in love.

The feature that loving, being analyzed, and being hypnotized share with masochism is "self-negation," or perhaps even the sacrifice of the ego. They are, of course, not quite the same experiences. One might rightly say that in both loving and being analyzed only part of the ego is sacrificed. But since Freud insists that being in love is separated from being hypnotized only by one "short step," then there always lurks the possibility of being delivered to total—masochistic—self-abandonment. This is a disturbing outcome for at least a couple of reasons.

1. The ordinary experience of being in love (such is the presupposition of common sense reasoning) should be in concord with the interests of the ego (since everybody loves or wants to be able to). The fact that the experience is so common (or normal) suggests that the interests of the ego should be those of the life instincts, of which love is only a manifestation. Love and ego working in support of each other equals "self-love," which explains the ontological primacy given to it in Freud's account of things. Thus, "self-love" comes first and "works for the preservation of the individual."[21] Love is always personal and conservative.

Love for others (persons and things) is what limits otherwise limitless self-love ("Love for oneself knows only one barrier—love for others, love for objects"[22]). Always faithful to spatial and territorial tropes, Freud insists that the ego finds its barrier in its love for others. Love for another is thus an interior force of self-crafting; it delineates the space, borders, and territory occupied by the ego and confirms the barrier of personal identity. Thus, it again serves the interests of self-preservation. According to this logic, once love for another becomes threatening to the ego, self-love should counteract in order to maintain the preservation. However, if in falling in love one can "always" lose one's ego, then it could be—could it not?—that the interest of life somehow runs counter to the interest of the ego.

2. If the loss of the ego is the interest of life (which then corresponds to the aims of masochistic perversion), then masochism is not a perversion; rather, the ego with its goals could be seen as a perversion of the normal egoless life (and the psychoanalytic imperative "where the It was the I should be" could be seen as a version of such a perversion).

Certain Animals, Humans, and Masochists

The essay "On Narcissism" (1914), one may claim, was supposed to answer some of the questions that will reappear in the "Group Psychology." In it, Freud had famously differentiated various forms of love and self-love. Perhaps the most important achievement of that essay, I am proposing, is in its effort to ward off, albeit tacitly, the dangerous subversive effects of the masochistic perversion.

At first sight, the distinction between ego-libido and object libido, to which Freud dedicates most of the discussion in that essay, seems to confirm early theses—from the "Three Essays"—and so to reinforce with what psychoanalysis had claimed about ego, love and selflessness up to that point. "We see also, broadly speaking, an antithesis between ego-libido and object-libido. The more of the one is employed, the more the other becomes depleted. The highest phase of development of which object-libido is capable is seen in the state of being in love, when the subject seems to give up his own personality in favour of an object-cathexis."[23] That one loses one's self in love is thus reasserted; love is still affirmed as an experience of selflessness, as the loss of personality and the process through which the ego becomes an object.[24] However, this time, the becoming object of the ego is seen as a type of self-loss that is narcissistic rather than masochistic. In this way, far from being a perversion, self-abandonment appears as a version of the ways in which the ego manages to reassert itself.

The loss of the ego in objects is now declared not to be the objectifying of the ego but the ego-becoming of objects. For sexual energy can be differentiated only on the basis of the object-cathexis (it is now persons who give form or birth to sexual energy and so form our "personal" aims): "not until there is object-cathexis is it possible to discriminate a sexual energy—the libido—from an energy of the ego-instincts." The very existence of the ego instinct (its distinction from object-cathexis) thus depends on the objects. If, however, there must be an object for the ego to exist then the object is constituted by an egoless sexual energy. There are two ways of understanding this process. One may say that both the object and the ego are only provisional formations of the impersonal (nondifferentiated "sexual energy"); or else one may say that even though the ego depends on the object to differentiate its instinct, it is nevertheless the ego that recognizes the object, which is why every object has to be narcissistic. According to Borch-Jacobsen, Freud opted for the second reading. As the former puts it, "up to now, the term libido has designated the sexual instinct *understood as desire for an object*. . . . At this point, even when I desire an object, it is myself that I desire in it. The object is a *narcissistic object*."[25]

However, as Borch-Jacobsen also suggests, "to say that ego libido manifests itself only by transforming itself into object libido is also to say that it can only be posited as transgressing the limits of the experience in which it is concealing itself from the start."[26] This is to say that in construing the ego in the way analogous to the way he produced the "pervert"—as a transgressor—Freud again faces the collapse of the oppositional divide he wanted to preserve in order to preserve the ego. The differentiation between the ego and its loss in the life of desire is now blurred by the very difference between ego and object-oriented libido. Like the passive masochistic ego that loses itself in the other (as if it were hypnotized or in love), the narcissistic ego vanishes in objects, now claimed to be its "narcissistic realm." And so it seems that the masochistic loss of the ego in the other becomes but a version of the narcissistic loss of the ego in the object-self. What is gained by this conceptual shift is not the ego but another possibility of thinking about the loss of the self, whereas Freud wants to preserve the ego.

Freud himself recognizes the ruse of his logic: "A strong egoism is a protection against falling ill, but in the last resort we must begin to love in order not to fall ill, and we are bound to fall ill if, in consequence of frustration, we are unable to love."[27] The choice seems to be bleak: either the illness of the ego, which works against its preservation, or its loss in the other.

Freud will thus introduce an elaborate distinction among narcissistic objects in order to multiply the ego's choices and so increase its chances. But there he will encounter another dualism: that between the need to preserve the ego and an ethics that values selfless love, which he wants to support. On one hand, it is necessary to recover narcissism (outline the firm limits of personal identity, thus differentiating the "normal" ego from the perverted one). On the other hand, and in spite of the interests of the ego, Freud will "morally" condemn the "narcissistic type of love," and that on the basis of its being narcissistic, which will come to mean—inhuman.

Human beings, Freud claims, are differentiated from animals on the basis of their original possibility to chose among two sexual objects, themselves and a nurse: "We say that a human being has originally two sexual objects—himself and the woman who nurses him, and in doing so we are postulating a primary narcissism in everyone."[28] Animals, ungrateful to their nurses, go on loving only themselves. But the species divide does not seem to be unbridgeable, since there are certain human beings whose humanity will be disqualified on the basis of their bestiality, that is because of the way they love. The "narcissistic type of love" does not make a shift from the self to the nurse in order to get attached to her, but remains fascinated by itself. It is practiced by perverts and inverts who "take as a model not their mother but their own selves," and by femmes fatales who "strictly speaking," says Freud, love "only themselves . . . with an intensity comparable to that of the man's love for them."[29] They are, Freud concludes, like certain "animals which seem not to concern themselves about us."[30]

But this psychology based on an ad hoc discourse of species now confronts Freud with even greater difficulty. For the whole process of recovering the ego ends up in finding it in animals. "Animals" become the model for the perfect ego: detached, self-centered, indifferent to others, nonvulnerable, an ideal of non-object-oriented narcissism. Animals (at least "certain" animals) are perfect humans, which Freud cannot say (as that would be against his "humanistic"/egoistic ethics).

He thus has to celebrate the other type of love, the human, by attachments, the perfect example of which is a man who loses himself in the woman who does not love him (for she is precisely like a certain animal). Passively entrusting himself to her and giving himself over to her cold and catlike charm, the attached man ends badly, like a dominated masochist. In the words of Borch-Jacobsen, narcissism "finds satisfaction in submission, in that peculiar 'voluntary servitude' that submits it to *itself* in the figure of the Lady. (But is that Lady, that *domina*, still a woman? Are we not faced with *domination* pure and simple, prior to any sexual characterization?)"[31]

The consequence of the analysis Freud undertakes in "On Narcissism" is a double bind: either one is an animal who may not be lost to itself but is lost to humans/humanity, or one subjects oneself to another in order to become attached, communal, ethical; either an animal and morally questionable detachment or a morally but psychologically unacceptable self-loss.

A whole series of troublesome questions arise here. If in the experience of masochistic perversion one loses one's self (in a more exaggerated but structurally similar way to the experience of love and hypnosis), then such a perversion could be seen not as a desire to enjoy pain but as a desire to "get lost," to die. On the other hand, if a desire to lose oneself is the way that life lives (as in love), then life itself might want its own death. This then puts in jeopardy the principal "a priori" category of psychoanalysis according to which the successful constitution of the ego is the "great health" of psychic life. The ethical aspect of the same dilemma is equally disturbing: if we have to support "human" ethics then we have to buy into something that is dangerously close to masochism. It is this series of questions that blurs the distinction between ontology, biology, and ethics that *Beyond The Pleasure Principle* wants to answer.

The Dead Turn

The double stance of the essay's argument (it is about both psychic life and what is beyond it) concords with the major confession on which the essay is based, namely, that psychoanalysis does not aim at any unity or mediation between mind and body but rests on a "straightforward" dualism of the Cartesian type. Dualism, not always quite clear up to this point (for, after all, the conscious could have been understood as a form of unconscious, and passivity in exposure to death as a form of life), becomes from now on the fundamental economy of metapsychology: "Our views have from the very first been *dualistic*, and today they are even more definitely dualistic than before—now that we describe the opposition as being not between ego-instincts and sexual instincts, but between life instincts and death instincts."[32] Everything is hereafter dual.

At stake in this dualism is the thesis that there is a separate existence for death drives, a properly "autonomous" labor of death working against life, in "opposition" to it and thus destroying it. But whenever Freud refers to this divide, it turns out that the dualism cannot be sustained. No matter how skillful the analyst is in going behind the back of life and death, somehow in Thanatos one always finds Eros, and life appears to be everywhere. Thus Eros wins the game but—unacceptedly—in an egoless way.

And so, in order to maintain dualism and to establish a clear distinction between life and death Freud finds himself forced to go ever more backward (toward "beyond"): "let us turn back then." The "back" that he wants to face is the thesis "that all living substance is bound to die from internal causes." Once that "back" is seen, everybody should be convinced of the existence of the death drive. Freud starts off with an anthropological orientation and faces the problem. For to believe in the "internal causes of death" is to believe in "naked" nature, a belief foreign not only to the "civilized" mind but to the primitive men too. Thus, we cannot quite rely on the "internal causes" of natural death for "natural death" is quite foreign to primitive races whose views we have to take into account if we are going back; "they attribute every death that occurs among them to the influence of an enemy or of an evil spirit."[33] Since belief in an "evil spirit" is a sure way not to prove anything, as Descartes's First Meditation testifies, Freud then turns to biology, citing many idiosyncratic sources.[34]

But it is Wilhelm Fliess's version of biology that gets special attention, and it is there that one witnesses a truly delirious moment in Freud's analysis. Fliess's biology refers to the "fact" that "all the phenomena of life exhibited by organisms—and also, no doubt, their death—are linked with the completion of fixed periods, which express the dependence of two kinds of living substance (one male and the other female) upon the solar year."[35] The appearance of two separate "living" substances conditioned by solar years does not seem to be "beyond" enough for Freud, precisely because substances are still alive, and there is no death yet on the horizon.

And so the solar years pass by, with Freud still going backward, moving within a kind of panoramic snapshot of eternity, arriving at the composition of bodies and decomposing them to cells. There, something like a "death" substance appears; there are two types of cells; bodies are made of mortal and immortal cells: "the mortal parts are the body in the narrower sense—the 'soma'—which alone is subject to natural death. The germ-cells, on the other hand, are potentially immortal, in so far as they are able, under certain favorable conditions, to develop into a new individual, or, in other words, to surround themselves with a new soma."[36] It is hard to translate from the language of this psychedelic biology, but it seems that the thesis distinguishes between "cells" that signify (or somehow form?) personalized matter—the body and its organs—and another group of cells which are immortal (something like a material soul), signifying life that keeps on living in its impersonal way. The personalized cells would thus die into a life.

No matter how far back he goes he always finds only life; or, more precisely, he finds that death is a form of life and not vice versa, Thanatos being only the "secondary" characteristic of life, as it were. This would suggest a reversal of his hypothesis: not only that life does not die of internal natural causes but, to the contrary, death has to be enlivened by an internal cause, which is life. Substance is thus one and alive (that is, anti-Cartesian), which clearly contradicts his thesis that there must be a dualistic distinction between life and death. For that reason, the death drive appears not as a theoretical or psychoanalytical concept but as a very mystical thing, a "positively mystical impression." Freud thus finds himself in a strange situation, having introduced concepts whose referents he is unable to trace.

Freud himself suggests that the interpretative situation in which he finds himself could be seen as embarrassing. And in order to find his way out of it, he employs a circular strategy: one of the things that was supposed to be proven by the existence of the death "substance"—masochism as the "originary" force driving life to death; the enjoyment in pain that can lead to destruction of the ego—is now used to prove the existence of the death drive. The "solution" is thus as strange as a "problem" and perhaps even stranger, as there was nothing in the argument advanced in the essay that pointed to masochism suggesting its originarity. Freud is clearly aware that nothing in argument can bridge the gap between solar year, male and female substances and masochism so that its introduction seems quite inexplicable, it even looks suspicious: "this way of looking at things is very far from being easy to grasp and creates a positively mystical impression. It looks suspiciously as though we were trying to find a way out of a highly embarrassing situation at any price."[37]

To demystify that impression, Freud now refers to other "scientific" papers that confirm the existence of the death drive. For he will now claim that he had studied the problem of masochism carefully and was convinced of the existence of the death drive by reading an extraordinary paper by Sabina Spielrein, a very "instructive and interesting paper, which however, is unfortunately not entirely clear to me."[38]

Demystification mystifies, for Freud claims he was enlightened by a paper that remained obscure to him. On the basis of this nonunderstanding—which somehow has to legitimize his position as the subject who knows—he claims that masochism is a destructive instinct, precisely the intrinsic cause of death he has been looking for. For whereas the sadist directs his aggression toward the external object and so preserves his own ego/his mortal cells (sadism appears as a form of the life instincts), the masochist is self-destructive; his instincts act against his ego in order to destroy him. Masochistic life turns upon itself in order to end in death. Such a turning of life upon itself is the action of the death drive: "Masochism, the turning round of the instinct upon the subject's own ego, would in that case be a return to an earlier phase [how many solar years earlier than sadism?] of the instinct's history, a regression. The account that was formerly given of masochism requires emendation as being too sweeping in one respect: there *might* be such a thing as primary masochism—a possibility which I had contested at that time."[39] Described as "a turn," death becomes a trope of life, which transports it beyond itself, into inorganic substance.

But what did Freud not understand in the essay written by his colleague and patient? What part of it was not clear enough?

Depersonalization and the Atmosphere of Pain (Sabina Spielrein)

Freud refers to Spielrein's paper "Destruction as a Cause of Coming Into Being" ("Die Destruktion als Ursache des Werdens," 1912).[40] Like Freud's essay on the death instinct, Spielrein's paper raises questions that transcend psychic economy, for she also treats life as an ontological and biological issue. Thus, in both instances—in Spielrein as well as in Freud—"instinct" sometimes signifies a "substance" and sometimes a biological principle.

The fundamental contrast between Spielrein and Freud is already suggested by the title of her essay. Whereas Freud is after something like "death per se," her main question is about life; more precisely, she focuses on the "moment" of coming into being, on the moment in which one being becomes another. Throughout her discussion, destruction is understood as a process of becoming through overcoming, as a paradoxical moment of destruction that constructs. Destruction is therefore identified as an experience of profound changes in one's identity that aim at its reformation. What she calls destruction is a version of the ancient—Ovid's—theory of metamorphoses. More specifically, her version of that theory of change is, as she herself claims, profoundly affected by Nietzsche's philosophy of metamorphosis; she thus explains the term "destruction" as synonymous with Nietzsche's "overcoming:" "The procreative act *per se* leads to self-destruction. Nietzsche's words illustrate this: 'Man is something that must be overcome,' teaches Zarathustra, 'in order for the superman to appear'. . . . The implication of these sentences is: You must know how to overcome (destroy) yourself. Otherwise, how could you create the highest, the child?"[41] (D, 170).

In Spielrein's understanding, self-destruction functions as an injunction proposed by a kind of a process-ethics; self-negation, which leads one to the brink of thought (the void, abyss, or nothingness), is necessary for becoming. In order to remain ethical, such a thinking—that negates itself in order to give birth to the highest in the self—has to be capable of repeating itself, thus incessantly enacting the overcoming of the self. This, she thinks, is precisely the "abysmal thought of eternal recurrence," which on many occasions threatens to die in Zarathustra, as he is seduced by the possibility of remaining identitarian and protecting his own self. "But he summons it to life," overcoming himself (D, 170). The point she is making by referring to Nietzsche is that self-destruction, like Zarathustra's metamorphosis, leads to the possibility of giving birth to the "artist," or the "child," a man with a different psychic economy: a man beyond revenge and appropriation. Another difference from Freud: she wants to perceive movements, whereas Freud wants to stabilize; or, what in her theory is "transitional"—self-abandonment—in Freud becomes death strangely detached from life; in Freud destruction somehow becomes autonomous.

Destruction as overcoming finds its analogy in biological life. But even when she talks weird biology (the first part of her paper is called "Biological Facts"), she is careful enough to bring it quickly back to the question of the psyche and to the problem of personal identity, which suggests that in her theory biology serves only as an illustration of a psychic economy: "The fusion of germ cells during copulation mimics the correspondingly intimate union of two individuals: a union in which one forces its way into the other. The difference is merely quantitative: it is not the entire individual that is incorporated, but only a part of it, at this instant, represents the essence of the entire organism. . . . An alteration comes over the whole organism; destruction and reconstruction, which under usual circumstances always accompany each other, occur rapidly. . . . It would be highly unlikely if the individual did not at least surmise, through corresponding feelings, these internal destructive-reconstructive events" (D, 157).

This "abrupt" change is only a fast-forwarded version of a rather ordinary process. For change is always diligent and even when imperceptible it destabilizes the whole structure, slowly affecting it so that at some point the changed part becomes the essence of the "whole organism." The organism is always exposed to its own destruction, which gives it a new life and marks the moment of its great health: "no change can take place without destruction of the former condition" (D, 174). Whereas Freud stops at the insight that the dissolution of "soma" cells is the death of the individual, Spielrein continues to follow the path of these now disconnected and disseminated "cells," because she identifies their dissolution with a precious and precarious moment of giving birth to yet another form. Destruction, in her vocabulary is a technical term signifying a twofold moment: a form (in the moment of its deformation), and the formlessness of life.

Ontologically then, her reality is always in transition. She conceives of being less as a substance than as a life in movement: shimmers, waves, intensities. Her image of the mother is not that of a figure or a person; to the Freudian nurse, following Nietzsche, she opposes water: "An ancient view of the mother as the sea (the motherly creative water from which all life springs)" (D, 158). It is also important to note that in Spielrein, water is not a primal organic unity (such as that Freud talks about in response to Romain Rolland, source of the "oceanic feeling") but signifies (inorganic) life as a wavelike drifting or floating on the surface. In other words, the surface of the water (formless life) becomes the image of life that sublates the difference between organic and inorganic. And it is this impersonal water that—because it is undifferentiated—becomes "potentially creative,

and, hence, an eternal living entity" (ibid.). "Eternal life" is depicted as
water that is ignorant of death because whatever dies in the water dies in
the potentiality of all forms. It becomes clear that Freud and Spielrein do
not share the same ontology. Whereas she understands being as becoming
(alive, energized, sexual but not necessarily personal), Freud feels at home
in the dualism of substances, being closer to the Cartesian idea of the
stable *res*.

It is on the basis of this ontology that she proposes a philosophy of
subjectivity that—one can only speculate here—might have seriously dis-
turbed Freud. The second part of her paper ("Individual Psychological
Observations") constitutes the ego as an instance that can be present to
itself only on condition that its thinking and experiences are in the past:
"The statement that we psychically experience very little in the present
strikes us as paradoxical and yet it is correct" (D, 157). The idea that one
cannot experience oneself in the "now" because the now is not self-reflexive is, of course, a major proposal of modern philosophy, from Descartes
on. But in contrast to that tradition, Spielrein does not say that the "I"
has to reflect itself as an image that it would appropriate in order to determine its own existence. Her idea of the "I-relationship" has nothing to do
with mirrors but rather with tonalities and intensities.

The "I" is not self-reflexively present to itself (is not a representation)
but is with itself only by triggering an "affective" memory (her proposal
is closer to Proust's involuntary memory). It is absorbed in the present
by becoming—in the "now"—something like a tone, tonality, quality or
"tinctura" that it once "was:" "An event is feeling-toned for us only to the
extent that it can stimulate previously experienced feeling-toned contents
that now lie hidden in the unconscious. . . . Thus we experience nothing
in the present since we project a feeling-tone onto a current image" (D,
157). But it is this "gesture" of toning the now (the current image) with
the past atmosphere that, paradoxically, adapts the current content (what
is flowing into us) to what has been and so makes the "I"; the "I" becomes
an affective tonality established between a memory and a current image;
only in that way does it fit the present: "Every content appearing in consciousness is a product that differentiates from other, psychologically
older, contents. The content is adapted to the present and contains a specific coloring that endows it with the character of its relation to the ego"
(D, 173). From the thesis that the "I" is an unstable "relationship" between two feeling-toned images rather than a stable form Spielrein's essay
draws, more or less explicitly, many radical consequences.

1. *Thinking.* If the "I" is an "ambiance," an immediacy of "color," then its thinking differs from the self-reflexive or even conceptual thinking. In other words, its thinking is not self-present, which is why both conscious and unconscious thinking have to become versions of an unconscious that is differentiated within itself (the psychic world is made of many layers).

2. *The language of thought.* Nonreflexive thinking thinks in a different language (something important to insist on if one keeps in mind that in Freud even instincts are concepts). Thus we have conscious and unconscious language standing in a relation of analogy to each other, but in the process of translation they lose their substance: "Analogous unconscious thoughts or images accompany every conscious thought or image and transform the products of conscious thought into a specific language. Silberer described this parallel train of thought in states of fatigue" (D, 157). The relationship between conscious and unconscious is one of self-doubling experienced in fatigue; when tired we follow our images or think certain thoughts but without really being engaged in them. That non-engagement—the absence of the feeling tonality, either of pleasure or pain—would characterize a "purely" conscious thought. A conscious self-reflexive subject is therefore always tired (withdrawn, absent).

What follows from this is a reversal of Freud. For in contrast to Freud, Spielrein's thesis suggests that we come to understand something not because we manage to translate it into conscious thought but rather the opposite, by transferring images into depths the unconscious the unconscious makes things "really" felt or understandable. Understanding works by being affected by images, feelings, or words, not through analysis of meaning; only when a "current image" coming from the outside gets successfully translated into the unconscious and "hits" an image existing there do we understand, and we do so from the "depths of our being."

For the unconscious is made of very private images which, of course, we translate into concepts all the time, but those concepts Spielrein calls only "portraits of an image" (D, 164), a phrase that suggests that concepts are also imagistic but too distant from the content to be understood. The ego is therefore a fragile instance that negotiates between obscure images and their conceptual representations.

3. *The pain principle.* If most of our thinking occurs in a "nonreflexive" way—in the form of the "I-relationship"—then pleasure and pain will likely be thought as tonality-images that do not necessarily belong to the ego. In order to name this divide Spielrein establishes a distinction between "pain-image" and "ego-image." The pain image exists in the non-ego consciousness and is not necessarily related to the "I." The evocation

of the "pain-image" "activates an "ego-image," and ego tends to distance itself from it by objectivizing the pain image into an "indifferent thing" (exaggerated and exemplary in dementia praecox, she claims). When the ego does not negate the pain by turning it into an "indifferent thing" but tries to face and cope with it, the pain image will be translated into a less painful word, image or symbol, one that, for not quite being an indifferent object, does not overly damage the "I" (D, 161). This process of handling the pain-image corroborates John Kerr's suggestion: "She grants that the unconscious is the source of pleasure and unpleasure, but she also depicts it as largely indifferent to the ego. Thus, if we view matters from the ego's standpoint, the unconscious does not really proceed purely on the pleasure principle."[42]

More precisely, Spielrein believes that the ego—not the unconscious—wants pleasure but she also insists that the ego is not where the interests of our psychic life reside: "Pleasure is derived from infantile sources. Now, however, we meet the problem of whether our entire psychic life resides in the ego. Do we not possess powerful drives that set our psychic contents in motion, untroubled by the welfare and misery of the ego?" (D, 159). In fact, she offers the answer to this question, in an oblique way, by proposing that the ego fluctuates and does not have steady interests: "Much advocates the idea that the ego is something completely inessential, continually changing, merely a momentary grouping of eternally living elementary sensations" (D, 160). Life—as the rhythm of pain and pleasure—is indifferent to the interests of the ego.

On the other hand, the unconscious that is turned into a rhythmic succession of pain and pleasure becomes a doubled unity for neither pleasure nor displeasure is more originary, both serve the "originary" interest of becoming. The pleasure principle is not the only or even the most important driving force of the psychic economy. But if the unpleasure principle is one of the constitutive moments of the unconscious, then masochistic desire could be seen as constitutive of life interests (rather than being regarded as the moment of transgression that contradicts them, leading life to its opposite, inorganic death).

4. *Depersonalization.* This interpretation is supported by the fact that Spielrein regards the ego, too, as a highly "private" contrivance; it is less private than the unconscious but too private for another ego to understand it, which is why it is in its best interest to depersonalize itself. The ego can be understood by another ego only if it is depersonalized. The process of self-depersonalization—which for Freud is perverted—is thus, according

to Spielrein, not only necessary, but also ordinary, as it conditions the common practice of communicating.

Translated from the obscure unconscious into conscious images, our thoughts are still accessible only to us, toned as they are with the atmosphere of highly private affects. Our self-understanding—thus our identity—is based on a private language. Hence the paradox: to convey that identity to others who can recognize it, we have to make it ever less private: "In each declaration of a thought, which is a portrait of an image, we establish a generalization in which words are symbols, serving to mould universally human and universally comprehensible ideas around the personal, i.e., the impressions are depersonalized. The purely personal can never be understood by others. It is not surprising that Nietzsche, a man of powerful ego-consciousness, concluded that the purpose of language is to entangle itself and others" (D, 164). Personalities are buried in their persons ("the purely personal can never be understood") or else, in order to live, they have to let themselves go on the current of language, which is the force of depersonalization. Even Nietzsche, with his powerful ego-consciousness, gave it up in order to entangle his thoughts with the thoughts of others in the impersonal ocean of language. The tendency of language is thus similar to the tendency of life: both tend "toward assimilation or dissolution."

The person exists only on condition that it depersonalize itself. We are thus in a paradox situation: we exist as the "I," differentiated from others but able to be recognized by them and to be born into the communal existence, only by giving up the private substance the "I" is made of. Such an assimilation does not quite mean that the "I" vanishes but it is put in an awkward situation: "If the personal experience is already transformed into a collective experience, we can only act as a spectator who perceives the experience when it transfers to an image" (D, 174). Everything we convey as ours, by the very act of conveyance, becomes staged. The "I" then becomes an "empty"—feelingless—instance of spectatorship (Spielrein suggests that the experience is similar to what happens in dreams). We are present to our life as if it were happening to others, we watch ourselves being buried in our selves or else living outside, with others but as if in the absence of our selves.

We become present to ourselves when conversing with others, and have to retranslate the content they convey to us back into very private images into which the "I" will sink, feeling itself: "Everything that moves us aims to be felt as important and understood. . . . When this differentiated product enters . . . [the] individual's psyche, a re-transformation occurs. . . . In addition to the conscious processing, the image falls into an unconscious 'working through'" (D,163). But this sinking of the "I" into feeling or tonality is again its depersonalization (the "I" is present to itself only on condition of self-abandonment).

The "I" exists either as a feeling of itself (without specular relation to itself); or as a fluctuating, changeable "I"-relationship that negotiates connections of images and thoughts; or as a thought communicated to others; or as a person (ego) buried in itself. In all cases it is absent from itself, given over to the process of "differentiation or assimilation."

Oaks and Amorous Assimilations

The differentiation process—which Spielrein always couples with assimilation and analyzes through the example of language—could be understood as the moment of individuation that works toward self-preservation. Even though such an understanding is not mistaken it does not account for the whole story. For self-preservation, like the "ego" itself, is a complex phenomenon that sometimes "works" only by subverting what it is supposed to preserve. Thus, similar to the way in which we get recognized by others only through the process of depersonalization, we preserve our "person" not by distancing ourselves from another but by falling in love, by growing closer or becoming another. Losing ourselves in the new "person" made by love attachments is, Spielrein claims, absolutely necessary for the health of the very ego that is nevertheless about to vanish in its own health. The vanishing she has in mind is quite radical; she calls it a "dissolution" of the Ego: "The instinct for preservation of the species, a reproductive drive, expresses itself psychologically in the tendency to dissolve and assimilate (transformation of the I to the We), differentiating a new form of the 'primal substance.' 'Where love reigns, the ego, the ominous despot, dies'" (D, 174). Differentiation (self-preservation) has to lead to the assimilation.

This sounds similar to what Freud had to say about love but is in fact quite different. For not only does Spielrein not see the assimilation as a pathological aspect of love (which would make it comparable to perversions), but she also regards the depersonalization as an ambivalent process (negative and positive at the same time, as she says). It is negative because a particular "I" vanishes; but what makes it desirable or positive is that it helps to strengthen the new ego created by such self-negation: "When one is in love, the blending of the ego in the beloved is the strongest affirmation of self, a new ego existence in the person of the beloved" (ibid.).

She has learned that lesson from Nietzsche. At first sight, his case is paradoxical inasmuch as he appears to be a person of a strong ego: "psychic autoeroticism can be easily studied in Nietzsche, for, throughout his life, his entire libido was turned inward. How did Nietzsche conceive of love, or, more correctly, how did he experience love? Solitude tortured the poet so intensely that he created an ideal friend, Zarathustra, with whom he identified. The longing for a love object forced Nietzsche himself to become man and woman, both residing in the image of Zarathustra" (D, 167). Thus Nietzsche formed a strange triangular couple. He created Zarathustra as a couple so that—remaining faithful to his habit of falling in love with couples—he could be in love with the double Zarathustra. The destructive images embedded in his philosophy (as the series of overcomings) and which correspond to the "pain images" our psyche has to handle, work to enable him to become Zarathustra, that is a "man" whose goal is to overcome himself and become woman in the process of becoming the sea and the earth. Destructive images there function in the service of forcing his ego to let itself go and start traveling from becoming a couple to becoming a woman: "We have, it appears, learned to understand much about Nietzsche. . . . Nietzsche has come to be this 'woman' in that he has identified with the Mother [represented by the love for the "earth" and the "sea"] in whom he can be engulfed" (D, 168). What Freud considered to be a "pathological" or perverted ego—the one that depersonalizes itself in the passivity of love, in masochistic becomings, in the neurotic enjoyment of suffering—is here seen as a process of creative alteration of identity (the Nietzschean becoming earth, sea, child, woman), which, through the process of falling in love, comes to be the very force of depersonalization.

If it is difficult to fall in love, as Spielrein suggests, it is because the ego is afraid of letting itself go, afraid of depersonalization. The fear of depersonalization is twofold: on one hand, it is the effect of a desire to confirm the boundaries of the ego; on the other, it is the fear of the pain of losing oneself and of coming into "new" being. The birth of new forms out of impersonal life is—she refers here to Anaxagoras—the source of pain: "With good reason, Greek philosophers such as Anaxagoras sought the source of *Weltschmerz* in the differentiation of being from primal particles or 'seeds'; this pain results when each seed of our being longs to retransform in its source so that a new coming into being may emerge" (D, 158). Hence, a circular motion of fear and longing: one longs for "new comings into being" that are painful, so one is afraid of what one longs for.

When this fear or when self-protection prevails, love fails. And it is this failure of love (of depersonalization) that now becomes the source of the destructive images. More correctly, love fails because the ego feeds its fear of letting itself go and nourishes its boundaries by producing images of destruction that prolong the fear and block its love attachments: "If love fails, the image becomes one of destruction or death, a psychic or physical alteration in the individual image under the influence of an exceptional power such as the sexual act" (D, 174).

In contrast to Freud, the ego that is not in love (separated, nondissolved, with its boundaries confirmed) represents in Spielrein the victory of death. Whereas he sees the confirmation of the boundaries of the ego as the picture of a "healthy" psychic economy, she sees its power of self-affirmation as the effect of a terrible fear, which makes it lifeless. Unable to love, such an ego is dry (there is no water or ocean in it), empty, ruined: the image of death. As Kerr formulated it: "she argues that *destructive imagery arises as the response of the ego to the threat of dissolution inherent in the sexual instinct*. It is the same threat that triggers repression, which represents the attempt of the ego to preserve itself and ward off the threat of sexual fusion."[43] Afraid of touch and terrified with love, the ego elaborates a torturous imagery; each of the images sends it a message: this can happen to you. As long as it remains afraid of the destruction inherent in love, it stays away from the pain of blending; and it remains assured of its separatedness as long as it can see the images of destruction. The ego does not enjoy the images themselves but the reassuring information that it is keeping itself preserved, untouched by the violence of destruction it sees. It enjoys the fact that the painful dissolution is, precisely, only an image. However, absorbed in the screen of its frightful images, the ego that does not blend necessarily dies from failing to depersonalize; it is outsmarted by its own self-preserving contrivance.

Thus, in order to negate the lethal effect of self-preservation the ego will now have to learn to overcome this fear of depersonalization; it will have to learn how to love and how to lose itself. It is here that masochism/sadism come into play. They are not, as in Freud, conceived of as enjoyment in pain or in infliction of it, but play a positive role by helping the person to act out the fear of letting itself go, thus freeing it for the possibility of losing itself in real closeness with another. Masochism and sadism can help the isolated and fearful ego to free itself of the destructive images by seducing it into acting out its dissolution. By so doing, the ego performs or stages its self-abandonment and discharges its fear. According to Kerr's reading of Spielrein: "Sadism and masochism, too, can be thought of as means of discharging the destructive component so that procreation can go forward."[44]

The point is crucial and marks a fundamental difference from the Freudian version of the masochist as the creepy producer of the images of destruction for his own enjoyment. Here, according to Spielrein's scenario, the destructive images belong not to a perverted Oedipal fantasy but to the self-protective ego, and masochism is seen as the practice through which such an ego learns to free itself from the imagery of pain, by exposing itself to pain. This pain is not, of course, enjoyable; what is enjoyable to the ego is the fact that it sees its capacity of sustaining the pain, its power to lose itself and so to regenerate itself. Neither masochism nor sadism is, therefore, a destructive perversion but the power of creation. More correctly, they correspond to the destructive aspects of the sexual instinct—to the process of assimilation—but because such a process is necessary for becomings and overcomings they are conceived of as powers of creation. This is a reversal of Freudianism as from this point of view they help the destructive ego—here called destructive because it does not want to fuse—to heal itself. They are thus the power of succor in the service of life, understood as strategies by which the ego teaches itself how to let itself go in order to learn how to love.

But is there a difference between sadism and masochism? The difference is profound and is related to different ways in which man and woman subjectivize themselves. As in Freud, women have a less straightforward path toward their femininity, but the path is fundamentally different from the one he proposed. Woman becomes a woman—without ever "simply" being born one—through a complex process of depersonalization, identification with other women, and self-objectivation.

In order to seduce a man, a heterosexual woman fashions herself according to the images of other women she likes; she crafts her personality based on women who had or would seduce her. As a result: (1) She turns herself into an object, which she constantly observes in order to reshape it. Being exposed to self-seeing the woman is the one who has "subject-images;" in other words, because of her power to subject herself to her own gaze, to become its own object, she is always more of a subject than man, who is straightforwardly an "object:" "Furthermore, in women, subject-images do exist; in men, object-images" (D, 169). The woman is more of a subject because—in order to subjectivize herself—she can strategically and quickly switch from the position of subject to the position of object.

(2) The fact that the woman can fashion herself only in accordance with the image of femininity she herself likes (or, the fact that she has to like herself as an object-image before letting herself become an object of desire for the one she wants to seduce) suggests that she must already have been seduced by images of other women. Women, Spielrein proposes, look at other women all the time, fishing for what they like in order to identify themselves with that. Each of the women they have liked represents what Spielrein calls their "wish-personality." In order to seduce a man, a woman first has to seduce herself into the image of a woman she finds seductive. In other words, in order to be seductive she must be seduced by women. (3) Woman is originarily homosexual. The mother, who in Spielrein is identified with the impersonal intensity of closeness, is not a sexually formed or gender-related body, which is why the relationship with the mother does not constitute, as in Freud, woman's primary homosexuality. But woman is constituted by an originary homosexuality that comes to her through other women she would like to be. Woman teaches herself how to be a woman only by loving other women.

Since loving other women is nothing other than an incessant becoming "wish personalities," woman's originary homosexuality is a process of constant becoming (women). Woman, in other words, cannot at any point simply become and stay a woman. In order to be a woman, she has to learn the art of becoming (how to become other women?). A woman is thus constantly in the process of leaving herself, objectivizing herself, creating her personality through identifications with other women; all of this is, at the same time, a gesture of depersonalization.

Because a woman is the process of overcoming or constant re-creation she is more of a strong "subject" than a man, who does not have to go through the process of loving other men. Afraid of losing his ego, his images are instead "object-images": "Through the destructive component of the sexual instinct, the more driven man may possess more intensely sadistic wishes. He wants to destroy the love-object, the woman whom he imagines wants to be overwhelmed" (D, 169). That is why he has more to learn about becoming a woman, more to learn about overcomings through love than a woman. She also has a lot to learn: namely how not to be what she has become but to continue becomings.

However—if one may judge on the basis of Spielrein's last will—the becomings of women, their overcomings, their creative loss of the ego transgresses the ideology of the human. Life lives everywhere, and everything is a possible self. Thus, in losing one's personality in death, one may become an oak.

Spielrein's last will: "Plant an oak tree and write: I was also once a human being. My name was Sabina Spielrein."

How Many Slavs?

Needless to say, interpretations are always singular, and Spielrein's theses are certainly complex. But even though it is quite credible that Freud could not understand all of her theses—for they are sometimes contradictory, and on other occasions rely on vague concepts, for example "subject-image," "object-image"—things are not as obscure as Freud suggested. One should hope that a person with his intellectual capacities of understanding could have done a better hermeneutical job. For example, even though her ontology is not well organized (she refers to Christianity, mythology, biological discourse, plus Nietzsche) the title of the essay, to say the least, is quite clear. It states straightforwardly that destruction will be treated as the "cause of coming into being," as the cause of *werden* thus the force of life. Destruction, still on the basis of the title, is the "beginning," the cause, not the end (death). How complicated is that?

The summary she provides (D, 173–74) is also straightforward. "Self-preservation" is a "static" drive; it protects the individual from foreign influences; so protected the individual dies out; foreign influences are therefore necessary; that is the basis of "biological" life and the logic of the preservation of the species: mix and confuse. At first sight it may seem that the absolutely private interest of the ego contradicts that of the species, while helping the person; it turns out that in doing so—in separating itself for the purposes of preservation—the ego contradicts the interests of life and ruins itself. On the other hand, when and if destruction—or even physical death—happens, it will be reabsorbed by the forces of life and serve to support other lives. This may sound too Nietzschean, or perhaps even more precisely, Spinozist. But no matter how vague it is, one thing is clear: Spielrein does not accept the thesis upon which Freud's essay is based, namely that life moves toward death for internal reasons, that its aim is death. In Spielrein the Freudian substance of death and the death principle simply do not exist. For her, death is a "destructive" form of life, but it is not autonomous from life and certainly not where life wants to go and be.

Another clear consequence for masochism follows. If the aim of life is not death but life, then masochism—primary, secondary—is not the force of the death drive; what is more, it becomes a strategy of finding a way to

live. However "weird" in its performance, such a strategy does not negate
its aim, which is to serve life, and for that reason it is perhaps not a perversion at all. With the exception of the last suggestion she makes all those
points quite plainly, which is why we may ask how Freud's confusion
arises. Is it possible that he could not follow the essay because he could
not absorb the idea of a world in which there would be only one substance,
namely life, and perhaps no perversions at all?

If he did not understand much of what she had written, was there a
reason for that? Was it because he was trying something else instead?
Should one raise the question of the ethics of reading? On the basis of the
documents Kerr cites and on the basis of the reading of "The Child is
Being Beaten" (1919), one may safely conclude that Freud understood
more than he admitted but used his interpretation of Spielrein for different aims.

Spielrein was Freud's patient, which was, Kerr suggests, her "chief relevance to [him]," because the main goal of analysis was to "free" her from
Jung's ideas and influence. For his part, Jung was not only her lover but
also her analyst: he treated her for perversion; Spielrein was a masochist
who had suffered "hysterical delirium." Jung wrote a paper about her case
and his treatment of it, which he presented at the Amsterdam Congress in
1907, with Freud's knowledge of the identity of the patient.

Spielrein left Geneva for Vienna not because she suffered hysteria or
masochistic perversion, but because she suffered heartbreak, which produced ambivalent feelings toward Jung. Freud undertakes his analysis of
Spielrein not only at the moment when she broke up with Jung, but also
at the moment when he parted with the latter for doctrinal reasons. To
cure Spielrein thus becomes a political question for him; the analysis is
not about "healing" her heart but about curing her from the bad version
of psychoanalysis since his main goal is "drive out the tyrant" Jung.[45]

But why refer to the biographical background? For no other reason
than Freud's own taste in literary theory. As it turns out, it was Freud who
never believed in the death of the author and considered theories to be
simply formulations of the psychic troubles of their authors. If one talks
about the dissolution of the ego into impersonal life and if that person is
undergoing analysis because she is a masochist, then her theory of the ego
has to be a theory of the masochistic ego. That is Freud's reading of Spielrein. Kerr gives a detailed account: "Spielrein presented part of her paper
to a meeting of the Vienna Psychoanalytic Society—Freud attended—on
November 29, 1911. . . . For her talk, "On Transformation," Spielrein

drew largely from the very difficult third part of her essay. . . . The following spring, on March 21 [1912], we find Freud writing to Jung that while he still has not seen the entire manuscript, he has nevertheless arrived at an appraisal: 'As for Spielrein's paper, I know only the one chapter that she read at the Society. She is very bright; there is meaning in everything she says; her destructive drive is not much to my liking, because I believe it is personally conditioned. She seems abnormally ambivalent."[46]

Everything she says is bright and charged with meaning, but such meaning is highly personal and abnormal. For that reason, she does not really theorize, but simply relates her personal situation, that of a masochist, through a theoretical narrative. And since she is abnormal and a first-rate masochist, the best thing for a theoretically oriented analyst to do is to somehow combine her "theory" and her "personality" in order to formulate a theory of masochism. This combination found its expression before "Beyond the Pleasure Principle" was written, in "A Child is Being Beaten."

The child being beaten is Spielrein: "Even prior to meeting her, Freud was well aware that hers was the case Jung had used in his historic defense of psychoanalysis at the Amsterdam Congress in September of 1907. Jung's description of her in that address . . . had been frank in its portrayal of her masochism: in her hysterical delirium, she imagined being beaten by her father and thereby derived voluptuous pleasure. Jung has also been frank about her anal-erotic trends, and, in the intervening years, anality had become inextricably linked with the reciprocal vice, sadism, in the evolving doctrines of psychoanalysis."[47] Psychoanalytical theory evolves around the fantasies of a masochist, which first served Jung in formulating his historical defense of it, and then Freud in defending it against Jung. As the theory gets more differentiated, Jung and Freud fall apart, and psychoanalysis is threatened by the dispute between those who had saved it.

In the middle of that dispute, the body of the masochist travels from Geneva to Vienna, this time to be analyzed by Freud; psychoanalysis will be defended once again, only this time the goal is somewhat different: to cure the patient from perversion by curing her from her perverse love for Jung. Kerr again: "Shortly thereafter probably in March but certainly by June [1912], she consulted Freud expressly for the purpose of resolving the painful problem of her simultaneous love and hate—for Jung." If the masochist can be cured from her ambivalent (masochistic) love for Jung, the latter's doctrines will be expelled, and psychoanalysis itself will be recovered and healed. As if a masochist were needed each time that psychoanalysis had to be defended.

In analyzing Spielrein's masochistic fantasies, Freud made another "transfer." Freud had connected, her watching herself/another being beaten by her father (to fantasize a little here: by that time, knowing about her and Jung, Freud must have himself been fantasizing heavily about Jung being the father in question) I am suggesting, with her thesis in the "Destruction" essay regarding the nature of the normal ego. There, to reassert the point, she argued that the "I" cannot live in the present other than through intensities (that is: feeling-tonalities), and that what we call the "I" (the specular, reflexive instance of representation) is the distant spectator of everything that actually happens to it. As long as it exists in the isolated form the "I" cannot really participate in what is happening to it, because it is isolated. In order to participate in its own life—to love, to be close to another, and so on—it has to abandon itself. Hence the idea of love as dissolution and of creation as destruction.

But in Freud's "A Child Is Being Beaten" her theory about the ego becomes his theory of the masochistic ego: "By the same process, on the other hand, the girl escapes from the demands of the erotic side of her life altogether. She turns herself in phantasy into a man, without herself becoming active in a masculine way, and is no longer anything but a spectator of the event which takes the place of a sexual act."[48] Only the ego that does not participate in its own dissolution but watches it from afar—thus preserving itself—is understandable to Freud, and that only on condition that such an ego be called masochistic (because the "normal" ego would not have the masochistic ambivalence of wanting to see its own vanishing). It is on the basis of this "specular" ego that Freud will, in the same essay on masochism, specularize the pain by turning it into the spiritual suffering of the feeling of guilt. In Freud, the masochist becomes a perverted sinner in the hands of the angry god of bad conscience and so is turned into the very ruin that, according to Spielrein, is overcome by masochism.

Nietzschean overcoming, which plays a crucial role in Spielrein's understanding of destruction as becoming, is not mentioned in "A Child is Being Beaten," but Freud returns to the question in an oblique way in "Beyond the Pleasure Principle." There, as Kerr explains, "Nietzsche, though not named, has been a target throughout, not only in the express attack on 'supermen' and in the mockery of the 'eternal recurrence,' but also in the very title of the essay. *Beyond the Pleasure Principle* takes the reader into the Beyond (*Jenseits*) no less than *Beyond Good and Evil* . . . except that for Freud what is Beyond turns out to be what was Before, and both are equal to Death."[49]

The eternal recurrence—even though no less silly than solar years and masculine and feminine substances—is mocked, I am suggesting, not simply because it makes a case for circular rather than reflexive thinking (and breaks the logic of causality upon which psychoanalysis relies), but because what has to be accepted through circular repetitions—as Nietzsche always insisted—is the recurrence of pain and suffering ("Yes-saying without reservation, even to suffering . . . even to everything that is questionable and strange in existence"). To see time and life within it as an ongoing repetition of pain; to call for an ethics that insists on exposure to it in the form of the Zarathustrian metamorphosis (for self-overcoming is always painful, as Spielrein points out), and what is more, to "ontologize" pain into the suffering of the earth, must have looked to Freud like an ontologization of masochistic perversion (beyond which, he insisted, can only be death).

Nietzsche understood the last words of Zarathustrian metamorphosis, those that would make of all science a gay knowledge ("If you have no more happiness to give me, well then! *You still have suffering*"), to be the words to what he called "the *Hymn to Life*," a gay song saying yes to pain and to its eternal recurrence. Freud understood the last words of Nietzsche's recurrence as well as of Spielrein's coming into being (based on her understanding of Nietzsche) to be death. Beyond the pleasure principle, beyond good and evil there is no impersonal life of earth and water but only death. Outside of the ego the world is dead.

Knowingly or not (it is of no relevance to my reading), by mocking and misreading Nietzsche's "highest formula of affirmation," and Spielrein's theory of coming into being, Freud was defying yet another Russian (whom he knew and with whom, like with Spielrein and Jung, he had a complex relationship). For the text of Zarathustra, Nietzsche explains in order to avoid misunderstandings, is not written by him, Nietzsche, at all. The conservative Freudian literary theory that sees texts as biographically driven is thus negated in advance by Nietzsche. *Thus Spoke Zarathustra* is written in one of Nietzsche's metamorphoses, when his person was not with him but he was somebody else, in the mood of another person's mind. It was written by a Russian woman, as a matter of fact: "The text, to say this expressly because a misunderstanding has gained currency, is not by me: it is the amazing inspiration of a young Russian woman who was my friend at that time, Miss Lou von Salomé."[50]

Nietzsche's friend had whispered in his ear what she had seen in her inspiration; his hearing of what she had seen caused his becoming-seer; he had to become his friend in order to write her vision. Nietzsche, a Russian woman, writes the highest formula of affirmation.

Beyond the pleasure principle Russian and Polish women (for often, especially when traveling, Nietzsche was leaving her Russian femininity and becoming Polish) and their masochistic theories travel through Europe, from Geneva to Vienna, from Genoa to Eze, from Rostov at Don to Berlin, being watched, treated, examined or simply mocked by the analysts who knew what was "beyond." Bodies and texts in becoming—with their minor theories and pains—are found working toward destabilization of what, from the very beginning, wanted to become a solid body of western knowledge. They almost form a pan-Slavic movement in which yet another of their members, Sacher-Masoch, was involved in his effort to promote the politics of "minority groups and revolutionary movements in the Empire," himself in a constant becoming, writing from various metamorphoses, in different minor languages, producing many minor literatures (hence his "Galician, Jewish, Hungarian, Prussian tales").[51]

That may be what so frightens psychoanalysis in masochism: minor, virus-like bodies and thoughts, micropolitical, imperceptible in their dissolutions, in their effort to be, as Nietzsche put it, "new, nameless, self-evident," like earth or water; Slavs becoming Nietzschean "ideal Mediterraneans," escaping all the interpretations of psychoanalysis. And arrayed against them, doctors, working on discursivity, on an ideosphere, on a doctrine, in order to tell us that beyond good and evil there is nothing but death, that we are doomed to the ethics we have, that we cannot become others, different, hence better, that there are no breaks in our identity, no auspicious beginnings.

Of Rats and Names

Gil Anidjar

The notion of a rat [*von der Vorstellung der Ratte*] is inseparably bound
up with the fact that it has sharp teeth with which it gnaws and bites.
But rats cannot be sharp-toothed, greedy and dirty with impunity:
they are cruelly persecuted and mercilessly put to death by man [*sie
wird von den Menschen . . . grausam verfolgt und schonungslos erschlagen*],
as the patient had observed with horror. He had often pitied the poor
creatures. But he himself had been just such a nasty, dirty little
wretch, who was apt to bite people when he was in a rage, and had
been fearfully punished for doing so. He could truly be said to find "a
living likeness of himself" [*sein ganz 'natürlich Ebenbild'*] in the rat.

FREUD, *Rat Man*, 54/G435 (quoting Goethe's *Faust*)

Our patient, then, had wanted to kill this Dick
[*Diesen Dick wollte er nun umbrigen*].

FREUD, *Rat Man*, 32/G411

This much could have been obvious: Rat Man was a Jew, and Freud's case
study on Rat Man, his "Notes Upon a Case of Obsessional Neurosis" tells
us much about anti-Semitism.[1] In the terms of the present volume, it tells
us that anti-Semitism[2]—like the response to it—is a fundamentalism, a
mode of reading and of responding that strives for the one, eagerly and
felicitously linking in an undivided line self and other (though not every
other), choosing and chosen. Everything occurs as if both were inevitably
related in the noncontingent structure of a call, an interpellation (one
sender—one text, one people—one addressee). Is that what is called fundamentalism? A legitimate question, no doubt, but not one that Rat Man
enables us to explore directly. Instead, with and after Rat Man, the following will appear more pertinent: what is called naming?[3] And more precisely who calls and answers to the name? Interestingly, like anti-Semitism
and the names it is called (as well, obviously, as the names it calls),[4] fundamentalism operates first and foremost as a name, an interpellation of sorts,
an identification, election, or derogation hurled at the other, more rarely
at the self. As a result, its descriptive function is (or should be) limited,

71

even if the kind of limitation thus evoked also ends up constituting an expansion, the increased reach of the matter in the name of a *generalized fundamentalism*. If there is such a thing, then, fundamentalism would only become recognizable from the manner in which its deployment stages a call and a response, gathering as if by magic, caller and called. Responding to a text (a word, the Word, or a slur—a blessing or a curse), fundamentalism would therefore be governed by a broad structure of interpellation that remains wedded to felicity. Such at least is my contention. Within the limited case that will occupy us here, that is, in Rat Man's case, it should at any rate becomes possible to discern the way in which anti-Semitism— like the response to it, the two yet having to be rigorously divided—is a fundamentalism.[5]

To be sure, Jews remain unnamed in the case as it was published in its final form, and it is unclear whether the association, made famous and infamous by the Nazis, had already been established, which irrevocably linked Jews with rats in the anti-Semitic imaginary. Still, Freud's text has everything to do with Jews (fathers, rats, and money, all of which were or became deeply entangled within a web of Jewish and anti-Semitic significance, which is to say that, as Freud puts it, "rats had acquired a series of symbolic meanings, to which, during the period which followed, fresh ones were continually being added").[6] And it has everything to do with the response one offers to the word or name that is called. Another way to learn about Rat Man's predicament in its connection to Jewishness and anti-Semitism is by considering that the case constitutes, in fact, a grand rehearsal of *Totem and Taboo* (the ghost of the dead father, the significance of the law and of ritual, indeed, of obsessional practice) and of *Moses and Monotheism* ("the great man," the power of the name, revenge and guilt). Minimally, then, Rat Man's case was about religion all along, about commands and prohibitions, superstitions, prayers, and fathers, dead or alive. It is also about prophetic dreams and belief in telepathy, hyperbolic trust in the power of thought and in that of the name, fear of punishment (in this world and for all eternity), the obsession of protection and apotropaic (protective) measures, strange Eastern practices, and life after death, which is to say, survivor's guilt. A deeply religious figure and the very image of devotion, Rat Man was a doctor of law (*doctor juris*). He was obsessed with revenge, and, not surprisingly, he was fond of biblical stories. He declared his religion—a difficult and personal blend of motives and actions in which belief and practice are not necessarily connected. He confessed it to Freud upon the very first (or was it the second?) meeting.

The only other piece of information that I obtained from him during this [first] hour was that from the very first, on all the previous occasions on which he had had a fear that something would happen to people he loved no less than on the present one, he had referred the punishments not only to our present life but also to eternity—to the next world [*in die Ewigkeit*]. Up to his fourteenth or fifteenth year he had been devoutly religious [*er war . . . sehr gewissenhaft religiös gewesen*], but from that time on he had gradually developed into the free-thinker that he was today. He reconciled the contradiction between his beliefs and his obsessions by saying to himself: "What do you know about the next world? [*was weisst du vom Leben im Jenseits?*] Nothing *can* be known about it. You're not risking anything—so do it!" This form of argument seemed unobjectionable to a man who was in other respects particularly clear-headed, and in this way he exploited the uncertainty of reason in the face of these questions to the benefit of the religious attitude [*frommen Weltanschauung*] which he had outgrown. (15/G394)

Today, Rat Man teaches us perhaps most about hate. Therefore, it teaches us about the hatred of the Jews—anti-Semitism—and its current policing. This may not come to full clarification in what follows, but it is hardly as obscure as it may seem, for the case readily introduces us to the question of words that wound and their failure, that is to say, more centrally, to the question of interpellation. What does it mean to be interpellated by anti-Semitism? What does it mean to consider oneself, to publicly declare oneself, the addressee of hate speech and of murderous acts? Much as Althusser will later demonstrate, Freud links the question of interpellation, and by extension, that of injurious speech, acts, and *actes manqués*, to the police. As is well known, the word *interpeller*, in French, has the technical meaning of "hailing, arresting, seizing" in juridical language. Interpellation here recalls insult, murder, and murderous injury. It produces or evokes subjection and identification. Strong affects are at stake, and so are mistaken associations, inevitably, as well as mistaken identifications. "We are not used to feeling strong affects," Freud explains as if that explained something, anything. "We are not used to feeling strong affects without their having any ideational content, and therefore, if the content is missing, we seize as a substitute [*und nehmen . . . als Surrogat auf*] upon another content which is in some way suitable, much as our police, when they cannot catch the right murderer, arrest a wrong one instead [*einen unrechten an seiner Stelle verhaftet*]."[7] Such failures may well constitute successes, Freud later makes clear, and some interpellers easily become interlopers who felicitously redirect everything their way and thus produce and fashion their own subjects. Like the proverbial customer, such callers may always be right. "So too the king cannot be mistaken; if he addresses one of his subjects by a title which is not his [*wenn sie einen Untertan mit einem ihn nicht gebührenden Titel angesprochen hat*], the subject bears that title ever afterwards" (56/G437) Rat Man—*le bien (ou mal) nommé*—is a story of interpellation. It is the story of hate and of its policing.

Were it possible, when speaking about Freud, the scene around which my reading will gravitate could be described as unforgettable. And indeed, who could forget the child? Who—granted even the slightest familiarity with Freud's corpus—could fail to recall the child who, still being beaten, struck back at his father by hitting him with the gift of prophecy? The latter responds to kin in kind, or at least with a blessing and a curse.[8] "The child will be either a great man or a great criminal!" Undoubtedly among the better known citations within the Freudian text, and much like the phrase "the talking cure" had earlier, this sentence (for it is a sentence, perhaps even a death sentence), which Freud himself never uttered but that he reported and wrote, came in a way to name or describe psychoanalysis. Naming the great man and the great criminal, hailing and calling them, as it were, the sentence resonates across the fields and disciplines that Freud affected and changed. An instance of that which binds and un-binds father to son—male sociability, in a nutshell—the memory of which is sustained by the mother, the sentence and the scene which it ties and punctuates essentially stages the social according to Freud, from art, religion and politics ("the great man") to normality and perversion, law and the police ("a great criminal"). The entirety of the "Notes upon a Case of Obsessional Neurosis" is, as I have said, dominated by hate, the hate of a child for his father, and that of a father for his ancestors.[9] As the event of a collective psychology, it is structured and governed by self-hate. But more importantly, the case is about hate as it is carried by speech, words of hate and hate speech, abuse, insults and curses, incantations that end or change, turn around, as it were, at the turning point of the case of the Rat Man. ("Things soon reached a point at which, in his dreams, his waking phantasies, and his associations, he began heaping the grossest and filthiest abuse [*aufs gröblichtste und unflätigste beschimpfte*] upon me and my family, though in his deliberate actions he never treated me with anything but the greatest respect. His demeanor as he repeated these insults [*dieser Beschimp-fungen*] to me was that of a man in despair" [48/G429]). Out of despair, then, but with the greatest measure of respect, insults, curses, and abusive words proliferate through the text. But the case is also an extended tale of hate, the story of a murder or murders, a staged repetition, many have remarked, of the tale of Hamlet who, memorably interpellated, witnesses his father's ghostly returns ("And although he had never forgotten that his father was dead, the prospect of seeing a ghostly apparition of this kind had had no terrors for him; on the contrary, he had greatly desired it"),[10] and subsequently seeks to avenge his father's murder—but we know, of course, who does the murdering of fathers ("Thoughts about my father's death, occupied my mind from a very early age and for a long period of time").[11] Rat Man is the case of an individual who, interpellated, places himself before the law, and who "spontaneously converts a given statement into a command" endowed with force of law.[12] It is a tale of interpellation, the story of a call among many others that, Avital Ronell has repeatedly shown, inscribes itself and runs through multiple channels and traditions, and media, from Abraham to Moses, from Heidegger and Levinas to Althusser and Derrida, Butler and Ronell herself.[13] The call, perhaps an insult, never reaches its destination. Minimally, it tarries and procrastinates, but more often than not, something happens, running penetrating interferences, something or someone inserts itself (rats, nots, impertinent laughter, or dead fathers, Freud himself, or an evil spirit. God even) and disrupts the call, whether it is a prayer call, or a call of prophecy (as if Balaam was not just like every other prophet, as if every prophet was not always already inverted, inserted), a blessing or a curse. The call, then, misses its intent. Or addressee.

> At the time of the revival of his piety he used to make up prayers for himself, which took up more and more time and eventually lasted for an hour and a half. The reason for this was that he found, like an inverted Balaam [*ein ungekehrter Bileam*], that something always inserted itself into his pious phrases [*in die frommen Formeln immer etwas einmengte*] and turned them into their opposite. For instance, if he said, "May God protect him," an evil spirit would hurriedly insinuate a "not." On one such occasion the idea occurred to him of cursing instead, for in that case, he thought, the contrary words would be sure to creep in. (35/G415)

The call addresses no one, no one in particular, yet it chooses and elects one—the chosen one—for the better and for the worse, and it apparently forces one, not just anyone but *that* one, to turn and respond: "Here I am!" To be more precise, and contrary to received opinion (the fundamentalism of doxa, or the doxa of fundamentalism), it is not just the One who answers so. It is rather that "the interpellation of individuals as subjects presupposes the 'existence' of a Unique and central Other subject."[14] Thus, through the failures of a monotheism that is nothing less than biblical, there is always more than one chosen people. To the contrary, chosen people are more like a dime a dozen: "one individual (nine times out of ten it is the right one) turns round, believing/suspecting/knowing that it is for him, i.e., recognizing that 'it really is he' who is meant by the hailing."[15] Every one among nine, nine out of ten, almost a *minyian*, a quorum which may be left hanging, like a jury without a prayer, if some one, when someone, the other one, interrupts or fails to respond, thus enabling the other others to say: "it's for me." Can one fail to respond? Could any interruption, even a noninterruption, fail to qualify as a response? The calls have been made, the blessing or the curse issued, the insult hurled, and the response, therefore, follows. Does it follow? Witness, at any rate, the force of interpellation, transmitted, says Freud—and what else did you expect? The Spanish Inquisition? Yes, well, we are talking about the Jews, and therefore about anti-Semitism—by way of the mother.

> To my great astonishment the patient then informed me that his mother[16] had repeatedly described to him an occurrence . . . which dated from his earliest childhood and had evidently escaped being forgotten by her on account of its remarkable consequences. He himself, however, had no recollection of it whatever. The tale was as follows. When he was very small—it became possible to establish the date more exactly owing to its having coincided with the fatal illness of an elder sister—he had done something naughty, for which his father had given him a beating. The little boy had flown into a terrible rage and had hurled abuse at his father even while he was under his blows [*Da sei der kleine Knirps in eine schreckliche Wut geraten und habe noch unter den Schlägen den Vater beschimpft*]. But as he knew no bad language [*keine Schimpfwörter*], he had called him all the names of common objects that he could think of, and had screamed: "You lamp! You towel! You plate!" and so on. His father, shaken by such an outburst of elemental fury, had stopped beating him, and had declared: "The child will be either a great man or a great criminal!" The patient believed that the scene made a great impression upon himself as well as upon his father. His father, he said, never beat him again; and he also attributed to this experience a part of the change which came over his own character. From that time forward he was a coward—out of fear of the violence of his own rage. His whole life long, moreover, he was terribly afraid of blows, and used to creep away and hide, filled with terror and indignation, when one of his brothers or sisters was beaten. (46/G426).

What does it mean to be the addressee of a massive death sentence? What does it mean to consider oneself the addressee of such death sentence? In Jean-François Lyotard's rendering, the utterance, by a Nazi, of

the word "Jew" could mean only one thing: "You are dead." Or, lacking
the basic structure of address, the call "Jew!" meant immediate death. Addressed to no one, the utterance does not permit, strictly speaking, a response.[17] This impossibility of response is tied to a peculiar, one could say
a *fundamentalist*, structure: the lack of address in the utterance (the absence
of a "you" would could thereby respond) is paradoxically defined by the
success of its reach. The utterance reaches its destination, its proper addressee—in this case (and perhaps in every case), the dead. Whose response is this? Again, no response is possible because there is neither time
("Jew!" is not a threat that would open the possibility of deferral, the possibility of time) nor a "who" or a "you," that is thereby addressed. There
is no time and no one to respond. Beyond the possibility or impossibility
of its utterance, if the "Jew!" of the Nazi provides the ultimate example of
the anti-Semitic utterance, the question nonetheless lingers: who responds
to the call? Who is the addressee of anti-Semitism? Where to locate the
possibility of a mistake? And who could possibly claim to be its addressee?
When? The death toll of Nazi anti-Semitism is not to be doubted. But
who is it that responds to this anti-Semitism? Whom does it reach? Rat
Man raises the possibility that the injurious calls of anti-Semitism—and
the response to them—are governed by symptoms of "mistaken identity."
The "recognition," the identification of Jews with incidents that are said
to target Jews, incidents said to be anti-Semitic even when they are fabri-
cated lies or simply mistaken, is based on the logic of interpellation such
as Rat Man exemplifies it, and that includes the strange foregrounding of
felicity where there are only multiple modes of failures.

Rat Man is about anti-Semitism because it is about interpellation, the
call that names and arrests, that identifies and injures, a call that, strictly
speaking, never reaches its destination but nonetheless operates and
wounds.[18] Interpellation, for Rat Man, was a familiar procedure, but it also
carried the risk of spectacular failure. In fact, the story of his father's death
(or, as Freud more rigorously calls it, "the story of his father's illness,
die Krankengeschichte seines Vaters"), is precisely the story of a remarkably
dramatic exchange, of answer and response in a time of crisis, a tale of
danger and the estimation of its passing (what does it mean for danger to
pass?). It is about the failure to answer to one's name, to answer to the
name called, to respond to that which calls. In this case, it was the sick
father who called, and Rat Man (Father, can't you see I'm resting?) had
just been burning to take a nap. Rat Man had gone to sleep.

> One evening, thinking that the condition was one which would come to a
> crisis, he had asked the doctor when the danger could be regarded as over

[*wann die Gefahr als beseitigt gelten könnte*]. "The evening of the day after tomorrow," had been the reply. It had never entered his head that his father might not survive that limit. At half-past eleven at night he had lain down for an hour's rest. He had woken up at one o'clock, and had been told by a medical friend that his father had died. He had reproached himself [*Er machte sich den Vorwurf*] with not having been present at his death; and the reproach had been intensified when the nurse told him that his father had spoken his name once during the last days [*der Vater habe in den letzten Tagen einmal seinen Namen genannt*], and said to her as she came to bed: "Is that Paul?" (19/G398)[19]

Paul? In order to reflect on this final primal scene, it may be important to note that it is far from untypical. Interpellation, and the failure of interpellation (call and response), had long been a matter, indeed, a procedure familiar to Rat Man. Later, for instance, memorably instructed that he will have to pay back postal charges (a packet had been picked up and handed to him, although at this point, Freud does not say for whom the packet was intended), Rat Man engages the procedure and puts it to work at that very instant. "At that instant . . . a 'sanction' had taken shape in his mind, namely, *that he was not to pay back the money* or it would happen—(that is, the phantasy about the rats would come true as regards his father and the lady). And immediately, in accordance with a type of procedure with which he was familiar, to combat this sanction there had arisen a command in the shape of a vow: '*You must pay back the 3.80 crows to Lieutenant A.*' He had said these words to himself almost half aloud" (14). Recasting interpellation as command, hearing in any utterance the force of a law,[20] Rat Man was as familiar with such calls of duty as he was with acknowledging reception in the form of mistaken identities. "He repeatedly addressed me as 'Captain,'" writes Freud.

The habit of interpellating was also well established in the Lanzer household and around it. Recalling the episode I quoted earlier and that still awaits our reading, Patrick Mahony calls attention to the chain of associations linking the names and proper names operating through Rat Man's narrative, the practice of interpellation, and the multiplication of mistaken identities that occupies us here. Freud's complete notes, along with the editor's explanation, do explain a number of things. First of all, Lieutenant A.'s real name was David. In Freud's notes, therefore, the command is "*Du musst dem Obltt* [Oberleutnant] *David die 3 Kr 80 zurück- geben.*"[21] Incidentally, David is the name that Freud *mistakenly* attributes to Rat Man's father, noting one month into the analysis, that "His father was not called David, but Heinrich [*sein Vater hiess nicht David, sondern Heinrich*]."[22] In the process of narrating his crucial story, Rat Man too follows the names (if not the money) and interrupts himself by beginning to complain about his previous physicians, those who had failed to understand him. He had called, if you will, and they had failed to respond (of course, doctors themselves are more in the habit of making calls). Rat Man singles out one famous Viennese doctor who, on call at the time, later went on to receive the Nobel Prize. His name was Julius Wagner von Jauregg, but Freud (and apparently Rat Man as well) refers to him simply as: Wagner. Elza Hawelka, who edited Freud's manuscript for publication, surmises that there is no interruption by a total work of art here but only a seamless association. The name David, she says, must have brought to mind the character of the first theatrical performance Rat Man had ever attended as a child, a comic opera by the other Wagner, namely, Richard: *Die Meistersinger von Nürnberg*. There, David is the name of a character—an apprentice shoe repairman, as well as a music student who happens to know, Hawelka writes, all the musical "commands."[23] David, it turns out, is constantly interpellated and is often mistaken in responding (he spontaneously answers, for example, when reference is made, in the conversation, to the *David* of Albert Dürer). His name ultimately seems to function as the very name of interpellation. Never sure when he is called, whether it is him who is being called, David also becomes the name by which others are called and elected (one character becomes the object of another's love because he is said to resemble *David*, that is, Dürer's painting. It is at this point, that David, the other one, thinks he is being called: *Da bin ich. Wer ruft?*"), unsure whether it is their turn, this time, to be called. David, then, is the name of the called (Wagner, not the doctor, may have ironically considered that David, King David, was said to be the ancestor of the Messiah, who keeps being called and insists on not coming, although another, more popular version of that story has him arrive only to be persecuted and ridiculed, abandoned). During the representation, Rat Man himself had heard "David, David!" explains Freud. Subsequently, "he had used the David motif as call in the family [*Das Davidmotiv hat er als Ruf in der Familie verwendet*]."[24] Who did Rat Man think he was?[25]

Judith Butler explained that, in and through interpellation, "there is always the risk of a certain misrecognition . . . The one who is hailed may fail to hear, misread the call, turn the other way, answer to another name, insist on not being addressed in that way."[26] Butler pursues this line of thought by further underscoring the importance of misrecognition.

Consider the force of this dynamic interpellation and misrecognition when the name is not a proper name but a social category, and hence a signifier capable of being interpreted in a number of divergent and conflictual ways. To be hailed as a "woman" or "Jew" or "queer" or "Black" or "Chicana" may be heard or interpreted as an affirmation or an insult depending on the context in which the hailing occurs (where context is the effective historicity and spatiality of the sign). If that name is called, there is more often than not some hesitation about whether or how to respond, for what is at stake is whether the temporary totalization performed by the name is politically enabling or paralyzing, whether the foreclosure, indeed the violence, of the totalizing reduction of identity performed by that particular hailing is politically strategic or regressive or, if paralyzing and regressive, also enabling in some way. (96)

Rat Man, in the scene that occupies us here, confronts us with the very elements that Butler raises, with the figuration of a scene in which all possibilities of responses are at once entertained or at least plausible, while the immediacy of responses, their inevitability, appears equally unquestionable—and thereby all the more doubtful in their felicity. The effects in the scene and of the scene are granted spectacular immediacy, made all the more vivid by the complex sense of memory and forgetting within which they are inscribed. All those involved are interpellated, hailed, and arrested by the scene in its occurrence (the historical accuracy of which Freud incidentally puts into question in an elaborate footnote) and its aftermaths. The scene is manifestly traversed by numerous instances of interpellation. It *is*, as a whole, constituted as an interpellation: a veritable *Gesamtrufwerk*. Consider its effects as they are reported in Freud's narration. Freud himself begins by confessing his "great astonishment [*meinem grossen Erstaunen*]." Rat Man's mother remembers the scene "on account of its remarkable consequences [*weil sich so merkwürdige Dinge an ihn knüpften*]." The father is "shaken [*erschüttert*] by such an outburst." And Rat Man himself believes that the scene had left an enduring impression (although not one he actually remembered). No less impressive are its effects on the father's behavior and on Rat Man's personality. Rat Man becomes "a coward" (although one wonders whether this particular description should not be read as the proliferation of insults, abuse and self-reproach).[27] His father stops beating him for good. There is therefore no question of the "success" of the multiple interpellations operating in and around the scene in which the child hurls insults at his father, where he himself is beaten and becomes the third-person object of a prediction that is at once blessing and curse, and on the mutual transformation undergone by each of the persons present at the time. If success is defined by efficacy, Rat Man's childhood provides us with an exemplary illustration of interpellation as the felicitous fashioning of collective psychology and of sociability.

A child, then, is being beaten. He responds to the violence inflicted upon his body by calling out insults. The father responds by calling upon him, in prophetic fashion, the chance or danger of an uncertain future. Each of their singular responses to the event are unsettling because they both assume the posture of recipient of a unique instance of violence, the violence of the child's rage, responding to it with a "here I am." Indeed, "out of the fear of the violence of his own rage," Rat Man becomes a coward (or, self-berating, comes to understand himself so), while his father stops beating him, stunned by the power the child demonstrates and which promises (or threatens) of great things to come. As Freud points out, the father was wrong on both counts, and the son became a great neurotic, not a great man nor a great criminal. What is most extraordinary about the scene, however, is that it reveals the absolute discrepancy between the word hurled as insult and its (highly disseminated) reception. It reveals the precise infelicity of success. For at no point did the father ever consider identifying with lamps, towels or plates (he did not proudly embrace or resignify any of the injurious terms, nor did he rise to the defense of the rights of towels). Never was the question of recognition or misrecognition ever at issue in the exchange, in the interpellation of the father by the son. We already knew all this since Derrida explained it, of course. The mark can only function by being torn from its context.[28] It is in this way that it never reaches its destination. No insult could ever be received in the way it was "sent." No insult could ever mean the "same" for sender and for addressee. This would mean that neither recognition nor misrecognition is possible (both are rather equally impossible) in the case of interpellation, indeed, in any case. Clearly, the father is affected. What he receives is the rage of the child, thus alerting us to the difference between hate speech and the speaking of hate (Rat Man speaks his hate, yet what he utters is anything but hate speech). But pain and injury, even to the point of death, do not determine meaning. Had the father died right at that moment ("God forbid!" would interrupt a benevolent spirit), he would not have died a lamp or a towel. The insult or the curse—interpellation—may therefore well be a death sentence, but this would not constitute felicity. Not quite to the contrary (since it is not infelicitous either), the interpellation fails a priori and *fundamentally* to function; it fails, in fact, to operate as the site or occasion for identification. It is from this originary failure, out of the impossibility of naming the other without the response of the other—that interpellation comes to function as a figure of subjection and of identification. Interpellation hails. But then what? Anti-Semitism hails. What name does it call? And who would want to answer? Who is it that must answer? Who is it that does? These questions are those that Rat Man puts to us. They are the sound of Rat Man calling. Out of rage.

Mad Country, Mad Psychiatrists:
Psychoanalysis and the Balkan Genocide

Dušan Bjelić

"Serbs are mad people . . . but Croats suffer from a castration complex,"
avowed Serb psychiatrist Dr. Jovan Rašković to Franjo Tudjman, the president of Croatia, on the occasion of a meeting in 1990 to resolve the growing tension between the Croatian government and the Serb minority in
Croatia. Responding to what he saw as a need for psychiatric supervision
in a political situation that was spiraling out of control, he became the self-
appointed purveyor of that supervision, ostensibly to achieve a *rapprochement* between the two ethnic groups—mad Serbs and complexed Croatians. However, during this same period, Rašković was proselytizing mass
gatherings of Serbs in Croatia with psychoanalytically based theories on
Serb "madness," fomenting resistance to the "rational delirium" he saw
as the legacy of Croat fascism and postwar communism. Both regimes,
according to him, suppressed the Serb unconscious desire for its mother-
nation. Rašković advocated the Serb "irrational delirium" as a political
force for the liberation of the ethnic unconscious, a kind of antipsychiatry
from the right. This same psychoanalytic rhetoric was, in turn, adopted
by his protégé Dr. Radovan Karadžić. In deploying psychoanalytic discourse and psychiatric expertise to justify ethnic separation as well as to
project the normality of mass paranoia, Rašković and Karadžić, as we now
know, actually laid the groundwork for the bloody conflicts to come. Both

have since gained notoriety as psychiatrist-politicians who attained political power through the social production of madness. Their rhetoric set in motion a dance of Eros and Thanatos that culminated in Srebrenica in 1995, when up to eight thousand Bosnian Muslim men were executed by the troops of Dr. Karadžić. Rašković died before the war ended.[1] Karadžić has been indicted by the International War Crimes Tribunal in The Hague, but he remains at large today.

Although the Balkan war of the 1990s was a major global media event, the significant role of psychiatrists and psychoanalytic discourse in generating the ethnic conflicts that ignited that war is not well known in the West.[2] This essay addresses that role, considering how the language of psychoanalysis, developed to articulate the emancipation of the individual subject, came to be deployed in the postcommunist Balkans as a political force for ethnic "emancipation" in the context of the ethnic mixture in the ex-Yugoslavia. I am not suggesting that this deployment of psychoanalytic discourse is entirely responsible for generating the ethnic conflict and genocide in the ex-Yugoslavia—rather that those who plotted and executed the conflict could not have accomplished this without psychoanalytic discourse.

I situate the psychoanalytic language so deployed in the context of the Balkan "discursive geography" (to use Edward Said's term) and the self-orientalization specific to the Balkan identity. "Discursive geography" encompasses the idea that space is not an external condition of a discourse but, as in the case of the Balkans and Eastern Europe, internally regulates the politics of signification, defines the other in terms of the space and sets the territorial boundaries of their representation. As historians have recently argued, Voltaire and the Enlightenment divided European space into the rational West and the irrational East, a division that has shaped Western discourse of rationality (including psychoanalysis) along the lines of colonial exclusions. Larry Wolff and Maria Todorova argue that the philosophy of the Enlightenment constructed Eastern Europe and the Balkans as the dangerous exterior, "the dark side of the collective Europe," the place of Europe's forbidden desire, of vampires, unruly feminine sexuality and tribalism.[3] That is, all that West had to discharge in order to become the center of the world—the Empire—was ascribed to the East as the constitutive dark counterpoint to Enlightenment. Relations here have traditionally been fixed by a sort of "cognitive paranoia," whereby the West, with its cognitive superiority, constructs the identity of the "other" part of Europe.[4] Lacking its own Enlightenment and corresponding Eastern European Cartesianism, this geopolitical "other" either submits to (and internalizes) the externally imposed identity or completely rejects it. The line between the established geopolitics of the European *Grossraum* and Freud's metapsychology, as we will see, blurs in the Balkans.

One expression of the relationship described here is *balkanism*, a discourse that represents the Balkans as the place between the opposing worlds, Europe and the Ottomans, West and East. Though similar to the concept of orientalism, balkanism actually extends that discourse because it accounts for discursive stereotypes as schemes of self-identification for the Balkan population. Ethnic groups in that population define themselves according to their relative positions vis-à-vis the West. For example, Slovenes see themselves as more civilized than the Serbs, who are farther East; the Serbs, in turn, see themselves as more civilized than the Albanians.[5] Thus, representational schemes based on spatial hierarchies have been internalized as if essential identities because they allow and justify exclusion of the other. Balkanism, then, works two ways, as a system of stereotypical representation of the Balkans as the in-between-place and as a mechanism for internalization of these very stereotypes as if essential ethnic identities. Given the propensity of the Balkans to self-orientalization with respect to the dominant geopolitical stereotype—to see themselves as represented by the dominant discourse and act according to it as if it were an essential identity—the latent geopolitics of psychoanalytic language became a useful tool in interethnic conflicts there. Oedipal structure imposed as a universal to every national subject does not, in fact, serve the analytic function of individual emancipation. Rather, because it is both the arbiter and symptom of modernity, it becomes a geopolitical tool in nations that aspire to rid themselves of the Balkan taint and identify themselves as European.

The geopolitical map of the divided and hierarchized Europe preceded, and influenced, the development of Freud's theory of subjectivity. When he constructed his theory of the Oedipal complex, translating the character of the mythical Oedipus to the fixed structure of a normal child in a bourgeois family in capitalist society, he was convinced that he had identified the very core of human subjectivity. Put very simply, he theorized that at a certain stage of development, the child experiences unconscious erotic desire for the parent of the opposite sex and homicidal feelings toward the parent of the same sex. Resolution of the conflict these feelings create is key to the child's development, and the Oedipal complex itself is axiomatic to psychoanalysis—as are the competing drives for sexual pleasure (Eros) and death (Thanatos). For Freud and his followers, Oedipalization became a universal civilizational standard and, given the development and articulation of the theory within the context of the cognitive map of Europe, this universal application was inherently problematic. The perceived absence or Oedipalization in a particular group or society became a hallmark of barbarity, despotism, and paganism.[6] Thus, Oedipalization, metastasizing from its conceptual origins in individual psychoanalysis, acquired the ancillary, pernicious role of defining imperial hierarchies and justifying cultural disqualification of the other in order to claim psychoanalytic universality.[7]

For Freud, the people directly to the south of his native Austria did not meet the Oedipal civilizational standard, as he makes clear in his response to Trieste psychoanalyst Edoardo Weiss's complaint that a Slovene patient was not responding to therapy. Freud, in a letter of May 28, 1922, declares, "Our analytical art when faced with such people, our perspicacity alone cannot break through to the dynamic relation which controls them."[8] "The dynamic relations which controls them" is not sophisticated enough to respond positively to the "perspicacity" of the "analytic art." Southern Slavs in general, Freud argued in his explication of the case of the "Rat Man," are anal.[9] Not only do they have a proclivity to sodomy, but they also dream of shit as a sign of gold and luck.[10] Freud had a special admiration for the Bosnian Turks. He held the view that they love sex more than life; when they are no longer having sex, life loses all meaning.[11] In 1898, Freud went to Herzegovina and visited Trebinje, a small Turkish town with an old harem in it. Historian Peter Swales reconstructs this visit, arguing persuasively that it took place during a particularly intense period in Freud's sexual neurosis. Under these circumstances, his visit to the former seraglio as a tourist can be construed as a pivotal moment when he might have imagined himself a sexual despot, a Bosnian Turk.[12] The proof that the Balkans eroticized Freud is in his analysis of dreams, where we learn that on that journey he had convinced himself to indulge in extramarital sex whenever he had the opportunity.[13] According to Ernest Jones, Freud's travels reveal his imaginary map of Europe as expressive of his own desires.[14] When going north, he would experience order and civilization; when going south he would find the less civilized but more sensual culture and people already marked on his cognitive map.

Freud was apparently unaware of the extent to which his theory of Oedipal subjectivity—and his own imaginary map—had been influenced by the prevailing philosophical geography of the time. Because of this parallel with the hierarchical structure of the European cognitive map, psychoanalysis, from its inception, was complicit in the creation and dissemination of ethnic and racial stereotypes. The correspondence between Freud and Jung contains many references to the ways psychoanalysis, in its early days, constructed and nurtured ethnic bias. For example, Freud and Jung attributed the ineffectiveness of psychoanalysis in Russia to a lack of proper individuation among the "Russian material." In a letter to Freud dated June 2, 1909, Jung reports to Freud concerning a visit by a Russian psychiatrist: "This Dr. Asatiani (such is his name) complains about the lack of therapeutic results. Aside from the imperfection of his art, I think the trouble lies with the Russian material, where the individual is as ill differentiated as a fish in a shoal. The problems of the masses are the first things that need solving there."[15] And in another letter to Jung, Freud writes, "The Russians, I believe, are especially deficient in the art of pains-taking work." He ends this letter with a paean to Jung, his family and their new house on a lake near Zurich: "With very special regards to you, your wife and children in your new house."[16] The tone of this letter somehow conveys that Freud is comparing the hapless Russians unfavorably with Jung and his family.

Even though many of his patients were Eastern European and provided Freud (whose father came from Eastern Europe) not only with accounts of their personal lives but also with a decent middle-class livelihood, he still saw them as unindividuated "material" ripe for exploitation, a psycho-analytic abject. As Freud writes to Sandor Ferenczi, "Patients are a rabble . . . they only serve to provide us with a livelihood and material to learn from. We certainly cannot help them. This is therapeutic nihilism, and yet by the concealment of these doubts and the raising of patients' hopes, patients do become caught."[17] Jung, for his part, also had an early exploit-ive relation to the "Russian material." As a married man, he maintained a sexual relationship with Sabina Spielrein, an eighteen-year-old Russian girl who was his patient. When her mother demanded of Jung more pro-fessional conduct, he responded that he should start charging her for her daughter's therapy at ten francs per session. His implication was clear: he had the right to sex with her daughter as long as he was providing analysis for free.[18]

According to Freud and Jung, not only does the "Russian material" lack subjectivity but also, apparently, even prominent psychoanalysts such as Max Etingon (a former student of Jung and a close friend of Freud) are suspect simply because of their Russian origins. On this subject, Jung writes to Freud as follows: "I consider Etingon a totally impotent gasbag—scarcely has this uncharitable judgment left my lips than it occurs to me that I envy him his uninhibited abreaction of the polygamous instinct. I therefore retract 'impotent' as too compromising. He will certainly never

amount to anything; one day he may become a member of the Duma."[19]
The Duma was known as an ineffective political body dissolved by the
Czar, and Etingon's putative sexual potency makes him, in Jung's view,
impotent in the matter of democratic institutions.[20] Jung's sardonic comment about the "polygamous instinct" is quite hypocritical, given that he
was sexually involved with Spielrein at the time. His hypocrisy in this case
is only symptomatic of general sexual pathologizing of the exploited other
by the Western analyst. It is interesting to note that Russian psychoanalysts did not question Freud's and Jung's geopolitical bias but have instead
internalized and made it into psychoanalytic theory. For example, Russian
psychoanalyst Lou Andreas-Salomé turns this exclusionary logic upon
herself, equating Russian nationality with sexuality. The heroine of her
novel can have sex only with Russian men.[21] To Andreas-Salomé, the cognitive map of Europe had been justified and mystified in and through her
understanding of psychoanalysis. In the West, she dedicates her life to
reason and sexuality, in Russia, to mysticism and femininity.[22] And, interestingly enough, the mysticism that Freud rejected in the case of Jung's
rejection of Freud's sexual theory appeared quite natural, attractive and
intellectually engaging in the case of Andreas-Salomé, perhaps because it
has geopolitical justification.[23]

The geopolitical undercurrent in psychoanalytic discourse surfaces
even in interaction and correspondence between Freud and Jung. For instance, Jung remembers Freud saying to him, "My dear Jung, promise me
never to abandon the sexual theory. This is the most essential thing of all.
You see, we must make a dogma of it, an unshakable bulwark." When Jung
refused the request, Freud, deploying clinical language, quickly moved to
denigrate him. In a letter to James Jackson Putnam he declares, "[Jung] . .
. has not outgrown his own neurosis."[24] Jung, writing in response that
"the majority of psychoanalysts misuse psychoanalysis for the purpose of
devaluating others and their progress by insinuations about complexes"[25]
is clearly implying that Freud has done the same. Freud acknowledges the
truth of this, but offers no reconciliation. He equivocates instead, writing,
"I do not know if there is any way of preventing this entirely."[26] This
exchange moves from clinical to racial insinuations, with Freud declaring
that his effort to unite "Jews and Goyim" in the service of psychoanalysis
has failed because "they separate like oil and water." He then writes to
Spielrein that he is glad she is cured of her "neurotic dependence on Jung"
and, hearing the news that she is pregnant by a Jewish doctor, he notes
approvingly that the child will be "born from the superior Jewish race."
Jung then takes up the Aryan point of view, implying that the grounding

of psychoanalytic theory in sexuality is the result of Freud's and Adler's Jewish origins. As he reflects, "Freud's and Adler's reduction of everyday psychic to primitive sexual wishes and power drives has something about it that is beneficial and satisfying to the Jew . . . these specific Jewish doctrines are truly unsatisfying to the Germanic mentality."[27]

Not only did the universal application of the Oedipal standard create a de facto civilizational hierarchy, but psychoanalysis also, as the ultimate arbiter of *individual* subjectivity, was inherently a discourse of power. As Foucault argues, new discursive power forms at many points of origin. With respect to contemporary psychoanalytic discourse on the Balkans, some of these points of power have been academic, as in the case of Slavoj Žižek (a Slovene) and Bulgarian native Julia Kristeva; some have been medical and political (as represented by the two Serb psychiatrists Rašković and Karadžić). But all, invoking psychoanalysis—as perhaps the ultimate representational scheme of civilization—have been aimed at the reconstruction of postcommunist subjectivity.

Slavoj Žižek was already an established psychoanalyst when he ran unsuccessfully for one of four places in the collective presidency of Slovenia in 1990—the first multiparty elections of the postcommunist era. However, his real platform is a discursive one aimed at the patriarchal reconstruction of Slovene national identity through Lacanian psychoanalysis. Žižek takes up the case of the failing Slovene Oedipus at the point where Freud leaves it in the letter to Weiss concerning the "nonanalyzable Slovene," Weiss's patient who is not responding to therapy. Instead of questioning Freud's implicit geopolitical bias and the limitation of psychoanalytic theory beyond the walls of Vienna, Žižek uses Freud's original dictum to assert the collective conditions of the Slovene Oedipus. Elaborating on Freud's diagnosis, he writes,

> The "immoral" Slovene mentioned does not just embody the paradoxical way enjoyment and the Law are linked, but hides yet another surprise, which leads to the key to the Slovene national fantasy, to the theme of the "maternal superego," to the theme of the mother (not the father) as the bearer of the Law/Prohibition.[28]

According to Žižek, Slovenes are excessively attached in their "national fantasy" to the Mother. The absence of the Father, the bearer of internal law/Prohibition, engenders a "national fantasy" formed around maternal prohibition of external pleasures and creates the "impediment" to subjectivity expressed in the Slovene's sexual impotence and immorality. Only the Symbolic and internalized Law of the Father, through inner prohibition, engenders enjoyment as a form of transgression. And, Žižek concludes, "we Slovenes—'unanalyzable'" according to Freud—had to wait for Lacan to find a meeting with psychoanalysis; only with Lacan did psychoanalysis achieve a level of sophistication that rendered it capable of tackling such foul apparition as the Slovenes."[29] In other words, Žižek accepts and perpetuates the "point of view of the dominating other,"[30] and Lacanian language as the site of national self-transformation—Slovenia becoming *Lacania*. And when subjectivity has been restored to Slovenia, what becomes of the "unanalyzable" identity attributed to it by Freud and Žižek? It may be transferred to the "other" Balkans via the Lacanian concept of the *Real*, the presymbolic world. Mladen Dolar, another prominent Slovene Lacanian, discusses Freud's visit to the Slovene caves in Škocije in 1898, where he unexpectedly met the notorious anti-Semitic mayor of Vienna, Dr. Karl Lüger. Dolar describes the cave as "this metaphorical abyss of the unconscious" where "the Master missing from the symbolic makes an unexpected appearance in the Real." The Balkans is the *Real*, Europe's unconscious where its repressed desires and violence emerge. And, as Dolar writes, "Finally it is the place of the unanalyzable." Because the Balkans is the *Real* to Freud then it must be to the Slovenes as well. The point being, through Lacanian intervention the Slovenes have ceased to be Balkans.

In this transition from the Balkan femininity to national emancipation through patriarchy, Lacanian language becomes particularly cruel. Žižek advocates a kind of discursive patriarchy as a way to cure his nation of its dangerous femininity by means of masculine "shock and awe." He writes that "male and female are not two 'races' of humanity in the same way as different ethnic communities are. Ethnic communities are structured according to the principle of group identification with the ethnic Thing."[31] The Law binds man and woman into causal relations, thus breaking up ethnic solidarity. But, Žižek argues, at the core of this "productive" antagonism of sexual differences lies woman's depression—as "the original fact," of her sliding, Parsifal-like "into the abyss of self-annihilation, of absolute lethargy."[32] And, he asserts, male aggression works as a "kind of 'electroshock'"[33] to lift the woman out of her depression and self-annihilation. This causal bond between the male's fist and the woman's face should transcend ethnic collectivization and ethnic antagonisms, replacing them with the real and productive differentiation based in the Name-of-the-Father.[34]

Žižek's argument regarding sexual and ethnic politics in the Balkans (that is, his view of woman as a "dark continent" and threat to the symbolic order of the Father) bears a certain similarity to the discursive location of the Balkans (the "dark continent," Europe's unconscious) in European geopolitics and is just as regressive. For example, the Serbs committed horrendous rapes of Muslim women and often sadistically forced the father to watch the rape of his daughter. Here is Žižek's effort to fit this ritualized sexual aggression into the Lacanian scheme, and to circumvent the question of ethnicity by focusing on the "Father Thing" in the cruelty of the rape:

> Because his desire is split, divided between fascination with enjoyment and repulsion at it; or, to put it another way, because the implicit knowledge that the victim is *enjoying* her suffering, the observer's ability to act—to rescue the victim-woman from the torturer or from herself—bears witness to the fact that he became "dupe of his own fantasy" (as Lacan put it apropos of Sade): *the blow aims at the unbearable surplus-enjoyment.*[35]

Žižek is actually presenting two aspects of the Father's enjoyment (Lacan's *Pere-Jouissance*) here. One is symbolic, the other a presymbolic, primitive manifestation of the Balkan *Real*,[36] which is activated by the Serb rape and is the actual source of the Bosnian Father's impotence and perversion. Once again, he offers only a discursive construct; he has no access to the father's actual thoughts. There is, in fact, no perverse desire in the Bosnian father's experience other than one in Žižek's own *joy of analysis*. Given the bond he suggests between the masculine fist and the woman's face, one wonders if the Serb rape of the Bosnian daughter should be seen metaphorically as curing her of a deep depression.[37]

Julia Kristeva, like Žižek, bases her discourse on the Balkans in the essential negativity of the feminine—both psychological and geopolitical. She designates the Balkans, her "maternal container," "a blank spot on the geographical map, somber Balkans pierced through by a lack of curiosity about the West."[38] Rejecting her Bulgarian identity and offering her own biography as an example of Oedipal resurrection, she prescribes for the Balkan subject a civilizing project of "Oedipal revolt" against the "archaic mother" (that is, the Balkans) and views the West (France, in particular) as the symbolic Father and agent of civilizing "rescue" from the Balkan bond. She rhetorically warns the Balkans subjects that their failed subjectivity will cause them to regress into a pre-Oedipal "maternal space" (her "chora"—corresponding to the Lacanian *Real*) with a subsequent rise of irrational and violent politics epitomized by "Serbian neo-Fascism."[39]

There the subject may abandon itself to the bond with the "archaic mother," and surrender to the carnage and violence endemic to the pre-Oedipal condition or commit psychological and geopolitical matricide (as Kristeva herself has done) and be reborn through the psychological superiority of the masculine. The historical exclusion of the Balkans by the West as an archaic and dangerous space foreshadowed the exclusion that would come with the Oedipal divisions imposed by psychoanalysis as the universal science of subjectivity. Infusing fresh symbolic energy into this exclusion, Kristeva, with her prescription of "oedipal revolt," in effect demands its internal continuation by the Balkan subject.

To every Balkan psychoanalyst belongs one Bosnia. From the perspective of Kristeva's own exilic identity, French immigrants and the Balkans are of the same unoedipalized ilk. While the Balkans symbolize the mad archaic mother, the immigrants are angry children, and both are a threat to the Father. Kristeva accuses Third World immigrants, since their arrival in France, of "Balkanizing the cultural, political, and economic forces of European people."[40] Indeed, she lays the blame on immigrants for the "gruesome course" that French civil society has taken since the French Revolution. Kristeva wonders about the anger of "these young people in French suburbs [French Algerians]" who "have a need to express their unhappiness."[41] Supposedly because of their refusal to assimilate, their unhappiness will grow and, "if you allow this unhappiness to enter Islam, people begin adhering to dogma."[42] In 1990, many French intellectuals signed a petition in favor of granting political asylum to illegal immigrants. Refusing to do so, Kristeva stated in her *Open Letter to Harlem Desir* on February 24, 1990, "Much as I am sensitive to the distress of the immigrants, equally I don't think it's desirable to give the deceptive impression that integration is possible for everyone who asks for it."[43] According to Kristeva, immigrants should have to completely assimilate into the French way of life in order to be admitted into French society. They should have to prove that they are Oedipal subjects who have resolved the maternal bond and solidly anchored themselves in the Law of the Symbolic Father. The clear implication is that immigrants who fail to do so should be deported. The symbolic city (Paris), divided into the Muslim (maternal) suburbs and the civilized center, replicates the structure of Oedipal conflict. Applied to the Muslim neighbors in Paris, Kristeva's psychoanalytic view that "powers of horror" force the subject to be reborn through cleansing itself of the abject invents a little Bosnia in the heart of Paris.

The carnage in the ex-Yugoslavia, ubiquitous in the TV news of the 1990s, worked to legitimize the texts of Kristeva and Žižek read in academic seminars, conferences, and journals in the United States. In addition, there were countless books devoted to the Balkans published in the last decade. With the violence in the ex-Yugoslavia everywhere on view, it was all too easy to find justification for Kristeva's call to "matricide," and to see the ex-Yugoslavia as the mad archaic mother ripping apart the region. And Žižek's concept of perversion as a political factor, a discursive construct that ignores the tragic consequences of interethnic violence, plays to nationalist politics in the same way that the perversion represented in David Lynch's films plays to an audience. But little has been said about how the language of Oedipalization fed into an overall discursive strategy of demonizing the Balkans and to what extent that language was itself part of this horror. Since the Balkans lacks any subjectivity, without which there is no democracy, the conditions of subjectivity must be imposed from outside as both Žižek and Kristeva seek to do. These are colonizing strategies, as Tzvetan Todorov clearly explained, that go back to the language of conquest and extermination, and the politics of psychoanalysis delivered them in the language of normality and madness.[44] Their language did not *cause* anyone to kill, but those who did may easily recognize themselves in that language constructed as Balkan subjects.[45]

Work such as that of Kristeva and Žižek, couched in an erudite register, ultimately lends an academic authority and protection to the same colonizing language of exclusion when it *is* used explicitly for political manipulation—as in the case of Jovan Rašković and his protégé, Radovan Karadžić. The respective political careers of these two psychiatrists clearly illustrate the tragic consequences of explicit politicization of psychoanalytic language in the Balkans. The work of Jovan Rašković is a strange fusion of ethnopsychoanalysis and antipsychiatry. According to his own account,[46] when he worked as head of a psychiatric ward in Sibenik, Rašković found "empiric" evidence that ethnic types conform to Freud's theory of character. Following psychoanalytic theory, on the basis of this finding he theorized that the collective narcissism of ethnic groups is likely to be exacerbated by their very similarity and to lead, sooner or later, to conflict. In my practice," he writes, "working almost thirty-five years on the intersection of the borders of the three republics belonging to the Serb, Croat, and Muslim populations, I have noticed that members of different ethnic groups act according to different characterological types."[47] Although he carefully notes that, in formulating these theories, he is referring only to tendencies, he invokes psychoanalysis to back up his "evidence": "If psychoanalysis is not a science, then my investigations have no scientific base either. But if we agree that psychoanalysis is a science, then all of my moderate investigations are perhaps scientific."[48] Despite this disingenuous reluctance to make scientific claims for his "moderate investigations," he nonetheless anchors individual consciousness into a predetermined group narcissism, "healing"—and, at the same time, stereotyping—large and heterogeneous populations along ethnic lines. He then makes a theoretical connection between Freud's "narcissism of small differences" and his own Oedipal ethnocharacterology:

> From the standpoint of psychological phantasms, one can conclude that there are not only Orthodox/Catholic or Orthodox/Muslim conflicts; in fact, there are conflicts of character between ethnic groups as well. This is a conflict between an ethnic group which, in its essence, is Oedipal, somewhat aggressive, inclined to change, and another group, which is castrational, is satisfied with the *status quo*. Thus, one ethnic group, the Oedipal, is always ready for change—ready to change its fathers, its rulers, and those who rule over its pleasures. And the other group fears any change at all because it might lead to castration. This means, speaking as a psychiatrist, that here we have a clash between the Oedipal and the castrational ethnic groups. . . .
>
> The connection between the Oedipal and castrational characters is very unpleasant, thus it should not be surprising that we have a situation of great, paranoia-driven ethnic hate between these two groups. The castrational group, which fears the aggressive Oedipal, expresses great hate toward that group
>
> The castrational character, preoccupied with fear of the aggressive Oedipus, displays a great hate toward him, so that extermination of the aggressive Oedipus is not regarded as wrong, nor does it cause any guilt.[49]

In formulating this typology of character, Rašković is naturally most concerned with the Serb "type." He claims, in *Luda Zemlja*, that the significant majority of Serbs whom he has treated and whose characterology he has studied, regardless of whether the patient suffered from schizophrenia, neurosis, tension, or deep depression, bear all signs of the Oedipal character. This character type exhibits moderate aggression, but also submissiveness. The Oedipal inner structure has two principal parts: one of these is strong loyalty, which is expressed as a complete loyalty to authority—that is, to the Father who rules all pleasures and holds all power. A second hallmark of the Oedipal character is the transmutation of loyalty to destructive rebellion if the subject is deprived by the Father of power and pleasures. Serbs, therefore, Rašković explains, inherit authoritarian features along with some elements of aggression. The Oedipal character is usually a very open one; it is not a character of darkness and shade, but of clearly manifested extremes. Another aspect of this character is its great dependence on the Mother, which represents a disorderly factor. However, "In the psychological sense," Rašković writes," the mother can be identified with the earth, and with the wider ethnic group."[50]

The castrational (Croatian) and Oedipal (Serb) characters, Rašković claims, can live in peace only if the castrational group submissively accepts the domination of the Oedipal. By this logic, Greater Serbia occupies a position of governance natural not only for the Serbs who are born to be rulers, but also for Croats and others for whom subordination is a natural condition. The common ground of the two characters is their anti-authoritarian stance, taken by the castrational character because he fears castration, and by the Oedipal because he is deprived of his pleasures. According to Rašković, it is inevitable that a rift will occur between the two ethnic groups precisely *because* of the similarity in their characters:

> This syndrome of small differences about which I have spoken before also has a deeper meaning. As in marriage, there is conflict because of small differences, and the more similar the characters of the two parties, the more likely is their eventual separation. This is because of the feeling on each side that it must claim and hold fast to what it sees as its own, precisely because there is so little actual difference between the two parties. This is a lesser form of paranoia, of the same kind that affects Serb-Croat relations in Croatia. In the case of language, it is precisely because the differences in the languages are so small that each group fears losing its own, and proclaims it separate and distinct from the other.[51]

"Small differences" seem, in Rašković's account, to be an unavoidable source of repressed aggression towards the one who is like you. In discussing language, he is referring to the Croatian government's refusal to allow Croatian Serbs to use the Cyrillic alphabet; this dispute over a small difference in language was the source of a violent conflict between the Serb minority in Croatia and the Croatian government, which may be seen not only as an example of the "narcissism of small differences," but also as a political performative of Rašković's interpretation of psychoanalytic concepts. In other words, it was not the spontaneous combustion of group narcissism erupting out of the depth of a dark collective unconscious that caused ethnic violence, but the effect of the psychoanalytic concepts appropriated by the psychiatrist as political rhetoric to ignite the conflict hoping that the mad side will win.

For Rašković, the Serbian nation was the Mother. He argued always that the communist ideology and political system, by suppressing the Serb unconscious desire for nation and denying and criminalizing the Serb Oedipal structure, gave rise to a madness of rationality. In contrast to the transparent rationality of class ideology, the Serb unconscious desire for nation is for the Serb Oedipus an ontological abyss over which the Serb nation levitates. Rašković proposed to counter the suppression of the Serb unconscious desire for nation with madness of the irrational as a path to the Serb Oedipal desire. As a parochial and anti-Enlightenment psychiatrist, he construes the Serb Oedipus as dark and mad, as is evident from the following quotation. In the hollow shell of the postcommunist subject, his ontology of the darkness of postcommunist identity echoed ominously:

> A man's essence is in the dark space of the unconscious. A man's essence is irrational. Thus man is always alone when he is closest to himself, surrounded by phantasms, idols and irrational constructs. All dramas of this layer are more difficult, more shocking and deadlier. This layer is the essence of being. There dwell all forms of suffering beings, pains and harms. This is the birthplace of madness; the irrational is the core of the human essence. This is why it is first and foremost hopeless, always open and wondrous. It is never the same and identical. It is always incomplete.[52]

Rašković paints the Serb Oedipal essence with dark shades. There is a poetic dimension to the irrational human being that contrasts with the rational, instrumental and despotic; it is the source of deep intuition about both the metaphysical and social aspects of life. In Rašković's context, this ontology of Oedipal darkness serves as a permanent resistance to modernity. So constructed, postcommunist subjectivity, now defined by ethnicity and not by class, had a constant need to understand its suppressed madness as its essence. The human subject in the postcommunist Balkans had to be put under the permanent supervision of psychiatry not only to explain, but also to manage it.

But, as Rašković makes clear in his writings, this political necessity is not without danger. He warns that opening up the deepest layers of the unconscious may be shocking and mortal, even genocidal towards other ethnic groups if not supervised by a psychiatrist. Bringing irrationality and healthy madness into collective life was, for him, a psychological process, which eliminates individual fear. The Serb fear was an outgrowth of the

Croatian genocide and communism and formed an obstacle to the unconscious flow into the ego consciousness. Thus Rašković saw the organizing of Serbs in mass gatherings as having a therapeutic effect:

The big "advantage" of masses is that they eliminate everything individual. The mass gathering eliminates individual fear. It destroys anxiety, thus it has a therapeutic effect for all who take part. Besides this therapeutic effect, the mass gathering has another effect, expression of the unconscious. In the mass, every individual act simply "flows"; the mass is where phantasms transform into facts.

The mass appears usually in the time of great crisis, in great fears and great uncertainties.

They appear when moral norms and moral forces upon which civilization rests weaken. The mass always appears at the end of a civilization or at the end of an ideology which has been dominant for a long time, and it represents a formal ending to both.[53]

Mass gatherings activate a group imaginary in which individuals find psychological catharsis at times of confusion and civilizational collapse. Clearly, Rašković combined the psychoanalytic theory of the unconscious with the specific political context of the postcommunist Yugoslavia in a way that mobilized the masses for the ethnic conflicts to come. He himself acknowledged that potential danger of this, warning that because of the Serbs' long history of suppression, getting in touch with their collective unconscious would create a shock—even a temporary regression and desire for revenge on the authority imposing the repression.

Serb myths have entered the Serb spirit, but with a dose of poison, spite, vengeance, regression. All of these threatening emotions need be controlled, to be made less poisonous, to have more truth, emotional establishment of the integrity of personality of one people, the integrity of one people's being, rather than to be full of poison which will be transferred as revenge onto other ethnic groups.[54]

Once again, the necessity of a psychiatrically controlled process of political liberation was affirmed. In moving from the influence of the imposed "rational delirium" to that of their ontological being, the Serbs would encounter challenges to their collective identity. In the absence of individual consciousness, people would fall under the submission to the collective will of the mob. This, Rašković points out, could turn into a dangerous and genocidal campaign of vengeance against the Croats and Muslims, a tendency that could be monitored and controlled only by a skilled psychiatrist in touch with the Serb ontological being. He saw himself, in this role, as a sort of shaman leading his people through the labyrinth of the unconscious and helping them avoid the temptations of violence. He sought, in the course of this guidance, to keep the masses always exposed to irrational delirium, the sentiments caused by being together; for when masses become aware of their political interest, delirium becomes rational and aggressive. We should not be afraid of irrational delirium-we should be afraid of rational delirium; irrational delirium, he instructs, is nonviolent only symbolic and spectacular. His constant message to the Serbs was, "Do not be aggressive do not be genocidal, be irrational in your Oedipal desire!"

And yet, despite these instructions, genocide did occur—precisely because of the psychiatric supervision of the masses turned into the production of madness. The rational logic of social institutions such as police, military, and mass media were all co-opted in psychiatric discourse, in the service of producing/supervising madness as an ideology of nation—resulting, as we now know, in ethnic cleansing and mass rapes. When Rašković declared to Franjo Tudjman, "The Serbs are mad people," he had already Oedipalized them. Through his psychiatric work, they were already coded and collectivized.

Rašković had regarded his political activity as the leader of the Serb minority in Croatia as a form of mass psychiatry.[55] To carry out this mission, he carefully produced a political cadre for his movement: two of his patients became prominent members of his party. One became Minister of Interior in the secessionist Serb government, and he nominated his former student, Radovan Karadžić, as leader of the Serbian Democratic Party in Bosnia. In fact, he ushered in a kind of psychiatric politics of madness and escalated it to the level of military action against Muslim and Croatian minorities and, subsequently, to ethnic cleansing. If politics is a human affair, Rašković seems to have reasoned, it must open itself to the ontology of darkness and madness just as psychiatry does. Madness, which he constructed as a new political force of ethnic collectivity, went unrecognized as such camouflaged in the context of the politics of Marxist "rational delirium." Politicians, Rašković made clear, should recognize that being out of touch with one's own madness leads to the supremacy of ego or pseudo-madness. The failure of the Croatian government to recognize this was, to him, a form of "rational delirium." And, if the Croatian government refused to acknowledge madness as a political category, he was determined that the Serbs would introduce it into Croatian politics. His notion that Serbs and Croats, under Marxism, had to repress their ethnic essence, moved the social reality of Yugoslavia into the sphere of the frag-mentations and conflicts engendered by the dubious psychoanalytic theory designed to produce "irrational delirium."

While Rašković's polemics elicited the Eros of nation, Karadžić empha-sized Thanatos, the death instinct, as the birthright of the Serbian nation: "I was born . . . to set fire, kill and reduce everything to dust." At the end of his life, Freud wrote that the burning of candles at both weddings and funerals are symbolic of the psychoanalytic precept that erotic desire pro-duces a death wish. If Srebrenica, the result of Rašković's eroticization of the Serb nation, became the fulfillment of Karadžić's death wish, then both psychiatrists have burned candles—Rašković to wed the Serbs with Oedipus, and Karadžić seduce them with death.

This dual celebration of death and sex as the full scope of life has its roots in the convergence of the psychoanalytic imagination with the cog-nitive map of Europe and the Eastern and Oriental periphery of Freud's Empire. For a long time Freud resisted the Eastern European influence on psychoanalysis, but eventually accepted it, acknowledging and univer-salizing the attraction to death (Thanatos) as a counterpoint to the attrac-tion to sex (Eros) originally theorized by Sabina Spielrein (referred to by both Freud and Jung as "the Russian material"). The catalyst in Spielrein's own realization of this principle was a violent confrontation with Jung, her therapist and lover, which she recounts in her diary. Jung, whom she deeply loved and with whom she wanted to have a child, was denying to Freud his relationship with her. Confronting him, she pulled a knife; he grabbed her hand and forced her to drop the knife, but not without lacer-ating her. Spielrein, leaving the bloody knife on the floor and her lover, teacher, and therapist behind her, went on to write an essay that would make her famous, in which she argues that death and destruction are con-ditions of rebirth.[56] Years later, Freud would acknowledge the influence of Spielrein's paper, "Destruction as a Condition of Becoming" on his own articulation of the Eros/Thanatos duality in *Beyond the Pleasure Principle:* "I remember my own defensive attitude when the idea of an instinct of destruction first emerged in psychoanalytic literature, and how long it took before I became receptive to it."[57]

The theory of the "death wish," then, entered the psychoanalytic canon with a geopolitical supplement—the special relationship between death and the "Russian material." American James Rice addresses this relation-ship, arguing that the theory of the death wish was generally accepted in Russian intellectual circles and was an important Russian contribution to psychoanalysis.[58] This is certainly true, but the question must still be asked

whether the desire for death is innate to the "Russian soul" or was discur-
sively implanted by psychoanalysis through its internal geopolitics. In the
case of Spielrein's violent scene with Jung, was she casting herself spontaneously in the role of self-destructive "Russian material" for which she
had been carefully rehearsed? Bruno Bettelheim argues precisely this, that
Spielrein viewed her involvement with Jung as "dirty" because Jung saw
it that way.[59] She took upon herself to act as "Russian material" just to be
with her master, "at present I am in league with the devil. May that be
true. My friend and I had the tenderest 'poetry' last Wednesday."[60] The
originary bond between the "Russian material" and the death instinct as
created by the psychoanalytic imagination was very personal for Spielrein.
On the other hand, whether the source of this bond was external, internal
or both, it lent her the creative force to develop her experience into a
seminal psychoanalytic theory and has assured her a place in the history of psychoanalysis. As Judith Butler writes, "what operates under the
sign of the symbolic may be nothing other than precisely that set of imaginary effects which have become naturalized and reified as the law of
signification."[61]

Since ego extends into collectivity and vice versa, does not the psychoanalytic concept of death and destruction as a condition of coming into
being converge with that of the Eros of nation? I argue here that it does
and that the writing and political career of Radovan Karadžić, architect of
the Bosnian genocide, is an example of this convergence. Massacres and
genocide followed his political deployment of the language of the "death
wish," and his own writing reveals the extent to which his project eroticized the idea of nation intertwined with death—as in this poem:

> I'm born to live without the tomb,
> this divine body will not die.
> It's not only born to smell flowers,
> but also to set fire, kill and
> reduce everything to dust.[62]

As the Turkish poet Akgun Akova writes, "Karadžić is a poet of holocaust.
He is a poet who places death in people's irises."[63]

After Rašković had created the dogma of the Serbian Oedipus and had
put in place a "desiring machine" to produce love for the Serbian *ethnos*,
Karadžić came to infer death from the ethnic *Eros*. In an extraordinary
piece of prose titled provocatively "Da li je ovo bio rat?" ("Was this a
war?") which he read at a conference dedicated to the *Philosophy of War*
(1995) he divulged the full extent of his fantasy about the Serb project of

death as the birth of a national subject out of destruction. Actual burning villages formed the backdrop of the conference, and the part of Karadžić in this psychiatric performative was ostensibly to evoke the Serb primitive past. In fact, he was creating the geopolitical future, the discursive territory formed around the simultaneous denial and enjoyment of death. The piece he read at the conference, quoted here, has strong overtones of Spielrein's writings on the creation/destruction dyad. In his apology for war, he argues that war is the ontology of the Serb national identity. At one point, he tells the story of a Serb soldier returning to his village:

> The village is wiped out, and no one can recognize it. Between burnt houses there lie unburied corpses. . . . Also all the domestic animals are killed, mutilated and scattered around. . . . Everything is murdered, mutilated and burnt. Birds on branches—some killed, some frightened. They also do not recognize the landscape. The young fruit trees on which they have landed are also plucked. The eaves have disappeared. . . . There's no church. There are only ruins. . . . The warrior knows quite well who has passed through his village. *He has known this for a few centuries.* He knows that *for the hundredth time* . . . his family, home, present and past are erased, and that there is nothing at all. . . . We do not have the possibility of asking ourselves whether it was possible or whether it is possible to be different. That can be done by others who live some other and different life. Who can allow themselves not to belong to their people, not to be Serbs, *not to be*, if they feel like it, anything.[64]

In analyzing this piece, Serb philosopher Branka Arsić proposes that the Serb self-spectralizing nationalism and its accompanying madness have been caused by not properly mourning death. Producing the Serb Oedipal desire towards the tribe, towards the Mother represented by language, myths, and territories, has produced collective madness, genocide and its denial. Relying on Derrida's spectral analysis, Arsić's essay "On the Dark Side of Twilight"[65] delineates the delusional interpretation of reality that has caused massive collective denial of genocide among Serbs. She shows why genocide could not be acknowledged by Karadžić or by Serbian nationalists, whose denial persists today. It is this that holds Serb national ideology in a no-man's-land between life and death where neither can be recognized or acknowledged. According to Arsić, the burned village described by Karadžić represents the world of death and the routine of murder and destruction deeply engraved in the Serb collective memory. It is this heritage of death that leaves the Serb no choice except to be the continuation of death and prevents him from living. While the French may enjoy cheese and wine and the Germans their forests, Serbs have no option of enjoying anything other than their own death. The soldier has survived the war but he is not alive; he can neither live nor die. In this twilight zone rests the homeland of the Serb collective memory as articulated by Karadžić, and Arsić offers the following analysis of his prose, which also explains the impossibility of the Serb nationalists' ever acknowledging genocide:

> The ideological profit of this nationalistic mobilization is enormous. First, since we are always already spectres, we are those who do not have our bare life either; we are those who do not live and who cannot live. Consequently, our "life" cannot be killed, because it was always already killed, always already half-killed, or, as it is sometimes said in Serbian nationalistic narration—slaughtered alive. However, if our own life is always already both alive and slaughtered, then it follows that the other can occupy only the place of life that works against our death. In this "screen play" the other is never a spectre since the projection failed, since we are spectralising ourselves, etc.) The other is repulsively and unpleasantly alive. . . . Furthermore, if we, as those who know the sad truth that it is impossible to die, go to some military conflict only in order to realize ourselves into the final death, we, then in fact, never kill, because there is no death, at least we know that perfectly well. It is clear: the question of guilt and responsibility completely disappears.[66]

Arsić's lucid analysis of Karadžić's "philosophy of war" explains the continuing delusional denial of genocide among Serb nationalists, and why photos of Karadžić and general Ratko Mladić, the butchers of Srebrenica, are sometimes still displayed with joy and pride in public during the Serb national and religious holidays. To the oedipalized Serbs, Karadžić and Mladić "never" killed because they were never alive.

Before Karadžič's arrest in July 2008, he was rumored to be hiding in the caves near his birthplace in Montenegro, as if he had returned to the site of Europe's *Real*. One is reminded of Freud's encounter with Karl Lüger—whose extreme anti-Semitic political stance was to serve as a model for Hitler—in the Škocjan caves over a century ago, when "the Master missing from the symbolic makes an unexpected appearance in the *Real*." The Balkans is still the *Real*, and "the national identification, the secret national enjoyment which surfaces in Europe in highly sublimated form, or at the most in a form of marginal excesses, emerges there in its outspoken and bare shape, as an insolvable antagonism . . . (this is the place to come across a figure of a Lüger nowadays)." But, as it turned out, he had spent most of his time as a fugitive masquerading as Dr. Dragan Dabič, an urban practitioner of alternative medicine, in a tavern called "Mad House" run by Bosnian Serb refugees at the edge of the urban jungle of New Belgrade. The constellation of signifiers here is in itself maddening. The mad psychiatrist, the "Mad House," refugees made into "mad Serbs," converge into two great projects: "greater Serbia" and what Laurence A. Rickels termed "greater psychoanalysis" in his three-volume work *Nazi Psychoanalysis*.[67]

Slavoj Žižek compares social reality to "walking through fantasy," and the manner of Karadžić's reappearance in the public space certainly bears out this correlation. Freud described the "Wolf Man," as 'a piece of psychoanalysis.' This might be said also of Karadžić. When he left prison in 1985, where he had served eleven months for embezzlement and fraud, he was heard to say that he had "read everything by Freud and Jung" while in prison. When he was arrested for far more serious crimes and imprisoned in the Hague—shaved and recognizable as the fugitive Radovan Karadžić—he addressed the court as follows: "I have stopped using a false identity, and it's time the court does the same." Radman Šelmić comments that, according to Karadžić's logic, because psychiatry has renounced the oppressive practice of criminalization, he in turn should expect flexibility from the courts.[68]

Žižek takes Hegel's statement, "What I think, the product of my thought, is objective truth," to mean that there is no difference between paranoid and idealistic thought, because in both instances the reality is a made-up supplement by subjectivity. He also endorses Lacan's claim that "normalcy itself is a mode, a subspecies of psychosis" and Schelling's that normal reason is "regulated madness." According to Žižek,

> the ontological necessity of "madness" resides in the fact that it is not possible to pass directly from the purely "animal soul" immersed in its natural life-world to "normal" subjectivity dwelling in its symbolic universe—the vanishing mediator between the two is the "mad" gesture of radical withdrawal from reality that opens up the space for its symbolic (re)constitution.[69]

But is not Karadžić himself an example of "the 'mad' gesture of radical withdrawal from reality"? Could we not classify Karadžić's madness as a psychoanalytic *performative*? This is borne out in his statements to the court referring to the "kernel of fantasy" that, he claims, underlies the legality and objectivity of the court. After all, he is the traumatic cause of the court formed specifically to prosecute crimes done by him. He, the "kernel of fantasy," is speaking to the symbolic authority of the court, reminding it of its causal dependence on his "ontological madness." As Sherry Turkle writes of Lacan, "he will not speak *of* psychoanalysis; his speech itself would be a psychoanalytic discourse . . . a discourse close to delirium."[70] Žižek promotes the psychoanalytic ethics of power, the politics of the traumatic kernel that "reality is never 'itself'" that "spectral apparitions emerge in this very gap that forever separates reality from the real."[71] And, he reminded readers in the *London Review of Books* (August 2008) upon Karadžić's arrest, that he was a poet (in addition to psychiatrist and ruthless politician) who exemplifies postmodern nationalism and in the capacity of superego incites mass transgression of ethnic enjoyment with rhymes such as, "Convert to my new faith crowd . . . nothing is forbidden in my faith."[72] Yet, Žižek failed to mention that Karadžić regarded himself also as a psychoanalyst—and that, in that capacity, he deployed psychoanalytic principles as performative schemes for carrying out crimes against humanity. His poetry is part of this scheme.

Madness, then , in Žižek's theory as well as Karadžić's practice, becomes the path to the psychoanalyst's subjectivity and to the subject's "symbolic (re) constitution." If Karadžić provides the traumatic infrastructure for "ontological madness," Žižek provides its superstructure (Žižek *avec* Karadžić). Karadžić alone is responsible for the legal consequences of his "madness," but he could not have carried out his atrocities without invoking Freud's theories. Fascism is not, in fact, "terrified by psychoanalysis."[73] To quote a Nazi psychotherapist: "We as doctors are able to say objectively that we cannot do without the work of that man (Freud), work which a politically aroused youth (from their standpoint, quite correctly) burn."[74]

Everything You Always Wanted to Know About David Lynch, but Should Be Afraid to Ask Slavoj Žižek

Kriss Ravetto-Biagioli

In a very precise way, things are *even worse* in psychoanalysis than in Stalinism. Yes, we do have to renounce the secret treasure in ourselves, the *agalma* that confers on us our innermost dignity—all those things so dear to personalism; we have to undergo the conversion of this treasure into a "piece of shit," into a stinking excrement, and identify with it. However—and this is why things get even worse in psychoanalysis—the analysand has to accomplish this conversion *by himself*, without the alibi of monstrous circumstances that can be blamed for it.

SLAVOJ ŽIŽEK

Slavoj Žižek has written about the most pressing political issues of the last twenty years—multiculturalism, terrorism, the clash of civilizations, sexual difference, the Balkan and Iraq wars. He has spanned the "high" and the "low," engaging with philosophical debates over the legacy of Freud, Lacan, Hegel, Kant, and Schmitt, while also writing about dirty jokes, popular culture, and film. While extraordinarily wide in scope, his arguments rely on a remarkably narrow range of interpretive tools hinging, ultimately, on a fundamentalist approach to psychoanalysis. Not only does he invoke Freud's law of castration and the paradox of desire's repeated failure to escape castration to account for such disparate things as sexism, racism, global economics, war, and even genocide, but he also does so by simplifying (even caricaturizing) Freud's categories and by denying the implications of the fact that patriarchy is not what it used to be. Žižek does acknowledge the expanding gap between the original context of Freud's model (the late-nineteenth-century nuclear family) and the collapse of patriarchal authority and the destabilizing of the subject, but presents it as a nonproblem. To him (as to Lacan) the father was never real—he was always imaginary. By turning the father into an imaginary figure, he renders it irrefutable and impervious to any change in family structure, gender dynamics, ethnic and global politics. This reframing turns Freudian theory into dogma.

In Žižek's hands, such dogma often slips over into misogyny. He claims that his sometimes "dogmatic," "orthodox," or "obsessive" readings of Freud and Lacan are radical in their description of the conservatism and misogyny of popular culture, but his readings of film offer neither a radical critique of social formations, nor do they challenge antifeminism. They actually seem to do the opposite. He often comments on violent antifeminist and conservative trends in liberal politics, but he still attempts to justify some of the most antifeminist dimensions of Freud and Lacan. As William Hart points out, he "adopts a reactionary rhetoric masquerading under the honorific label of Left."[1]

The Idiot's Imaginary

At the beginning of the television program *The Pervert's Guide to Cinema*, Žižek declares: "there is nothing natural about desire . . . we have to be taught to desire, Cinema is the ultimate pervert art, it doesn't give you what you desire, it tells you how to desire." He does not, however, simply posit that cinema instructs us how to desire, he also suggests that cinema represents the secret truth of "our" desires. The question remains: If reality resides in illusion (cinematic spectacle), how then does such illusion constitute a "secret truth?" It turns out that it is only through the figure of what he calls the "imbecile" that he can hold onto a fundamentalist reduction of all truth to castration truth, and maintain the centrality of the phallus.

Žižek takes cinema to be the ideal form of popular culture to illustrate the law of castration and the paradox of desire and subjectivity, because it unknowingly stages them. In *The Metastases of Enjoyment*, he writes, "I am convinced of my proper grasp of some Lacanian concept only when I can translate it successfully into the inherent imbecility of popular culture."[2] But such an act of translation—like the identification of Oedipal structures in popular cultural productions—is disingenuous. If he is dismissive of popular culture as an "imbecilic medium" because of "its radical refusal of initiating secrecy" of castration truth and man's failed desires and failed subject identities, then how can he claim to find any truth in these imbecilic narratives?[3] Alternatively, if these Oedipal tropes are so evident that even an imbecile can see them, then why continually point to the obvious? He treats both the spectator (who allegedly blinds himself to the obvious secret of castration) and the medium (that allegedly cannot help but make the spectators see the truth of castration) as idiotic and ingenious at the same time. Žižek suggests that the "imbecilic" medium that produces a surplus of fantasies about circumventing castration is governed by the law (of castration) and therefore automatically externalizes the most profound internal secret of the idiot (that he is castrated and still guilty of incestual desire) regardless of whether he is a consumer, a producer, a critic, or and analyst.

Žižek has turned the figure of the idiot into what Deleuze and Guattari call a "conceptual persona." They argue that the idiot can be traced to the "reaction against the 'scholastic' organization of Christianity and the authoritarian organization of the Church" found in the works of Saint Augustine, Nicholas of Cusa, and Descartes. It later reappears in the work of Dostoyevsky. For Deleuze and Guattari, the idiot of Descartes and Dostoyevsky are not the same persona: "the old idiot [of the cogito] wanted truth, but the new idiot wants to turn the absurd into the highest power of thought."[4] The new idiot does not just demand the absurd (impossible) in the abstract, but demands the recovery of everything lost and the revenge for every immoral act. Žižek seems to want to combine the two (incompatible) idiots—one that demands indubitable truths (accountable to reason) and the other that absurdly demands the recovery of everything that was lost (accountable to potentially everything, and therefore to nothing).

By collapsing the two idiots Žižek performs a series of extraordinary metonymic slips, reducing all subjects, through a process of substitution, into imbeciles: the man-self is likened to the "two idiots, the two average men who stand in for the big Other"—a term that slips from symbolic Father into the dead (obscene) Father, Master-signifier (through the phallus), only to be displaced onto a series of nonsymbolic (castrated) others, including the Woman who is both every thing and nothing, excess, excrement, and God.[5] In the transference of "inherent imbecility of the big Other" (the imbecile who believes he is not castrated) to what he calls "the inherent imbecility of popular culture," he reduces complex narratives to fixed Freudian theoretical assumptions. Images of all kinds (including sound-images) are absorbed into an idiotic public imaginary and into a symbolic order that is both extremely individual and generically universal.

I will not engage directly with Freud or Lacan, only with the conceptual personae of "Freud" and "Lacan" appearing in Žižek's work, since he often speaks for them without quotation, paraphrases, and sometimes even modifies their texts to fit his purposes.[6] He literally treats them like dummies that he speaks through. Instead, I take issue with his suggestion that popular culture serves only to expose men's notorious private desires—the desire to cover up the secret truth of castration embodied in the figure of woman. As Derrida, Irigaray, Butler, and many others have pointed out, positing all social, political, and metaphysical truths as castration-truth only serves to reprivilege the phallus as the master-signifier. It is a claim that positions femininity as the truth of castration, because in the logic of the sexual signifier woman has already been castrated, thus turning man's paranoid anxiety into woman's reality. Such an essential connection between truth and castration-truth only forecloses interpretations of texts and works that are not reducible to "real" and "irreal" truths,[7] such as *La femme n'existe pas*" (~~The~~ woman does not exist), "*il n'y a pas de rapport sexuel*" (there is no sexual relation), "woman is subject," and "masculinity is fake." But Žižek's reading of film for the purpose of illustrating a dubiously pervasive castration-truth only exemplifies, I argue, what he calls the "already low cinema studies standard" he attributes to film critics.[8]

Lynch in the Form of Phallic Fundamentalism

Because Žižek has written extensively on David Lynch—particularly *Blue Velvet* (1986), *Wild at Heart* (1990), and *Lost Highway* (1998)—I want to show how these films are far more resistant to the obvious or imbecilic truths than Žižek allows for, and to show how his readings do not just explicate psychoanalytic concepts, but are reactionary representations of the popular culture that Lynch evokes. I will try to reveal not only the substantial misogyny of such readings, but also how such readings normalize (if not celebrate) misogyny at the same time they treat it ironically. I do not argue that irony is necessarily a conservative trope (as others have), but that when combined with the logic of failure it becomes the keeper of the law of castration and symbolic social ordering that goes with it—the protector of the imaginary penis, the phallus—which ironically is attributed to the figure of woman.

With the films of Lynch, Žižek does not champion the role of the male protagonist as a voyeur but rather castigates the unwillingness of woman to play her proper role of bridging the gap between violence and *jouissance feminine*. Žižek argues that in these films the place of woman has changed from a male fantasy—"woman does not exist" but becomes a subject only by realizing that she is a victim—to the femme fatale—"woman is a symptom of man" and represents men's resistance to the father, who is himself an impostor. Finally, woman returns in the place of the depressed, which Žižek describes as a "withdrawal-into-self, the primordial act of retreat, of maintaining a distance towards the indestructible life-substance, making it appear as a repulsive scintillation."[9] In the world of traditional film noir, "Woman is not an external, active cause which lures Man into Fall; she is just a consequence, a result, a materialization of Man's Fall. So when Man purifies his desire of the pathological remainder, Woman disintegrates in precisely the same way as a symptom dissolves after successful interpretation, after we have symbolized its repressed meaning."[10] His reading of film noir accentuates the Lacanian adages that "woman is a symptom of man," and "woman does not exist." Yet in the context of *Blue Velvet* and *Wild at Heart*, woman is treated as already a subject par excellence. By her retreat into depression, woman threatens to disrupt the relationship between cause and effect, depression and the indestructible life substance. She threatens man's subjectivity.[11]

It is not surprising that Žižek points to Lynch's films as an example of a disengaged sexual or romantically debunked relationship. These films often invoke what have become conventional psychoanalytical interpretations of the American family, deep-seated American racism, the romantic heterosexual couple, and gender and its relation to power. Such issues allow Žižek to treat films like *Wild at Heart*, *Blue Velvet*, and *The Lost Highway* as symptomatic of a general cultural malaise. What is surprising is that these surrealist films come to represent the real of feminine desire (depression) as opposed to other neo-noir films that instead challenge gender power relations. Ironically, Žižek refuses to analyze neo-noir films like *The Last Seduction* and *Body Heat*—films that feature female protagonists who exemplify Žižek's and Jacques-Alain Miller's definition of the "true woman." This is a woman who is characterized by "a certain radical ACT, the act of taking from man, her partner, of obliterating, destroying even that which is 'in him more than himself,' that which 'means everything to him' and to which he holds more than to his own life, the precious *agalma* around which his life turns."[12]

Žižek dismisses these "vulgar, cold manipulative bitches" as "too real" because they challenge sexual difference altogether. This is because, according to Žižek, such neo-noir femme fatale characters point to a "brutal self-commodification" that does not "create sex as the mysterious, impenetrable entity to be conquered." Or as he more succinctly puts it, "it does not provoke us violently to take her and to abuse her."[13] His choice of

Lynch over neo-noir, is itself telling. Žižek seems unable to recognize that the simulation of 1950s patriarchal culture is presented by Lynch as a thin disguise for 1980s and 1990s issues of domestic abuse, the irony of family values in the age of divorce and rising single parent households. Lynch's satire of 1950s cultural representations and icons juxtaposes the facade of a wholesome image of American culture to its seamy underside (or reality).

In *Blue Velvet*, the wholesome blonde (and bland) Sandy—who fits the image of innocent 1950s teenage girls—is juxtaposed to the dark-haired, sexualized Dorothy—who is a mixture of images from the Dorothy of the *Wizard of Oz*, the exotic Italian woman of 1950s film, a heavily made-up drag queen, and a porn star. Similarly, Sandy's father, who plays the role of a policeman in a 1950s television show, is so one-dimensional that he even wears his gun at home. Frank, on the other hand, is the obscene and excessively violent angry white man who blurs the lines between infantile and adult, aggressive heterosexual and homosexual behavior. The façade of the 1950s is so fake—all the way down to the stuffed robin at the end of the film—that it only accentuates the hypocrisies of American culture of the 1980s that marked a return of images of machismo and nostalgia for the 1950s, but at the same time exposed the dark underside of the American family, including widespread domestic violence, drug abuse, and an emphasis on private gains rather than the common good.

Žižek argues that man has retreated from his patriarchal role and is interested only in the commodified image of woman, but he is unwilling to address narratives where women expose this imaginary order as only a function of capitalism—commodity fetishism. He is invested in keeping woman in the place of seduction, mystery and sexual difference. The erasure of these neo-noir films because they "mock" and "violate" the "rule that evil is to be punished," and expose what is "traumatically too real," makes one think we are hearing not a cultural critic but a call for the reinstatement of the Hayes Production Code. The Production Code provided a rule (the censorship of sexual and violent content, miscegenation, anticlericalism, enforcing the rule that "evil is to be punished"), which could then be programmatically subverted by fostering the viewer's "dirty imagination" while simultaneously abiding by the Law. According to Žižek, it is the Law that "needs the obscene supplement to support it."[14] Yet, the Production Code was neither a product of the Law, nor of a generic Big Other. It was rather procured by a specific group of politically organized Catholic bishops who rallied Protestants and Jews against what they saw as the immorality of Hollywood. There was nothing transcendent about that. Žižek believes he is advocating the Law when he rejects neo-noir, but fails to realize that he is simply reifying a historically contingent notion of morality.

Driven by his fundamentalism, Žižek argues that the neo-noir fatale is not as subversive as the fantasmic fatale, that is, the fatale of 1940s and 1950s film noir who either dies or is made to pay for her and man's transgressions. But this assumption clashes with the structure of *Lost Highway*, since there we find the two versions of the femme fatale—Patricia Arquette, who plays both the triumphant blond Alice as well as Renée, the fantasmic brunette murdered wife. In order to simplify things for himself, Žižek reads both incarnations of Arquette as fantasmic, an assumption that forces him to radically misread the second half of the film (where the protagonist—Fred Madison—is substituted by, transformed into, or just imagines himself to be Pete Dayton) as a "shift into psychotic hallucination in which the hero reconstructs the parameters of the Oedipal triangle that again make him potent."[15] If so, then Pete's virility must also be fantasmic. But if that's the case, then Žižek has no ways to draw the line between impotence, potency, and fantasy. *Lost Highway*, instead, is not clear about such demarcations and actually seems to enjoy questioning them. There are so many fantasies and uncanny events embedded in dreams and fantasies that it is hard point to one part of the film that is more realistic than another.

But Žižek is so invested in the Oedipal narrative, castration truth, and Fred's potency that he suggests that Fred is made potent at the precise moment when Pete becomes Fred again—that is, at the moment that Pete is rejected or symbolically castrated by Alice who tells him "you'll never have me" before she disappears. Symbolic castration is therefore turned into a sign of virility. But that same castration truth drives Žižek to treat Renée as a fantasmic figure in Fred's psychotic hallucination, even though he treats Fred's murderous rage over his sexual inadequacy and jealousy as all too real. That we end up with a real murder of a fantasmic figure says something about the problems with Žižek's logic. Only by treating Renée as a fantasmic figure can he get away with reading the significance of the film as restoring Fred's virility as opposed the film's blurring the lines between psychic hallucinations and real events like murder.

Rather than recognize that *Lost Highway* challenges narrative structures (including his simple psychoanalytic ones), Žižek insists on narrativizing the film by treating it as a symptom—not of male impotence or feminine depression, but of failed romantic narratives. This return to the myth of Oedipus (Fred) as a figure of every man masks the violence of Žižek's own criticism—his demand for catharsis (man's purification) castration-truth, over any notion of moral righteousness.

Whose Metastasis?

By harking back to a despotic model of discipline and punishment where transgressive or sexually aggressive women are put back in their place or just killed off, Žižek attempts to reimpose order, redefine individuals vis-à-vis a symbolic language, and reassert the authority of a patriarchal society even while simultaneously admitting that it is in crisis, if not already completely bankrupt. This contradiction is evident in his readings of *Blue Velvet*, *Wild at Heart*, and *Lost Highway*. While his analyses hinge on what he calls symbolic paternal figures (Frank Booth, Bobby Peru, Mr. Eddy, or Dick Laurent), none of these figures is exactly paternal.[16]

In *Blue Velvet*, Frank Booth kidnaps Dorothy Vallen's husband and son, cuts off her husband's ear, and coerces Dorothy into sadistic sexual games. While he wants to be called "daddy," he acts like a baby and an adolescent psycho rebel without a cause. Besides anger, Frank's only display of emotion is triggered by sentimental 1950s music (Roy Orbison's "In Dreams," and Bobby Vincent's "Blue Velvet"). Bobby Peru is equally unpaternal in *Wild at Heart*. An ex-marine who massacred civilians in Vietnam, he violently forces himself on Lula (only to reject her once she submits). He then sets up Lula's boyfriend, Sailor, to rob a bank (while planning to kill him afterward), though ends up killing himself instead. In *Lost Highway*, Mr. Eddy (or Dick Laurent) is a pornographer with ties to the mob, the sex trade, and various sub rosa dealings.

The closest Mr. Eddy comes to enforcing the law is in his reaction to an act of road rage with a more extreme form of rage by ramming the perpetrator's car, forcing him out at gunpoint, cursing him, beating him, while berating him with statistical information about road conduct—"Do you know how many fucking car lengths it takes to stop a car going 35 miles an hour?" This scene, which is actually quite comical, draws attention to the absurdity of his appeal to the law and the driver's safety manual, since while he intimidates the other driver to abide by the "fucking rules," he also beats him unconscious. Breaking the rules of the road would seem trivial as compared to Mr. Eddy's transgressions. Surprisingly, not only does Žižek demand we take this scene seriously, but he also defines Mr. Eddy (like Frank and Bobby Peru) as figures of "excessive, exuberant assertion and enjoyment of life," figures that "are beyond good and evil, but are at the same time the enforcers of the fundamental respect for the socio-symbolic law."[17]

Žižek confuses the law with its transgression. Frank, Bobby, and Mr. Eddy are criminals: rapists, murderers, bank-robbers, pornographers. But if these figures are "fantasmic defense formations—not the threat, but the defense against the true threat," then what precisely is Žižek defending?[18] Reducing transgression to an articulation of the law—the symbolic order—has the result of foreclosing readings of Lynch's films that could instead acknowledge subversive dimensions in the actions of Jeffrey Beaumont, Sailor Ripley, Fred Madison, or Pete Dayton. By repeating the cycle of repression and resentment, Žižek ultimately inscribes man (Jeffrey, Sailor, Fred, and Pete) in a narrative of failure, failed desires, failed communities, and dysfunctional families. He asserts, for instance, that the key point in *Lost Highway* is the "inherent failure" of sexual relationships: "It is crucial that both [sexual acts], end in failure for the man, the first directly (Renée patronizing pats on Fred on his shoulder), while the second ends with Alice eluding Pete and disappearing in the house, after she whispers into his ear, 'You'll never have me!'"[19]

Although Žižek never clarifies why failure is crucial, it becomes obvious that it is crucial not only to his own reading of Lynch's films, but also to confirm his assumptions about the causes of much broader political problems such as racism, nationalism, and even genocide. Sexual failure is the paradigmatic example of the necessary "displacement from reality to fantasy." If we are to grasp the logic of this failure, it must be externalized in the form of fantasy. In this displacement from reality to fantasy, "the status of the obstacle changes: while in the first part, the obstacle/failure is IN-HERENT (the sexual relationship simply doesn't work), in the second part, this inherent impossibility is EXTERNALIZED into the positive obstacle which from the outside prevents its actualization."[20] What is too real, it turns out, is male impotence, not the *femme fatale*.

Just because Fred is unable to complete the sexual act does not make the first half of *Lost Highway* any more realistic than the second half, as Žižek states. Fred's hallucinations or the appearance of the mysterious stranger, the bizarre videotapes, and the narrative ellipsis that omits any diegetic (real) visualization of the murder of Renée, or the sudden exchange of Fred with Pete clearly place the film well outside of the genre of realism. And if fantasies about women are the criteria for men's understanding their own subjectivity, then the second half of the film is equally a failure. The only difference is that Pete is symbolically castrated by Alice, rather than presented as impotent like Fred. Hence, Alice can be blamed for not loving him—disappearing into thin air once he realizes that she is just an object of desire—while Fred has no such excuse other than his jealousy, insecurity, and inadequacy.

Raising Oedipus

Lost Highway presents us with a remarkably complicated narrative structure that cannot be adequately described in a text. The narrative's complexity questions its own point of departure by presenting itself as infinitely repeatable and open to different possible outcomes. The film begins and ends with the line, "Dick Laurent is dead." In the first instance it is Fred who hears the statement via the house intercom from an unknown messenger. In the second instance it is Fred who delivers the message over the intercom to an unknown recipient at the very same house. Other such confusions or transformations occur when Fred is seemingly jailed for allegedly murdering his wife Renée. I emphasize the ambiguity of these occurrences since the film has already blurred the lines between reality and hallucination, the fantastic and the marvelous—a filmic imaginary or Fred's imaginary constructions.

The appearance of the mysterious stranger, played by Robert Blake, whose face first appears in the place of Renée's, marks the departure from reality. This transformation or hallucination occurs just as Fred awakes from a nightmare only to find out that he is still dreaming. Fred encounters this stranger once more at a party. The stranger's conversation with Fred seems to occur outside of the diegetic space and time of the film. All background action stops and all background noise disappears. It is here that the mysterious stranger confronts Fred, demonstrating his ability to be in two places at the same time—both with Fred at the party and inside Fred's house. Even more disturbing than his ability to bilocate is the fact that Fred and Renée have been receiving videotapes from a mysterious stranger who has recorded them as they sleep (from inside the house). It is this tape, shot by an unknown cameraman, that is entered as evidence when Fred is eventually accused of murdering Renée. Just how this "evidence" ends up in the hands of the police remains a mystery.

Fred's expressed dislike for video images simultaneously seems to implicate him for denying reality (seeing is believing), and to cast doubt on whether seeing can in fact amount to believing (that some trick of cinematic montage maybe indeed be involved). Even Fred's recollection of the murder is influenced by the video. His memories are initially of the video images, not of facts. He seems to witness himself in the act rather than remember performing the act of killing Renée. The video fills in the gap in the narrative between Fred's attempt to protect Renée from an intruder in the house and her violent murder. We are ultimately left to wonder if the mysterious stranger is an actual (paranormal) figure who can read Fred's mind, watch and videotape him, or whether he is just the personification of Fred's (and later Mr. Eddy's) id. Or could he be the personification of a camera, limited to a perverted point of view?

Once in jail, Fred suffers from violent headaches. After one such episode he disappears from his cell, only to be replaced by Pete, the young auto mechanic, who gives the impression of knowing nothing about Fred or about how he ended up in the cell. Pete's connection to Fred is indirect, constructed by visual analogies and duplicities that begin with his affair with Renée's blond double, Alice. Alice shares some friends with Renée (like Andy) as well as an association with Dick Laurent. The next narrative interruption coincides with the abrupt end of the affair between Pete and Alice. During the sexual act, Pete tells Alice he wants her, she responds by saying, "You'll never have me." It is at this moment that Pete is transformed back into Fred. Pete, like Alice, is literally dropped from the narrative, and Renée returns, but only to the Lost Highway Hotel, where Fred sees her having sex with Mr. Eddy.

Rather than appreciate the complexity of the film and the impossibility of making narrative sense of it, Žižek boils *Lost Highway* down to the "impossibility of the hero [Fred] encountering *himself*, like in the time-warp scenes of science fiction novels where the hero, traveling back in time, encounters himself in an earlier time. . . . The temporal loop that structures *Lost Highway* is thus the very loop of the psychoanalytic treatment in which, after a long detour, we return to our starting point from another perspective."[21] But if indeed the line between reality and fantasy is blurred beyond repair, what does allow Žižek to identify Fred as the hero? How can he locate the slippage of "reality" into "fantasy" in the moment in which Fred is substituted by Pete? How can he reduce an exceedingly complex plotline to Fred's obsession with his wife Renée? Žižek takes that obsession to lead Fred to kill her—an obsession that continues even after he has killed her. Having stated that, Žižek then decides the rest of the film is simply the visualization of Fred's fantasmic, imaginary constructions wherein Fred replaces Renée with Alice and himself with Pete. Allegedly, this will lead him away from his overidentification with the Law and back into a "healthy" Oedipal economy.

It seems, therefore, that Žižek wants to read *Lost Highway* as the reverse of *Vertigo*, where the sublime object of desire appears after the death of its object-cause. Like Judy, Renée is the "gift of shit" (the remainder of the real) and Alice, like Madeleine, is the sublime object of desire. But this would mean that what Žižek reads as a the return to a "healthy Oedipal economy" in *Lost Highway* is, at best, an unconscious form of denial or, at worst, Fred's conscious erasure of his culpability in Renée's murder. Although Scottie obsesses with Madeleine while Fred is more obsessed with his self-image, both *Vertigo* and *Lost Highway* stage a play of doubles that leads to confusion and dissimulation rather than to truth of the Oedipal or castration variety. Both Hitchcock's and Lynch's films are much more about transgression (of narrative structure, identity, perspective, subjectivity) than about enforcing an a priori "idiotic" Law of castration. If *Lost Highway* were indeed about a return to an Oedipal economy, then what are we to do with the fact that the figure that Žižek assigns to the Law (Mr. Eddy) makes snuff films, or that Fred ends up the subject (if not hero) of such a film? In the words of Mr. Eddy, Fred can easily "out ugly those sons of bitches," thus aligning Fred and Mr. Eddy with trangression, not Law. The nature and genre of Oedipus changes from tragedy to something much more sinister and desperate.

Symptomatic Entrapment

In *Wild at Heart*, almost every time we see the extreme close-up of a match lighting a cigarette, Lula appears to have a painful, possibly traumatic memory often accompanied by a hallucination of the Wicked Witch of the West from *The Wizard of Oz*. These reactions are followed by diegetic visualizations of her memories and the appearance of the witch (pictured as Lula's mother) riding a broomstick. What we see, however, does not always match what Lula tells Sailor, her lover, about her symptomatic associations. When she tells Sailor that her mother gave her "the talk" about sex at age fifteen, she is reminded by Sailor that she was raped by her uncle Pooch at fourteen. And while she tells Sailor that her mother never knew anything about her uncle Pooch, she remembers or fantasizes that her mother walked in, catching Pooch just after he raped her. Lula, therefore, does not reveal the truth or internal "workings of her mind" to Sailor, depriving him of the causal link between her visceral reaction to a match lighting a cigarette and her verbal explanations.

Similarly, the sound of laughter triggers in Lula the traumatic memory of what she believes to be her father's suicide. Yet it is the sound of a woman's laughter—her mother's—that provokes that reaction, thus suggesting that her father's death might have been a murder. By coding the trauma of the father's death as a response the mother's laugh, Lynch posits that this trauma has a nonsensical effect that questions the symptom, which is supposed to occur once reality has been done away with. At the same time, Lula's linking the mother's laugh to the father's death is given validity later in the film when we discover that Lula's mother, Marietta, murdered her father with the help of her lover, Marcellos Santos.

Against Lynch's complexities, Žižek manages to reduce Lula's unwillingness to divulge causal links to her knee-jerk reactions as "Woman's breaking the causal chain asunder," which amounts to a repetition of Sailor's dismissive response to Lula that "the way your mind works, peanut, is God's own private mystery." Similarly mysterious is how Žižek's disregard of the fact that Sailor withholds information from Lula—an occurrence that, were Žižek to follow his own logic, should indicate that Sailor is "breaking the causal chain asunder" as much as Lula. Sailor, for instance, does not tell Lula that he knew her father, that he worked for Marcellos, that Lula's mother hit on him (in the opening sequence of the film) and then, once rejected by Sailor, threatened to kill him for what she believed he might have seen the night she and Marcellos murdered her husband.

Like Lula, Sailor also represents a certain social parody—a conglomeration of specifically white male sex symbols and rock & roll fantasies from impersonations of Elvis Presley to heavy metal music of the 1980s and 1990s. Sailor exemplifies the paradox of rock & roll images that are seriously macho and ridiculously sentimental at the same time. He teaches a lesson to a man who hits on Lula at a heavy metal concert, only to break into song (Elvis's "Love Me Tender"). Figures like Sailor and Lula reveal the contradictions in American popular culture icons that are created by coexisting demands for violence and tenderness, depth and shallowness, individuality and co-dependence.

Žižek's interpretation of "woman's inability to fully submit to the causal link" is rooted in the failure to recognize the inconsistencies of Lynch's male protagonists (Jeffrey is both a "detective and a pervert"; Fred is both impotent and homicidal; and Sailor is both exaggeratedly violent and emotionally immature) as well as of any reason why women (who for the most part play secondary roles in Lynch's films) might be depressed. Rather than address Lula's anxiety about being pregnant and stranded in

Big Tuna, Texas (an emotion shared by Sailor), or Dorothy's abusive marriage (demonstrated by the fact that when Dorothy asks Jeffrey to hit her, she addresses him as Don—her husband's name), and an obviously abusive relationship with Frank (evidenced by the bruises on her body), Žižek reads woman's depression as a primal act rather than as something possibly having a connection with specific material circumstances.[22]

Lula's recurrent dreams are turned by Žižek into an illustration that the real (or the present) does not possess the truth, that the truth always slips away either into some ominous future or abyss of the past—that blinding look into the void from which we have sprung. But if the truth vanishes on the horizon of the future and the real disintegrates into the unreachable and unrecoverable past, then what becomes of our sense of political and sensual presence? Žižek would like us to believe that we are forever barred from it, which of course would render us incapable of reacting to those "great many distinct regimes," which Foucault describes as "breaking the body down into the rhythms of work, rest, and holidays."[23]

Žižek shifts the focus from a political economy to a personal one. He glides from the idiot to the eternal hero of the psychoanalytic narrative, the mythic figure of Oedipus, who like a detective searches for truth (or so Žižek claims). And yet, Žižek's hero is not the Oedipal figure but the maniacal father who beats or rapes woman back into her proper place. The Oedipal figure is simply the benefactor of such patriarchal exuberance. But even Sandy (*Blue Velvet*) is not sure if Jeffrey is a "detective or a pervert." (Ultimately he will prove to be a bit of both). If it is man's identification with Oedipus that ensures his equality with other men, and if we use *Blue Velvet* as a model for all men, we must then liken them to perverts. But if we include Fred from *Lost Highway* in this list of Oedipal figures, then the universal man is also a murderer who denies his actions and escapes into fantasy. Ironically, it is Žižek who seems to construct such equivalences by reading characters like Frank and Jeffrey in *Blue Velvet* as working out their Oedipal fantasies on Dorothy, who stands in for the universal Mother/ whore. Yet ultimately Frank must play father to Jeffrey so that Jeffrey can kill him, and transfer his love from Dorothy to the more wholesome Sandy. Dorothy's private mystery is treated as Jeffrey's secret Oedipal longings. The real truth behind the modern Oedipus is not his transgressions against authority, since authority is already absent in such narratives. The modern Oedipus serves as a means of internalizing the law of submission and repression, and relinquishing of desire as to not upset the order of things.

Žižek explains this movement as a crossing from the experience of sensual presence to the feeling of lostness inherent in the act of representation: "The moment we enter the symbolic order, the immediacy of the pre-symbolic Real is lost forever, the true object of desire (the mother) becomes impossible-unattainable." The problem with this picture is that "every positive object we encounter in reality is already a substitute for this lost original," what Žižek calls "the incestuous *Ding* rendered inaccessible by the very fact of language—that is symbolic castration."[24] The very law that binds all men alienates them from their d(esir)ing agencies but also confines them to the jurisdiction of the family where "the production of desire" will be domesticated and shunted into a particular order of representation.

Žižek infantilizes the ego or the position of the subject as an eternal child who desires his (her) mommy or her (his) daddy, but he also installs the institution of the family as the framing device for all institutions. But what can he then do with figures like Frank who claim to be mommy-daddy-me at the same time? He can only wipe off his lipstick, stuff him into the role of the law, symbolic meaning, and physical agency, and recast Dorothy (in her red shoes) as the Mother of all objects of desire, the body, passivity, negativity, and nothingness. That is, he can only reduce her to a mere tear in the fabric of the order of things, or to a tear in her blue velvet robe—the very sign of her violation.

Even his reading of feminine depression is not original, as Žižek's analysis appears to be a long quotation from Michel Chion's 1995 *David Lynch*.[25] What is original in Žižek's reading is that Dorothy does not slide into depression simply because depression is not something a woman can slip into. As he puts it, "what is of crucial importance is the universal, formal structure at work here. The 'normal' relationship between cause and effect is inverted; the 'effect' [depression] is the original fact."[26] Depression is transformed into a transcendental a priori form, and yet it cannot produce the "proper" causal link since it is seen as a form of "absolute negativity." It is a universal noncausal cause, an original fact with no effects that are worth pursuing.

The Joys of Repression

The specter of feminine depression serves a dual purpose: to resurrect an image of moral authority, and as a means of deterrence through a reinstallment of the spectator in the economy of self-censorship. This moral panic reflects the need for allusions to morality in order to protect the spectator from witnessing the radical dissimulation of symbolic authority, of the Law of repression itself. The mixing of what Gayatri Spivak calls "semantics with semen" serves to make up for man's imaginary phallic desire for his mother with the means to gain access to Žižek's "neutral [neutered] medium of language" or the patriarchal symbolic community.

Žižek interprets Dorothy as representative of depression. Given that she has to pay for the ransom of her husband and son in sexual favors, one might be inclined to consider her a victim. Žižek, instead, casts her as a threat to the symbolic order. She is "an unwholesome sexuality permeated with the rot of death," or "the black hole, the tear in the fabric of reality, the body stripped of its skin."[27] Ironically, Žižek attempts to patch up what Lynch has peeled off—the snakeskin jacket that in *Wild at Heart* Sailor claims to be a "*symbol* of my personal freedom and individuality." Is Žižek resurrecting the division between surface and depth as a means of containing what threatens man's personal fantasy of individualism?

Although Jeffrey does not psychically threaten Dorothy, she perceives his entrance into her house and his voyeurism as acts of violence, and responds by demonstrating violence. But Žižek interprets Dorothy's pulling a knife on Jeffrey as a sign of her overidentification with masculine aggressiveness. By identifying with aggressive sadistic sexuality, she threatens to deterritorialize what Žižek takes to be the property of men. Lynch's representations of heterosexual and homosexual relationships are problematic in and of themselves, but at least they cannot be reduced to a simple perversion of aesthetic gender codes. It is also an exaggeration of those codes that points to the very artificiality and violence that underlie such cultural productions.

If nothing else, Žižek's identification with Frank (rapist and kidnapper) places him under the auspices of the gaze of the "Real" within the ethos of an aggressive male sexuality. Žižek obsesses on hygiene, on woman's seeping through the surface of the symbolic, which he fears will collapse the symbolic into the real. What could be considered Lynch's attempt to reveal a dark underside of normal sexual relationships is read by Žižek as an indication of woman's "suicidal propensity to slide into permanent lethargy."[28] He thus reads Frank's rape of Dorothy as an attempt to restore woman to the depths of the real, arguing that Frank, "far from being the cause of her malaise is, rather, a desperate therapeutic attempt to prevent the woman from sliding into the abyss of absolute depression"[29]

What disturbs Žižek is not the fact that woman is sliding into some irrecoverable black hole, but that she is sliding onto the surface of man's screen, disrupting his desire to put her in her proper place, so that he may confirm his own sexual and social dominance. Although this scene appears just after the alleged "symbolic rape" of Jeffrey by Dorothy and right before a more intimate or compassionate exchange between Dorothy and Jeffrey, Žižek decontextualizes it and (apparently unaware of the fact that he reads Dorothy as a potential rapist, Frank as a defender of the Law, and Jeffrey as a victim) dismisses more complex alternative readings that would address the violence of symbolic language itself. One such reading would pay attention to the image of the knife, often used as a metaphor for the phallus, which in this scene changes hands—from Dorothy to Frank, and potentially to Jeffrey. In the context of sexual relations, the knife signifies not only a cultural perception of male sexuality as violent, but could also function as a commentary on reactionary feminism's capacity to read all forms of penetration as rape. (Dorothy, of course, would have to be included in this sadistic phallic economy.) Another reading would be to question the very language that allows "rape" to slip into consent by the eroticization of violence. Here one might want to reflect on Lynch's including references to, if not overly parodying, the porn industry.

Žižek does not allow the women any means of subjective identification, not even through the male subject position. Women are returned to the economy of sexual and social stratification, where power is determined by the implementation of pure agency, causing the object through which power affirms itself to disappear. This indifference to the object which empowers the self's pure agency is illustrated in Freud's translation of orgasm into a discharge of tension which thereby effectuates the disappearance of the object of desire. It is the installing of desire into the logic of singularity (the construction of a bounded individual) that heightens the self as the sole agent of desire who acts on objects, thus reducing desire to object relations. In this instance, the psychoanalytic model tips over into sadism. Similar to de Sade's institutionalization of power, Žižek conspicuously makes the law, as well as reason, serve his ends. The purpose is not to reinforce moral narratives (symbolic meaning) but to remind us that "the project of psychoanalysis is to make us identify with the shit that we are."

In order to inscribe repression into a moralistic discourse of transcendence, Lacan recodes the act of repression as a symbolic act of sacrifice. He states that "the only thing we can ultimately be guilty of is giving in to our desire; there is no other good than that which can serve to pay the price for access to desire."[30] Repression becomes the model of the good, and within this model woman serves as a vehicle for man's transcendence.

In other words, man can only approach self-recognition from a distance, as if he were a third party. Otherness becomes essential in the process of setting up the cognitive distance, a neutral zone from which the subject can become conscious of himself. Man, therefore, chooses a woman who will excite his desire for repression, the woman who will not give in to his advances, who will make him suffer. Žižek's formulation of courtly love merges with the sexual economy of masochism, whereby the man enters into a contract with the Lady, submitting to her punishment as to circumvent his submission to the Law of the Father (castration). Although Žižek takes the model of courtly love to signify man's transcending woman, when he comes to exemplify the theoretical relationship of man to woman, he withdraws man from his designated role of masochist, turning him into a pure transcendental thought process where mind triumphs over matter. The theatrical roles of the masochistic game are ultimately played out by women. Women are both the cold, cruel, indifferent objects of man's desire, and at the same time the object of humiliation.

The masochistic relationship that traditionally places woman as dominating and humiliating man, frustrating his desire and yet prolonging his desiring agency, is transformed by Žižek into two distinct moments. First, the man kills the real woman and replaces her with a completely artificial automaton so that he may repel his own narcissistic desire through her. Second, she is symbolically humiliated—which Žižek describes as "an unexpected gesture of refusal." More than symbolizing man's triumph over sexual desire, this refusal marks Žižek's own sadistic model of interpretation:

> There is no greater violence than the subject who is forced against his or her will to expose to public view the object in him or herself and incidentally therein resides the ultimate argument against rape—even if in a sense, male chauvinism is right—even if some women somehow and sometimes do want to be taken roughly—for that very reason there is nothing more humiliating than to force a woman, against her will to comply with her desire.[31]

This is precisely how he reads the scene in *Wild at Heart* where Bobby Peru forces Lula to say "fuck me."

Taken Roughly

Žižek collapses "rape" and "being taken roughly," but if the two were really interchangeable then there would be no difference between Bobby's "rape" of Lula and Lula and Sailor's "rough" onscreen sexual encounters. Strangely enough, Žižek seems to ignore Sailor. His image of Bobby is also unclear, probably because it represents a slippage between "non-castrated raw phallic power" (what Chion calls more plainly a "dick-head") and a "cuntface" or "vagina dentata" that "provokes Dern to 'fuck me.' "[32] According to Žižek, "the uneasiness of this scene, of course, lies in the fact that the shock of Dafoe's [Bobby Peru's] final rejection of Dern's [Lula's] forcibly extorted offer gives the final pinch to him: his very unexpected rejection is his ultimate triumph and, in a way, humiliates her more than her *direct rape*. He has attained what he really wanted: not the act itself, just her *consent* to it, her symbolic humiliation. The fantasy is forced out, aroused, and then abandoned, thrown upon the victim."[33]

Over and over, Žižek reads submission as consent. Ironically, he does not extend such a reading to Jeffrey's submission to Frank. That is because it is Frank who first claims (without waiting for Jeffrey's submission) that he "can make [Jeffrey] do anything he wants," and that he "will fuck anything that moves." After that, he begins to treat Jeffrey more and more like Dorothy, calling him a "fuck," telling him not to look at him in the eye, and finally then pulling a knife on him as he hyperventilates into an oxygen mask. But if Jeffrey is left humiliated and abandoned, shouldn't this count as "symbolic rape" in Žižek's own terms? And how do we draw the line between "direct rape," "successful rape," "actual rape," "symbolic rape," "staged rape," "symbolic humiliation," "the fantasy of being raped," "the desire to be taken roughly," and good old masochism? Are all forms of rape, with the exception of "direct rape," a form of consent?

Why does Žižek grant Lynch such insight into "real" women's fantasies without even acknowledging that characters like Lula and Dorothy are complex fictional constructs instead of simple foils for secret (unconscious) urges? Even if one were to reduce these scenes to representations of unconscious urges, shouldn't one also consider that fantasies of rape may be partly a male fantasy, or a fantasy projected by either mainstream media or porn? This question is particularly relevant, given that Žižek situates sex and desire within an Oedipal economy where woman's fantasy is read as purely a reflection or mimicry of her suitor's. So how can it be that Bobby Peru and Frank remain in the realm of representation, while Dorothy and Lula come to represent the gaze of the Real—real women's fantasies about sex and, allegedly, about sexual violence?

Even if this were to be Žižek's own form of shock therapy designed to make women react, his persistent disassociation of woman as an object ends up embracing the logic of sadistic subversion. He uses woman as a means of moralizing or resolving his theoretical projects, killing the real woman in the process. The feminine other is always made of some impenetrable stuff, but also of a visceral ooze that erupts through the skin, disturbing what man has considered his private property, his place in the world, his symbolic exchange value, his very individuality—like Sailor's snakeskin jacket. Yet this cosmic feminine sludge resurfaces and elicits a hypochondriacal compulsion to quarantine it, allowing man once again to buttress the walls of his own being. By disavowing the Other, this alleged man defines himself.

Žižek's orthodoxy to Freudian and Lacanian dogma is far from clear-cut. He has performed extraordinary feats, bending philosophical concepts, texts, contexts, films, popular culture, and current events just to reaffirm the simple truth of castration as a defining negativity. My question is: What could ever come of this fundamentalist model other than some of the most violent ways of seeing, representing and reacting to fellow (wo)man, all done in the name of a conceptual order that Žižek himself calls imbecilic?

Fictions of Possession:
Psychoanalysis and the Occult

Lecia Rosenthal

Sigmund Freud's interest in the occult, along with the charges of occult-ism that it threatened to inspire, has long been of great concern to biog-raphers, critics, and followers of the "founder" of psychoanalysis. Ernest Jones's well-known objection to Freud's "conversion to telepathy," along with James Strachey's attempt to frame Freud's work on the occult as mere "miscellany,"[1] demonstrate the anxiety occasioned by Freud's on-going refusal to define psychoanalysis "proper," and along with it the proper fields of psychoanalytic inquiry, in strict opposition to the occult. Whatever it is, the occult, like psychoanalysis for Freud, borders on and proliferates "improper" subjects, charged lines of fascination and inquiry which, for some of his disciples and detractors alike, represent only anachronistic returns and fanciful remainders of outmoded, now merely outrageous beliefs. Such subjects would include, in addition to the very question of belief, the dangerous subjects of telepathy, transference, and the unconscious.[2]

Freud's writings on the occult, and on telepathy in particular, are best understood as part of the metapsychological Freud and the continued in-terest in psychoanalysis as a mode of theorizing the unconscious in its unverifiability. Over and against the staunch repudiation of the occult by his more empiricist and conservative disciples, Freud resists the resistance to the occult. Even as he declines any positive affirmation of the "existence of telepathy," he acknowledges that the occult, whatever it might be, has in common with psychoanalysis several productive, if explosive and unresolved, points of interest.[3] To the extent that both are marginalized by "official" institutions of scientific knowledge, the occult and psychoanalysis, as Freud argues in "Psycho-analysis and Telepathy," have a common share "in opposition to everything that is conventionally restricted, well-established and generally accepted."[4] If, in the penumbra of doubt cast by the sanctioned purveyors of truth, psychoanalysis is itself often dismissed as an occulted and occulting discourse, Freud insists that its future lay not with similar self-consolidating negations of "impossible" occurrences, but in a persistent critique of the very limits ascribed to the possible, as well as of the received oppositions between belief and science, the archaic and the modern, religion and psychoanalysis.

Telepathy: Freud's Thoughts on the Subject

From the beginning, the question of the occult was, for Freud and his readers, tied to a desire to know what Freud himself thought about the subject. In "Dreams and Telepathy," his second "fake" lecture devoted to the "enigma of telepathy,"[5] Freud begins by raising and putting down some "very definite anticipations":

> At the present time, when such great interest is felt in what are called "occult" phenomena, very definite anticipations will doubtless be aroused by the announcement of a paper with this title. I will therefore hasten to explain that there is no ground for any such anticipations. You will learn nothing from this paper of mine about the enigma of telepathy; indeed, you will not even gather whether I believe in the existence of telepathy or not.[6]

Anticipating his audience, stating their "very definite anticipations" for them and before they will have said any such thing, Freud inscribes the occult, here represented by the possibility of telepathic transmission, as a problem of linkage. Between sender and receiver, author and audience, founder and disciples, transmission is neither a one-way affair nor the assurance of a shared mutuality. Structured by the anticipation of the desire of the other, transmission, here the transmission of Freud's own beliefs about "the existence of telepathy," presupposes and performatively enacts a kind of telepathic transfer, a circuit along the lines of what Avital Ronell has called a "telephonic logic."[7] If telepathy, or the unverifiable reception of the silent voice of the other, posits the possibility of thought-transmission across psychic, spatial, and temporal distance, Freud's anticipatory and preemptive response to this voice figures and indeed confirms such an operation.

One would be tempted to say that Freud *knows*, perhaps even that he knows *fundamentally*, that he is playing with this structural analogue, the inevitable rhetorical and conceptual linkages whereby telepathy has begun to operate as the anticipation of the anticipations of the imagined other. But on the subject of what Freud knows, particularly what he knows about telepathy, if we are to take him at his word, we will have crossed a limit. Freud ends the essay with a denegation: "Have I given you the impression that I am secretly inclined to support the reality of telepathy in the occult sense? If so, I should very much regret that it is so difficult to avoid giving such an impression. For in reality I have been anxious to be strictly impartial. I have every reason to be so, since I have no opinion on the matter and know nothing about it."[8] Telepathy, or rather telepathy in the occult sense, stands, for Freud, on the other side of what he will have professed and acknowledged himself to know. As Derrida comments, "everything, on our concept of knowledge, is constructed so that telepathy be impossible, unthinkable, unknown."[9] Whatever we may imagine Freud to have thought about it, whatever definite anticipations the enigma of telepathy will seem to have aroused in him, Freud has, and he himself says so, no such "secret" inclinations. As if in response to the possibility and impossibility of a telepathic communion with his audience, Freud voices a caveat: on his end of the line, in the space where his affirmative thoughts on the reality telepathy would be kept, and moreover kept in "secret," Freud offers instead the affirmation of a dead-end.

What message is the master putting out here? Suspecting his audience of wanting to hear a secret and be given access to a domain of hidden prejudices, Freud broaches and evacuates, opens and closes off what one might call his "private" thoughts on the matter of telepathy.[10] Left to imagine what we have been told we are not to know (and, as we will see in a moment, Freud did have something to say about the "imagination" and the still open question of what a psychoanalytic approach to telepathy might look like), we might be tempted to speak *with* Freud about all that he has said, and indeed all that he may have left unsaid, on telepathic lines. As if such posthumous colloquy were possible.[11] Indeed, it might not be possible to isolate telepathy from other, seemingly less occult modes of reception, such as, for example, that homely mode of overhearing that would claim to transmit an author's intentions or fundamental beliefs. Whose voices are we hearing when we claim to speak not only with Freud, but also for and against him, about this or any other subject? How to speak for another, and how to speak for ourselves, without broaching upon the telepathic and its occult powers? Far from merely fanciful, such questions can be asked of any claims to speak in the name of a founder, a master, those authorizing presences divine and secular whose thoughts we appeal to when seeking to grasp the truth behind words.

Psychoanalysis of the Occult

What, then, is the occult, and, moreover, what is the occult for psychoanalysis? The problem of cordoning off the occult, of defining its boundaries and containing its peculiar allure, suggests the way in which the occult threatens to contaminate distinctions and take over even the wariest of observers. For what is the occult if not a prolific blurring of the lines between, on one hand, the "dark" practices of witchcraft, magic, and other vestigial reminders of a prescientific age, and, on the other, "enlightened" discourses of scientific rationalism, materialism and empiricism, along with their claims to have supplanted such embarrassing remnants once and for all?

The charge of occultism often carries with it a critical appraisal of popular or commonly held beliefs, prejudices, and inclinations. This is perhaps nowhere more evident than in the rhetoric of the occult as a matter of "tendencies," or claims that diagnose the occult in terms of regression, atavism, and other characterizations of a backward movement within, and in resistance to, the supposed gains of modernity and science. Such assessments assume a narrative of linear, if nonetheless fragile, partial, or incomplete, historical development, a progressive logic for which the occult, along with its tendential allure, represents a threatening return to prior stages and past beliefs. Thus, Ernest Jones views all credulity towards occult matters, including and most notably Freud's, as "relics of a more primitive type of thinking," a diagnosis that he goes on to associate with "the fantastic beliefs of savages" and "uneducated people."[12]

Writing the occult as a species of the return of the repressed, Jones reads in its resurgence the occasion for "shame."[13] A troubling remnant, or the reappearance of the (historical, evolutionary) past within the present, the occult thus becomes legible only and precisely in its exteriorization, or the recognition of a contingent failure, a momentary and contained lapse into obsolete modes of thought. It is this structure of isolation through exteriorization that makes the recognition of Freud's interest in the occult so troubling not only for Jones, but also for Freud's other disciples and inheritors. If the occult can only appear in its repudiation, how to read and locate Freud's inclusion of the occult within the interests and sphere of psychoanalytic inquiry?

Introducing Freud's essay, "Dreams and Occultism," Strachey brackets the lecture as part of the "miscellaneous" Freud that deals with "topics only indirectly related to psychoanalysis" and that, "moreover," deals "with them in what might almost be described as a popular manner."[14] Striding a simultaneous excess and diminishment, the occult, as Strachey would have it, takes on the opprobrium of the *too* popular, common, and widely shared, and therefore the insufficiently rigorous, critical, analytic. Intimating that Freud might have confined himself to more rarified, one might even say more occulted, discussions of the occult, Strachey circumscribes the properly psychoanalytic as a mode of reserve, an essential resistance in which psychoanalysis would, at bottom, remain closed-off to the vagaries, reductions and misreadings marked by popular assimilation.

Strachey's comment points to the paradox of the occult as a hermeneutic and structure of initiation. On the one hand, the occult, whatever it is, suggests a realm of hiddenness, a secret knowledge kept by and for initiates, those insiders who are the possessors, guardians, and transmitters of truth. On the other, to the extent that it is possible to reach this inner sanctum, the occult, like a certain fundamentalism, would place the truth, however distant and occulted, at least theoretically within reach.[15] Yet what does it mean to arrive at the truth of the occult? And what marks the domain and the mark of the occult as such? If the profession, institution, and disciplinary practice of psychoanalysis posits itself as a gateway to an otherwise hidden field of knowledge, does it thereby become not only a discourse of or about the occult, but also an occult and occulting discourse?

Drawing strict lines between psychoanalysis and the occult, and indeed between a psychoanalytic approach to the occult and psychoanalysis as an occult practice, Jones and Strachey push for a model of assimilation without contamination. Like the notion of the present as an assimilative overcoming of the archaic substrate represented by the "primitive," psychoanalysis as science would account for the occult without being affected by its dark powers. Taking in the occult without being taken in by it, psychoanalysis would both account for and keep the occult at bay. Such a neat incorporation would make the occult submissive to a psychoanalysis unchanged and unthreatened by its object. In this sense, psychoanalysis of the occult not only requires and relies upon analytic discretion (as in the maintenance of proper and putatively stable distinctions), but also is itself a discreet processing.[16] Subsumed but not digested, assimilated yet discreet, the occult remains a site of trouble precisely because it is neither fully rejected nor entirely at home within the establishment of psychoanalysis.[17]

The stakes of staving off the charge of occultism relate not only to the problematic status of psychoanalysis as a science, but also to the uncertain status of its analytic *powers*. The links between occultism and fascism, theorized by Adorno and others,[18] point to a similar danger for psychoanalysis: that its "discovery" of the unconscious, along with its questionable power to hear thoughts unspoken, lend themselves all too easily to a host of abuses. These might include, in broad sketch, the mythologies and ideological meaning-making tendencies of metaphysics; the nostalgic consolations offered by omniscient leaders and self-appointed hierophants; the arrogation of the right to speak for others who putatively do not or cannot yet know their "own" thoughts. Adorno's summation of occultism as "the metaphysic of dunces" and "the complement of reification,"[19] provides a useful counter-point, and one from outside of Freud's immediate psychoanalytic circle, to Freud's willingness to take on occult matters. If Freud saw these matters differently, it was not necessarily because he was blind to the ways in which the occult provided a compensatory and consoling substitute in the face of loss.[20] Rather, for Freud, to the extent that psychoanalysis, like the occult, offers consolation, its work depends upon the suspension and rewriting of the oppositional difference between the "ways" of the imagination and science.

The "Ways" of Psychoanalysis: Telepathy, Transference, Imagination

Freud simultaneously endorses, encourages, and limits the occultation of psychoanalysis. While he is wary of any precipitous consolidation of psychoanalysis with the "unscientific" claims of occultism, and although he aligns the occult with "primitive" religion and mysticism,[21] Freud nonetheless repudiates the so-called danger to psychoanalysis posed by any interest in the occult, particularly his own. Rather, he argues,

> It does not follow as a matter of course that an intensified interest in occultism must involve a danger to psycho-analysis. We should, on the contrary,

be prepared to find reciprocal sympathy between them. They have both experienced the same contemptuous and arrogant treatment by official science. To this day psycho-analysis is regarded as savouring of mysticism, and its unconscious is looked upon as one of the things between heaven and earth which philosophy refuses to dream of.[22]

The citation of Hamlet's remonstrance to Horatio repeats the structure we have already witnessed in which telepathic transmissions operate neither as mutual nor as unilateral transmission. The occult, like the unconscious, is excluded and refused, "looked upon" as external to philosophy, as well as affirmed in the anticipation of a ghostly return. Hamlet's words, as appropriated and reissued by Freud, transform psychoanalysis into a call for welcoming the unconscious as the voice of a ghost, a spectral presence that, as in the telepathic transfer, would speak and be heard, but only and always from afar, from a distant "other world" whose lineaments and location are always, at least in part, on the run.

"Mysticism, occultism—what is meant by these words?" Freud's query at the beginning of "Dreams and Occultism," his last text devoted explicitly to the subject of psychoanalysis and the occult, notes the joint state of exclusion that attends these words and marks them for a space "beyond." His own definition, which seems only to reiterate a received emphasis on the nebulous, tracks a territorial language. "You must not expect me to make any attempt at embracing this ill-circumscribed region with definitions. We all know in a general and indefinite manner what the words imply to us. They refer to some sort of 'other world,' lying beyond the bright world governed by relentless laws which has been constructed for us by science."[23] Rejected by philosophy, denied by the established lights of science, it is this "other world" that Freud holds out as a field for psychoanalysis to test its conclusions and challenge the very certainties upon which it founds and differentiates itself as science.

It is alongside his ongoing elaboration of a theory of the unconscious that Freud's work on telepathy becomes so crucial. The word Freud uses most often for telepathy is thought-transference, or *Gedankenübertragung*, linking it inextricably, if problematically, to transference, *Übertragung*. In "Psycho-analysis and Telepathy," Freud defines thought-transference as the transfer of "knowledge" from one person to another "by some unknown method which exclude[s] the means of communication familiar to us. That is to say, we must draw the inference that there is such a thing as thought-transference [*Es gibt Gedankenübertragung*]."[24] The link between transference and thought-transference is further established in "Dreams and Occultism," where rather than a transfer of "knowledge," or *Wissen,* Freud argues that what are transferred are "mental processes":

> There is, for instance, the phenomenon of thought-transference, which is so close to telepathy and can indeed without much violence be regarded as the same thing. It claims that mental processes in one person—ideas, emotional states, conative impulses—can be transferred to another person through empty space without employing the familiar methods of communication by means of words and signs.[25]

How are we to read this connection between telepathy and transference, that most fundamental of Freudian of "concepts," one that similarly involves the transfer and transmission of "ideas, emotional states, and conative impulses" across psychic, spatial, temporal and no doubt other lines of difference? Certainly, telepathy cannot simply be extricated from or neatly opposed to Freud's discussions of transference and his defense of it as analytic treatment's "best tool, by whose help the most secret compartments of mental life can be opened up."[26] Long after Freud has made his break with hypnosis and suggestion therapy, distinguishing and denouncing them as "hackwork" whose distance from science recall "magic, incantations and hocus-pocus,"[27] telepathy remains a powerfully alluring, if unproven, possibility, one that Freud sketches as a mode of transference that links psychoanalysis to the imagination.

In "Dreams and Occultism," Freud emphasizes this link as an imaginary and imaginative road-making, a paving of the physico-psychic ways produced by psychoanalysis. He argues, "It would seem to me that psycho-analysis, by inserting the unconscious between what is physical and what was previously called 'psychical,' has paved the way for the assumption of such processes as telepathy. If one accustoms oneself to the idea of telepathy, one can accomplish a great deal with it—for the time being, it is true, only in imagination [*nur in der Phantasie*]."[28] Thus the psychoanalytic achievement of paving the unconscious as a path, backward and forward toward all kinds of "assumptions," including that of telepathy, is itself not yet complete. If only "for the time being," psychoanalysis remains bound to the imagination, that quasi-instrument through which it reflects upon and extends its limits.

Etymologically, *telepathy* designates feeling or suffering across distance. Conceptually, it points to the possibility that what may seem to be one's "own"—one's own feelings, thoughts, psychic life—may actually be transmitted to or sent from another. And therefore no longer one's own. This aspect of telepathy introduces a structural dispossession into the subject's self-belonging; rather than an autonomous or auto-generating set of affects and thoughts, the subject becomes a kind of input-output device caught in a larger relay of transmission, a network of exchanges and influences for which no definitive origin or endpoint can easily be determined. In this version of telepathy, the subject is linked to others, and therefore no longer self-same. Yet, even as the idea of telepathy threatens to dissolve the boundaries differentiating one subject from another, it also lends the promise of overcoming distance and resolving difference. Emphasizing unboundedness over perspectival limitation, seamless access over mediated relationality, this version of telepathy underwrites a fantasy in which alterity no longer exists because the other is always exposed and available to the unfettered transmissions of the tele-work.[29]

These versions of the telepathic hook-up implicate competing theories of the constitution of subjective life. In one, the subject is articulated through acts of reception and transmission he or she neither controls nor anticipates. It may even be that telepathy takes place without any notice or recognition on the part of the sender or receiver; if we are capable of overhearing the thoughts of others, and if they are capable of intercepting ours, then how to determine that any one thought as opposed to another is an effect of a distinct telepathic transfer or an identifiable point of origin? In this sense, by calling into question the identifiability of the agent "behind" thought, telepathy generalizes the psychoanalytic notion of a nonunitary self, a subject not governed by the sovereign cogito or the determining will, but inhabited by and effected through all sorts of others, including that "internal" (given telepathy, the very idea of internality becomes problematic) other of the unconscious. For the latter version of telepathy outlined earlier, in which blurred boundaries and interconnectedness mean an unmediated encounter with the other, the implied model of the subject ultimately becomes one of wholeness and totality; hooked up to an infinitely inclusive field of others, the telepathically enabled subject would transcend time and place to achieve a kind of godlike omniscience. Here, the very idea of the unconscious, or indeed of any site of resistance to the tele-technological's penetrating reach and fine-tuned receptivity, becomes almost nonsensical, at least from the point of view of the telepath who would know, encompass, catch all.

These two versions of telepathy—one transmitting to and from an alterity that cannot be reduced to an external or internal other; and one for which transmission is ultimately unnecessary because everything is already revealed—are indeed difficult to disentangle, as both are at work within the idea of telepathic transmission, that peculiar notion in which the mind might "communicate" in unfamiliar ways and on channels unknown ("without employing the familiar methods of communication by means of words and signs"). The idea of an "unfamiliar" medium or technology of communication gives telepathy a charge of epistemological uncertainty and a stealth appeal; below the radar of recognized and recognizable communication, telepathy offers another path, one that can be deployed to resist and critique official knowledge and the outputs of the recognized, hegemonic media.[30] Thus a capacity for telepathy might constitute the condition of a community within the community, a group of internal others apart from and at odds with the rest. At the same time, the potentially subversive function of telepathy as an "unfamiliar" means of communication renders it a "supplement" in the Derridean sense of a critical addition: adding to and critically displacing the dominant, telepathy, like the supplement, "is an adjunct, a subaltern instance which *takes-(the)-place* [*tient-lieu*]" of the already known and normalized conditions of knowledge, truth, language, and belonging.[31] Imagined and hypothetical as it might remain, it is precisely in its function as a critical addition to the "means of communication familiar to us" that telepathy for Freud becomes charged with so much danger and critical potential.

Telepathy, like transference, introduces previously unrecognized possibilities for the "transfer" of psychic material across time and place. But whereas telepathy would appear to convey such material without mediation or resistance, transference, Freud argues, is necessarily bound up with and constituted through distortion and resistance.[32] Still, because the idea of telepathy suggests an evasion of censorship and the overcoming of various forms of resistance to "receiving" the other, it intersects with what Freud lays down as the "fundamental rule" of psychoanalysis: the dual, if asymmetrical, responsibility of physician and patient to "transmit" the patient's unconscious.[33] In the following passage, Freud's account of telepathy looks very much like a description of transference: "The application of analysis to this case . . . teaches us that what has been communicated by this means of induction from one person to another is not merely a chance piece of indifferent knowledge. It shows that an extraordinarily powerful wish harboured by one person and standing in a special relation to his consciousness has succeeded, with the help of a second person, in finding conscious expression in a slightly disguised form."[34]

Yet Freud never allows that any "telepathic" access to the unconscious is possible, and to the extent that telepathy articulates a fantasy of direct and unbridled access to the "mind" of the other, Freud is critical of its seductive allure. Bound up with his comments on the occult's indiscriminate tendency to posit transcendent beings that can offer "ultimate explanations of everything," Freud's critique of such explanations is also an attempt to distinguish psychoanalysis from religion and to differentiate the "imagination" of one from that of the other.

Skeptical of any claim that would obviate the difficult, interpretive work of analysis, including that of receiving and reconstructing the unconscious, Freud criticizes the occult for promising to bypass unsolved problems with the "old religious faith" and explanations ascribed to "spirits": "It is a vain hope to suppose that analytic work, precisely because it relates to the mysterious unconscious, will be able to escape such a collapse in values as this [Freud has just been speaking of the "collapse of critical thought, of determinist standards and of mechanistic science"]. If spiritual beings who are the intimate friends of human enquirers can supply ultimate explanations of everything, no interest can be left over for the laborious approaches to unknown mental forces made by analytic research. So, too, the methods of analytic technique will be abandoned if there is a hope of getting into direct touch with the operative spirits by means of occult procedures."[35] Comparing analysis to the occult in order to distinguish the former from the false claims of the latter, Freud uses the occult as a way of thinking the differences of psychoanalysis.

Entertaining the possibility of telepathy, a "transfer of thought" by other than the "familiar" means, Freud does not reverse the hierarchy that privileges science over the occult, but rather charges psychoanalysis with an aleatory wager in pursuit of yet to be accepted possibilities. Freud's definition of telepathy echoes that put forward in 1882 by Frederic Myers, who is credited with coining the term.[36] Yet, Freud's work on telepathy, far from a validation of Myers's theories, points forward toward the possibility of the new, the unknown, the still to be discovered. He condemns the "world of occultism" to mere repetition of prior and extant "religious" beliefs, themselves dubious products of the "imagination" of a prescientific age: "there is nothing new in the world of occultism. There emerge in it once more all the signs, miracles, prophecies and apparitions which have been reported to us from ancient times and in ancient books and which we thought had long since been disposed of as the offspring of unbridled imagination [*ungezügelter Phantasie*] . . . it is hard for us to avoid a suspicion that one of the secret motives of the occultist movement is to come to the help of religion, threatened as it is by the advance of scientific thought.[37] Even as he condemns the current surge of interest in all things occult as symptomatic of the concomitant demise and defensive return of religion, and even as he condemns its "imagination" as overly expansive and out of control, by suspending his disbelief ("proceed[ing] as though I believed"[38]) and allowing for telepathy, Freud grants the occult a place within psychoanalysis—if only, for the time being, in the imagination. Neither "just" another religious "fantasy," nor strictly differentiable from the religious resurgence he disavows, Freud's attempt to test the conclusions of psychoanalysis on the occult represents a belief in the future, the future of belief, the future of psychoanalysis.

Freud's ambivalent speculations about the "existence" and "reality" of telepathy can be plotted as a vacillation between two positions, each of which he tentatively adopts in relation to the other. On one hand, he maintains an unwillingness to reject the possibility of telepathy altogether, such that, "One arrives at a provisional opinion that it may well be that telepathy really exists and that it provides the kernel of truth in many other hypotheses that would otherwise be incredible."[39] On the other hand, as argued above, Freud's nondenial of the possibility of telepathy amounts neither to an affirmation of its existence, nor to an endorsement of the claims made by those who would find in certain dreams, visions and voices evidence of a telepathic power or event. Rather, Freud repeatedly argues that such claims are usually best understood as "beliefs" subtended by a nonfamiliarity with or failure to understand the explanations and helpful relief provided by psychoanalysis. Thus, in his discussion of one case of purported telepathic experiences, Freud finds an "illusion" that would be fully cleared up by a psychoanalytic explanation (primarily the "female Oedipus complex" and wish-fulfillment). The claimant, Freud acknowledges, "would naturally firmly reject our attempt at explanation and would hold to her belief in the authenticity of her [telepathic] experience. But she could not do otherwise. She would be bound to believe in the reality of the pathological effect so long as the reality of its unconscious premises were unknown to her. Every such delusion derives its strength and its unassailable character from having a source in unconscious psychical reality."[40]

In these latter passages, it would seem that psychoanalysis, through its diagnostic insights, replaces the "occult" explanation of events. But Freud insists that psychoanalysis must go beyond merely relying upon and seeking to confirm already established conclusions. By claiming truth for itself, its revisions of occult "illusions" become inadequate, even potentially "deceptive": "With a person who so easily and so early in life lost touch with reality and replaced it by the world of phantasy [*Phantasie*], the temptation is irresistible to connect her telepathic experiences and 'visions' with her neurosis and to derive them from it, although here to we should not allow ourselves to be deceived as to the cogency of our own arguments. We shall merely be replacing what is unknown and unintelligible by possibilities that are at least comprehensible."[41]

Between a suspension of scientific disbelief and a challenge to the finalities of scientific comprehension, Freud's approach to the occult is always at the same time a commentary on psychoanalysis. As a science and a mode of (dis)belief, psychoanalysis, whatever it is, finds itself in relationship to an "occult" other, or those beliefs, prejudices, and tendencies that Freud never fully externalizes from nor dissolves into the borders of his discursive edifice.

What remains is the question of how psychoanalysis, and with it Freud as its leading and founding voice, writes the occult as a word for an unveiling and final revelation that never arrives. Psychoanalysis, Derrida has said, has not arrived.[42] Telepathy, and the occult, may be the name of this nonarrival. If transference designates the condition of possibility for "translating" and "carrying what is unconscious into what is conscious,"[43] then telepathy, and along with it the occulted truths of psychoanalysis as a science and structure of initiation, shadow the event of this transfer as unverified and unverifiable. The delivery and receipt of thought-transference are subject to the fictions of the imagination, the paving of imaginary ways. So, too, are the fundamentals of transference and the unconscious, those Freudian concepts we are still trying to receive and translate today.

Religion and the Future of Psychoanalysis

Jacob Taubes

I

Freud insisted time and again that psychoanalysis is not a philosophy but a therapeutic method. Nevertheless, this method, which developed out of the study of some cases of hysteria, drew into its orbit the arts and the humanities, philosophy and religion. For psychoanalysis as a therapeutic method carried far-reaching implications for the understanding of man.[1]

A revolutionary doctrine such as psychoanalysis could make its way into the general public only against the powerful resistance of current ideologies and established institutions. The resistance to the psychoanalytic method should not surprise the historian. What should astonish us is the rapid success that analytic method has achieved in recent decades. Did the resistances against psychoanalysis break down before the success of a therapeutic method, or did the theory and practice of analysis undergo a change? Did psychoanalysis adapt its theories to the established ideologies? Did the post-Freudian development of psychoanalytic theory obscure its critical implications for the life of society? Does it now serve to reinforce our existing institutions?

Prior to World War I, it was religion that represented the stronghold of resistance to the claims of psychoanalytic theory. And this opposition on the part of religion was not accidental. Freud had committed psychoanalytic theory to the premises of atheism. Beyond a general acceptance of atheistic views current in the late nineteenth century, Freud and his followers studied religion in terms analogous to the study of individual neurosis. Religion became a supreme instance of a primordial neurosis of mankind.

Freud belonged to the avant garde of "free spirits" anticipated by Nietzsche, who were sensitive enough to discern that with the decomposition of theism in the West the foundations of our morality had collapsed. Far from being tormented like Nietzsche by the greatness of the event, Freud took the end of religion for granted and dared to prophesy that the abandoning of religion will have to take place with fateful inexorability of growth and that we are just now in the middle of this phase of development. It must make us suspicious that within two decades of Freud's death,[2] psychoanalysis and religion now exhibit such marked signs of friendship.

Many reasons mingle to account for this shift. Surely one of them is the challenge and collapse of socialist Messianism in the West. Faced with the challenge of secular chiliasm, theologians and clerics have found in psychoanalysis a secular version of the doctrine of original sin that helps undercut the claims of the Marxist chiliasm.

When the hopes that the Western intelligentsia had invested in the transformation of the social structure were bitterly disappointed, Freud's anti-eschatological view of man and history could be used as an argument against the "illusions" of all chiliastic hopes that expected the transformation of men through the transformation of the societal structure. Even in the new society, man remained the old Adam possessed by his drives and instincts, unredeemed from his lusts and therefore even more apt to stumble into barbarism when the conservative fences around the political order were removed. While Marxism as secular version of chiliasm interpreted the history as a transitory stage of man on his way to the "reign of freedom" in the future, Freud insisted that man can never jump over the shadow of his past. As much as the early years of childhood exert a decisive influence on our adult life in a way that later events oppose in vain, likewise the past of our collective history turns the progress of history into a farce. Man moves in history as in a circle, reproducing in many versions "the same old story."

Once this conservative element in psychoanalysis became obvious, the ice of resistance in our society against psychoanalytic theory and practice melted, and Freud's discoveries about man's conduct and motives turned quickly into the most recent syllables of the divine. Religion and psychoanalysis equally stressed the authority of the past and could join in the affirmation of the past as a guide for human conduct on an individual as well as on the societal level.

II

Religion is a Latin term, which originally designated the civic cult of the Roman polity. Biblical literature does not know the term. Still the congregations whose experience is reflected in the books of the Old Testament as well as in the writings of the New Testament are classified as "religions." This is not a small philological detail, of interest only to the linguist or to the exegete. The fate of Christianity is embedded in this shift of language as in a nutshell. What was once a way of salvation, a hope for the redemption of man, has become an established religion in the realm of the world. In the term *religio*, Rome was victorious over the hope of redemption. It is impossible at this stage of history to break the ambiguity in the term religion, which comprises two contradictory elements: religion as a civic cult and religion as a way of salvation, redeeming man from the authority of the powers and principalities of the world.

A way of salvation is, as the Latin adjective *salvus* or *salus* indicates, concerned with redeeming man from the powers that break and disrupt his life. Man's life is threatened by forces from without and by forces within man. A message of salvation professes to heal the break in human existence, to redeem it from the burden of guilt under which man is breaking down. The conflict between religion as a way of salvation and psychoanalysis as a therapy focuses on the notion of salvation as a way of healing, as a way of redeeming man from his guilt. While psychoanalysis and religion as a civic cult could easily come to terms in the stress on the authority of the past, the relation between religion as a way of salvation and psychoanalysis as a therapy freeing man from the burden of his guilt is a more complex one.

While in *The Future of an Illusion* Freud makes use of the ideology of progress as developed in the age of Enlightenment to combat religion, his theoretical writings reveal an insight into the indispensable role of religion in the genealogy of guilt. And since the genealogy of guilt presents also the story of the origin of human society, Freud is forced against his ideology to describe the crucial role of religion in the origin and history of society. The edifice of society is built upon an original crime and the perennial rites and customs symbolizing atonement. "The totem was, on the one hand, the corporeal ancestor and protecting spirit of the clan; he was to be revered and protected. On the other hand, a festival was instituted on which day the same fate was to be meted out to him as the primeval father had encountered. He was killed by all the brothers together (totem feast, according to William Robertson Smith). This great day was in reality a feast of triumph to celebrate the victory of the united sons over the father."[3]

Even if the original fate of the primeval father certainly became forgotten in the course of thousands of centuries, the original act lives on, according to Freud, in veiled and repressed forms in the unconscious of humanity. Since this original act has occurred, guilt haunts man, and "it is not really a decisive matter whether one has killed one's father or abstained from the deed: one must feel guilty in either case."[4] The history of mankind is thus turned into a story of man's "original guilt." Society must foment an ever-increasing sense of guilt. "That which began in relation to the father ends in relation to the community. If civilization is an inevitable course of development from the group of the family to the group of humanity as a whole, then an intensification of the sense of guilt . . . will be inextricably bound up with it until perhaps the sense of guilt may swell to a magnitude that individuals can hardly support."[5]

III

Never since Paul and Augustine has a theologian taught a more radical doctrine of original guilt than Freud. No one since Paul has so clearly perceived and so strongly emphasized the urgent need to atone the act of original guilt as has Freud.

It is not a matter of sheer speculation that Freud conceived his work, his theory and therapy, in analogy to the message Paul preached to the gentiles. "Paul, a Roman Jew from Tarsus, seized upon this feeling of guilt and correctly traced it back to its primeval source. This he called original sin; it was a crime against God that could be expiated only through death. Death had come into the world through original sin. In reality, this crime deserving of death, had been the murder of the father who later was deified. The murderous deed itself, however, was not remembered; in its place stood the phantasy of expiation and that is why this phantasy could be welcomed in the form of a gospel of salvation (evangel)."[6]

Freud penetrates deeply into the dialectic of guilt and atonement that is the central motif of Paul's theology. He endows Paul with a "gift for religion in the truest sense of the phrase. Dark traces of the past lay in his soul, ready to break through in the regions of consciousness."[7] While the Mosaic religion did not progress beyond the recognition of the great father, Paul, by developing the Mosaic religion, became its destroyer. The Mosaic religion had been a father-religion, while Paul became the founder of a son-religion. Paul's success "was certainly mainly due to the fact that through the idea of salvation he laid the ghost of the feeling of guilt."[8]

It cannot be accidental that whenever Freud discusses the message of Paul, he takes the Apostle's side and "justifies" his message of salvation. In the religion of Moses (which represents for Freud the paradigmatic case of religion as authority), there is no room for a direct expression of the murderous father-hate. Therefore, the religion of Moses and the Prophets came only to increase the guilt of the community. "Law and Prophets" have burdened man with the sense of guilt. It therefore seemed significant to Freud that the lightening of the burden of guilt proceeded from a Jew. "Although food for the idea had been provided by many suggestive hints from various quarters, it was, nevertheless, in the mind of a Jew, Saul of Tarsus, who as a Roman citizen was called Paul, that the perception dawned, 'It is because we killed God the Father that we are so unhappy.'" Surely, Paul first formulated this "historical truth" in the delusional guise of the glad tidings. In Paul's message of salvation, "the murder of God was, of course, not mentioned but a crime that had to be expiated by a sacrificial death could only have been murder." Original guilt *and* salvation from the burden of guilt through the sacrificial death of the Son of God became the basis of the new religion founded by Paul. "The strength which this new faith derived from its source in historical truth enabled it to overcome all obstacles."[9]

What fascinated Freud in the message of Paul was the implicit confession of guilt contained in his good news. The evangel was at the same time a dysangel, the bad news of the original crime of man. The delusional form of the news is the "good" news that this guilt is expiated in the sacrificial death of the Redeemer. For in this form the confession of guilt is still veiled. Freud considers himself the first to break the spell and to dare spell out the secret guilt that haunts man. What Paul could only acknowledge in the illusion of a "good news" was spelled out by Freud without illusion. Guilt cannot be expiated through the sacrificial death of a son of God; it can only be acknowledged. By the conscious acknowledgment of guilt, man liberates himself from its blind bondage. Freud did not conceal to himself in serious moments that his "theories amount to a species of mythology, and a gloomy one at that." In this context, Freud's tract on *The Future of an Illusion* may take on some unexpected meaning. It may turn out that this seemingly "progressive" humanist tract really pits the tragic and the eschatological interpretation of man against each other. While the tragic consciousness can only go as far as man's awakening to his original guilt, the eschatological consciousness expresses man's hopes to overcome his guilt. While in the tragic consciousness man can never be absolved but can only bear the burden of his guilt in a heroic gesture, the eschatological man stakes his hope in a future reconciliation and atonement. For the tragic man, the hope in a future is an illusion. The future can only repeat the past, perhaps on a more conscious level, but never can man break the cycle of history.

It is no accident that the mythical numina that Freud calls to the fore are named with Greek names: Eros and Thanatos, Logos and Ananke. There is no hope for redemption from the powers of necessity, from the claws of death. History is caught in an eternal cycle of constructing and destroying. It is illusory to hope for man ever to break the cycle.

IV

The atheistic premise of Freud's psychoanalytic theory and therapy is not simply a residue of bourgeois optimistic humanism that lingered on among educated classes of the nineteenth century, but belongs within the history of tragic humanism since Nietzsche. The death of the Christian God proclaimed by Nietzsche through the mouth of his prophet Zarathustra inaugurates the rise of new mythologies. Nietzsche was well aware that the question revolved around where to lay "the greatest stress": on the eternal return or on the eschatological history. In the dionysiac-tragic horizon, "the eternal hourglass of existence is turned over and over, and you with it, a dust grain of dust." On the eschatological horizon, history does not turn around and around but comes to an end.

Nietzsche, who styled himself as "Antichrist" and as "the last disciple of Dionysos," has best put the ultimate difference between the eschatological and tragic view. Both Christ and Dionysos figure as suffering gods. What separates them is the sense given to their suffering, whether eschatological or tragic. "In the first case suffering is the road to a holy mode of existence; in the second case existence itself is regarded as sufficiently holy to justify an enormous amount of suffering."[10]

Freud's psychoanalytic method develops in the horizon the tragic dionysiac humanism. If there is progress, then it is solely toward opening man's eyes to the tragic structure of reality. Thus, the difference between religion as a way of salvation and psychoanalysis as a therapeutic method rests in the hope for reconciliation. Is human life "hopelessly" lost to the process of construction and destruction, or can it nourish the hope to overcome all destruction? The young Nietzsche, in a paper written while still at college, summed up the issue under the title "Fate and History." Freud's theoretical writings and practical therapy presuppose fate as the ultimate category. Even the patterns of evolutionary history (that are really the residue of nineteenth-century anthropology and sociology) are bracketed into an overreaching cycle of eternal recurrence. Freud, like Nietzsche, was convinced that the end of the Christian religion will lead the way out of two thousand years of falsehood and illusion. Religion was an illusion because the hope for reconciliation, for the atonement of guilt, is ultimately an illusion. Guilt cannot be overcome but only acknowledged.

Surely the psychoanalytic critique of religion can serve as a critical measure to discern all magical elements in the eschatological hope. Insofar as religion acts as a magic operation of atonement in which the person seeking reconciliation is not regenerated and transformed, it falls fully under the severest judgment of Freud. In the struggle between the priestly-magical and prophetic-personal element in eschatological religion, psychoanalysis can help to unmask the. retrogressive forms of magic manipulation that replace the regenerative and revolutionary act. But is the eschatological hope itself an illusion? If the eschatological hope is illusory, then the future itself turns out to be an illusion. This last difference between faith as hope and faith as illusion emerged already in Paul's confrontation with the Stoic philosophers. "Mankind," says Léon Bloy, "began to suffer *in hope* and this is what we call the Christian era."[11] With Nietzsche and Freud, this very hope is put under the suspicion of illusion. The success of Freud's psychoanalysis thus indicates to the historian, if such indications were still necessary, that the West has entered into a post-Christian era.

The Contribution of Psychoanalysis to Understanding the Genesis of Society

Cornelius Castoriadis

The subject of this talk[1] is the possible contribution of psychoanalysis to the understanding of the genesis of society. My response, you will see, is especially critical. However, permit me to say: first, I presuppose, at the very least, that we share an elementary knowledge of the psychoanalytic perspective; second, I will not speak of psychoanalysis as such but precisely of its possible contributions to the understanding of social phenomena. Moreover, I emphasize that whatever I am to say will refer to the work of Freud himself, and I will not take into account theories that developed later, based on Freud or reworking or exploiting Freud.

The talk will be especially critical. But this does not mean that I underestimate in any way Freud's enormous work; on the contrary, I think that without it we would be unable to make even a single step toward the understanding of the human psyche. But we can only make further steps if, on every occasion, we stand critically before those who preceded us, even before our own selves in the previous stages of our own thinking.

From this standpoint of looking at Freud's work there is a great difference, as far as I am concerned, between his primarily psychoanalytic writings, concerning the unconscious and the individual (if you will) psyche, and writings pertaining to the emergence and organization of society. In the first—let us say, psychoanalytic—works, exists a series of foundational notions that I consider outmaneuverable: the discovery and exploration of the unconscious, the interpretation of dreams, the theory of repression and of drives, and a whole lot more—much of which we can revisit, reinterpret, extend further, but cannot ignore. In the second—let us say, psychosociological—domain, the matter is less clear and certainly less rich, and this is not to criticize because Freud's primary work is psychoanalysis and writings that concern society or religion are in some ways tangential.

Whatever might be the significance of these texts to the understanding of society—I am referring to the well-known books *Totem and Taboo*, *Group Psychology and Analysis of the Ego*, *The Future of an Illusion*, *Civilization and Its Discontents*, and *Moses and Monotheism*, as well as a great number of essays that include tangents of this kind—Freud's contribution is certainly important but cannot be said to be outmaneuverable. These works are primarily provocations to further thought, while at the same time being, as far as I am concerned, examples of the insufficiency of a purely psychoanalytic theorization of the social-historical domain. This is what I will briefly attempt to demonstrate today.

Of course, what one would expect to hear in a lecture on the contribution of psychoanalysis to the understanding of certain questions posed by society would ideally involve the response to, or at least the examination of, the following four questions: What has psychoanalysis to say on the issue of the genesis or emergence of human society? This is roughly the same with the question: "What has psychoanalysis to say on the issue of the humanization of primates?" Second, what has psychoanalysis to say regarding the issue of history? Is history perhaps, from the psychoanalytic theoretical viewpoint, simply an epiphenomenon, and if not, why not? Third, what has psychoanalysis to say regarding the structure and content of social and political institutions, and especially phenomena of power over society, that is, the division between those who have power and those who have not, the issue of sovereignty, the inequality between the sexes, and possibly the conditions pertaining to labor and to knowledge? And fourth, what has psychoanalysis to say concerning the possibility and desirability of a transformation, reformation, or radical alteration of existing institutions—or to put it otherwise, issues concerning the rightful institutions of a society?

Freud confronts the question of the genesis of society as a question of the genesis of two enormous prohibitions: in other words, the question as to why incest is forbidden and why murder is forbidden—not any murder, but endotribal murder. (You understand what I mean: no society has ever forbidden murder as such, especially the murder of others, those who belong to other societies, but every society does forbid, at the outset, murder *within* it, except on those occasions when the existing instituted power permits the state, or those who govern, to murder on its behalf.) Parallel to these questions, another question emerges inevitably: How is the socialization of the psyche—that is, repression, the denial of drives—conducted? Now, parenthetically, one of Freud's gravest blind spots, which we will address later, is that he does not quite perceive that the socialization of the psyche is not merely "negative"—prohibitive or counterbalancing/palliative. It is also "affirmative" in the sense that it consists of receiving infinite elements that are necessary to the formation of social life, both subjectively and objectively. These elements are either themselves meanings (notions, if you will) or are replete with meaning. And this Freud does not see from the beginning, or only sees partially, as on the matter of religion, to which we shall also return.

One thing that has not been quite noted is that there exists a curious complexity—one might also even say, confusion—in Freud's efforts to give an account of society's origins, of the genesis of society as such. Of course, the main text in this regard is *Totem and Taboo* (1912–13), which is more psychoanalytic than the one that follows it thirty years later, *Moses and Monotheism*. In between the two fall two publications, *The Future of an Illusion* and the book about civilization and the misfortune it brings about, both texts providing a very different image than the one in *Totem and Taboo*, even though the two images are not at all contradictory or incompatible.

Totem and Taboo is a myth (Freud himself in later texts calls it a scientific myth) and, as you all know, it begins with a cyclopean family in which an omnipotent father wields power over all the females and kills, castrates or exiles all the born males until the alliance, at a specific moment, among the exiled brothers, who perform the famed murder of the father and, after the murder, establish the two basic prohibitions: from now on, no one is to have all the females in the tribe and no one is to murder, at least not within the tribe, within the horde. Later, at another moment, overtaken by guilt and compelled by their ambivalence of affect, the brothers raise the murdered father to the status of totem, that is, a protective but also terrifying animal or other object, which may grant its name to the horde and perhaps the subdivision of the horde. Meanwhile, as Freud claims following the theories of his era, the totem's destruction is prohibited except every so often or once a year, let us say, when a performative murder of this animal takes place as well as a symbolic repetition of the scene of the father's murder, his dismemberment and the subsequent cannibalization. In this, let us say, annual feast, the brothers kill, dismember, and eat the totemic animal, whose destruction at all other times is prohibited.

If we look now at *The Future of an Illusion* and *Civilization and Its Discontents*, we find a significantly different approach to the issue, a more sociological and, in this respect, perhaps less original approach, reminding us rather of theories already established in the history of philosophy and sociology. Here we find Freud's emphatic certainty that civilization is supported centrally and substantially by the repression of drives. The civilizational process is exclusively the work of minorities, which naturally gain from this process, since it is executed in the form of privileges extended to them, and it is only these minorities (according to Freud's texts) that are capable of enjoying the higher pleasures (that is, art and other cultural phenomena) via sublimation, while the masses—Freud says this explicitly—hate civilization because it forces them to deny or repress their drives. In both these texts, Freud almost speaks like an anarchist because he expresses great sympathy for this hatred of the masses against civilization. He says that they certainly have every right to hate it because the repression of drives they undergo is much too great, and only at one juncture does he concede that the masses may possibly elevate themselves, up to a point and via their identification with the controlling minority power, to the domain of sublimation that would allow them to enjoy the works of civilization.

Meanwhile, around 1920, on foundations already laid out before, Freud makes another crucial contribution to the theory of society and socialization: the introduction of the notion of identification, which he began to work on around 1910 and developed especially well in *Group Psychology and the Analysis of the Ego* (1920). I will not address this book at all here, but I will return to this notion of identification later.

What can we possibly say about the scientific myth in *Totem and Taboo*, which Freud after all repeats, in another fashion, in *Moses and Monotheism*? The problem with this myth is naturally—because Freud knows it is a myth—not any empirical or positive repudiations of it: meaning, things did not quite happen this way (although I will say something about this matter regarding primates). The problem is whether this myth actually helps us understand the genesis of society. I think that the myth in *Totem and Taboo* (the myth of the murder of the father, and so on) does not perform this understanding simply because it presupposes what it must produce, or it presupposes what must appear (or be constituted) at the end of the myth as outcome of what happens in it.

First of all, one could ask *why* the prohibition of endotribal murder and *why* the prohibition of incest. Regardless of what may seem to be the case, to this *why* the myth of *Totem and Taboo* responds exactly as a myth, that is, by positing an event: incest and endotribal murder are prohibited because at one time an event took place whose outcome produced these prohibitions. But if we look deeper into this matter, what does the prohibition of endotribal murder presuppose? It presupposes that there is a tendency in humans toward this sort of murder. No one prohibits human beings from flying. No one prohibits them from anything they do *not* desire to do. It prohibits things they *would do* because they desire them and because they can do them. Now, we naturally know rather extensively why there is this desire to kill one's neighbor. Where does it come from? The murder of the neighbor, of an individual of the same biological kind, is first of all unknown to any biological species before the human—or at least, unknown as noninstrumental murder. The stories of Konrad Lorenz and other scholars of animal customs about the battle among wolves, for example, are famous. When wolves battle among themselves—and they can battle with great violence—the one that is defeated or knows he is about to be defeated stops battling and presents his neck to the teeth of his victorious opponent, who at that point automatically ceases the battle. When there is battle among primates, especially chimpanzees—for whatever reason, and it can be greatly violent—the that who is defeated or knows he is about to be defeated presents his behind, for obvious reasons, since sodomy exists among chimpanzees, and the other stops the attack. Between humans, fortunately or unfortunately—unfortunately, I would say—this does not happen. That is, from the moment one is apparently weakened, the other becomes even more violent and finishes him off. But this refers us to something extremely important: in the human species, we have another sort of psyche that *tends* to the murder of one's own kind.

On this issue, incidentally, one could present a pseudo-neo-Darwinist response. That is, if we suppose there were a hundred hordes of primitive primates in the process of humanization, in those hordes where the repression against killing one's own kind disappeared, there emerged a handicap in the battle for survival and control of ground and thereby they vanished; only the ones who by chance, as according to all neo-Darwinism, fell upon the right solution, that is, prohibition, survived. This neo-Darwinist solution is pseudo-neo-Darwinist, for the simple reason that all neo-Darwinist responses as to why a given species presents given characteristics presuppose species changes to be inscribed in the genes, while we know very well that such transformation does not occur in humans, that, instead of species transformation, the transformation happens at the level of social institution, which can never be genetically inscribed. No one inherits the language or society of his parents, if we remove him from his society during the first day of his existence and take him three thousand kilometers down the road to another society.

Second question: why the prohibition of incest? Which incest? This is extremely interesting because in Freud's myth the kind of incest that should have been forbidden should have concerned all the females that derive from the same grandfather, let us say, the murdered father, or women who would have been the father's wives, daughters, nieces, granddaughters, and so forth. As is well known, however, all totemic prohibitions of incest, or rather totemic prohibitions of endogamy, go much further than that. In other words, where there is real totemism and exogamy exists, the prohibition of endogamy extends to all members of the same totemic horde, regardless of any blood kinship between prospective spouses or lovers. And yet we know that there is a grave tendency toward incest among humans, which actually takes place quite often, especially among siblings, but also vertically, and, more easily than statistics claim, between fathers and daughters. In this matter there can be no response, not even a pseudo-neo-Darwinist response because, regardless what has been claimed on occasion, the prohibition against incest does not serve *any* biological reason whatsoever.

Now, what Freud has in mind in this myth is essentially—and he says so—what Darwin wrote in his book on the origins of humanity based on his views on the customs of gorillas. Among gorillas there is indeed a cyclopean family, which reminds us of the cyclopean family in *Totem and Taboo*, that is, an extremely powerful father gorilla, who possesses all the females of the horde, as well as whatever females he can abduct from elsewhere, and who banishes the males when they reach a certain age and can survive on their own. And these males wander off until the moment when they can build their own horde, abducting females or perhaps, when the archgorilla gets old, returning to the tribe and taking over his place. But, of course, in this case neither is incest prohibited subsequently nor is endotribal murder.

What biologists tell us these days is that, according to the chromosomatic clock, closest to us humans are not gorillas but chimpanzees, among whom, however, groups of tens of individuals may exist who practice polymating or all-around mating, and there is, of course, no negative biological result. We know it; we see it; it is confirmed: the prohibition of incest is not due to biological reasons. I say all this so that we can properly situate

Freud, who surely spoke according to the parameters of his day. We are not interested in such repudiations, nor do we originate from chimpanzees. As you all know, the human species is divided from primates *before* the subdivisions among them to gorillas, chimpanzees, orangutans, and baboons, and by this token, human beings could easily reassume the customs of gorillas and such. I say this merely to add to our context of information.

So, let us accept Freud's scientific myth, that is, his cyclopean hypothesis. What does this myth tacitly presuppose? Freud himself says that perhaps the brothers forged an alliance at a particular moment *and* by virtue of a new technological discovery or invention. This is a superfluous hypothesis, as Hobbes and La Boétie, not to mention the ancient Greeks, already knew. No such technological invention was needed because if fifteen individuals of the same sort can put away one of their kind, even if stronger, no single person can resist, except if psychical factors intervene, but then we depart from Freud's presuppositions. This notion of a technological invention is superfluous but is also curious, because any such invention would already belong to the social and humanized realm.

But the myth *mainly* presupposes the alliance among the brothers with aims that are exo- and antibiological. We do know for sure about alliances among animals, but herding animals, ants, chimpanzees, or baboons that live in groups are hardly all the same. These alliances are biologically instrumental; they serve purposes that are posited by the species in its biological constitution. In the human case, however, we have a condition where, by presupposition, the biological status quo is the cyclopean family. Such an alliance—the alliance of the brothers for a nonbiological cause—is, of course, itself an institution, a primary institution, which also presupposes another institution, language. Finally, the oath that the brothers share is also itself an institution. (Incidentally, the sisters are entirely ignored in Freud's text, which is not surprising considering his patriarchal position.) The brothers' oath is the creation of institution—there is no oath among animals—and this institution establishes the double prohibition. It also establishes the totem. I will not discuss what ethnologists who revise Freud (justifiably, but this does not interest me) claim: namely, that the issue of totemism is much less ubiquitous than Frazier (or others whom Freud followed) believed, that totems are not always animals.

What concerns us here is what Freud says about ambivalence in relation to the totem. In the first and second chapters of *Totem and Taboo*, he describes the ambivalence of human affect. What is this ambivalence about? Surely, it is the positive and negative simultaneously, that is, hatred against this horrific father, which leads to murder and cannibalization, but simultaneously, as Freud says explicitly, a love-worship toward the father once murdered. Such ambivalent feelings—I do not believe they are known in animals—presuppose a biologically anomalous development of the human psyche and naturally go hand in hand with the tacit supposition that institutions already exist. I am suggesting that guilt is surely inconceivable except as consequence of transgressing a prohibition. One could possibly say, as stated in psychoanalysis, that guilt exists not only as consequence of transgressing a prohibition, but as consequence of a certain act against a person we love, or against a person whose love we want, or both.

This presupposes sentiments of love toward the father who is the object of murder. Now, what does love mean in this case? When we speak of animals, we speak of sexual instincts, we can speak of motherly instincts or motherly and fatherly instincts, or if we set aside primates and go to birds or other animal species, where there is a real sense of family, we can speak of instinctual "spousal" arrangements and the like—but we cannot say there is love. But Freud speaks of love. And he speaks of guilt, and these two presuppose that there exists *already* a human sort of *psyche*.

If we go now to the other two of Freud's works from the late 1920s, where, as I mentioned, Freud speaks of minorities that play the civilizing role, the first question that comes to mind is "where did these minorities spring from?"—in other words, the matter is simply displaced. Second, this idea about civilizing minorities is actually unfounded in real terms because, without supposing that some sort of primitive communism had existed at one time, we know very well that the division of primitive societies (those at least we know something about) is not asymmetrical and antagonistic. It is rather an articulation of the various subdivisions of the pertinent social unit, and in this sense we cannot speak of any minorities that play a civilizing role. This is established by the work of various ethnologists. I will merely refer to the best known: the work of Pierre Clastres on certain Indian tribes in South America, where there is no power separate from the tribe itself—there is merely a chief in whom power is "diffused" in some manner. Parenthetically, I note that this idea of civilizing minorities contradicts the admission one finds in *Totem and Taboo* that the first societies after the father's murder, wherein exists the oath among the brothers as well as prohibition and guilt, were societies of "primitive democracy." But this does not really concern us here; these contradictions are superficial, and the matter in this entire story is significantly more profound.

The picture formed by these two of Freud's efforts—*Totem and Taboo* and the works from the late 1920s—suggests that human beings are mobilized and determined exclusively by their drives (*Triebe*—not instincts, this is significant) and that these drives are essentially sexual or always related to a source of pleasure, which, in the first phases of psychic development, according to Freud, reigns without limits.

First aporia regarding this matter: Animals have extremely strong drives and something even stronger than drives since they have instincts. And these instincts, in a way, are similar in purpose to human drives—sexual satisfaction and self-preservation, or hunger, let us say. Why, then, does there not exist a multitude of animal societies, in the strictest sense of the term? Why aren't there totems and taboos among tigers or apes? Why, in other words—and in what terms—did human animals become human or humanized?

To this, Freud gives an implicit response that explains nothing and gives a potential possibility, if I may say, of a response, which I think has remained still unexplored.

The implicit response in which Freud recognizes the main enigma of any psychology—or one of the main enigmas of any psychology and, of course, of psychoanalysis itself—is the existence of consciousness. But this does not lead us anywhere. If we take consciousness simply as consciousness, that is, as the quality of being conscious of certain psychic phenomena, it is merely a passive quality, if I may put it this way, which is merely added to such phenomena. In order to produce a difference, the existence of consciousness must refer to an active consciousness, that is, a kind of active and acting rationality. We know these two things are entirely different. Animals are surely much more rational than humans, instrumentally rational. Animals do not make mistakes; animals do not eat poisonous mushrooms; animals do not stumble—horses occasionally stumble because they are denaturalized by humans. While, we humans do not know what is edible and what is poisonous; we learn it only if we are told. And we know that, as humans, we have consciousness and yet, simultaneously, we are monstrously nonrational—we see this every day, in our own life, in the life of others, in the life of the whole world. And, most important, if drives are the only force that mobilizes the human being, then this consciousness, whether rational or nonrational, would produce always the same thing, except perhaps for molecular changes of adjustment to external conditions. In other words, there would be no difference between societies; there would be no history. This matter of history is, in some ways, the black hole of psychoanalysis, and it pertains to the second question I posed at the outset, which I will not address today.

The unexplored potentiality of a response is given by Freud in the 1915 text "Instincts and their Vicissitudes." Freud does not elaborate on it—he does not even suspect it—but this text, in my opinion, includes the answer to the question of the characteristics of humanization. I think the answer is the following, along strictly Freudian lines: drives (for example, the sexual drive) trace their source to the body and purport a satisfaction of a certain need. As we said, this need is, to begin with, or primarily, or in-between, the pleasure that comes from the relief and the serenity that follows satisfaction. The action or energy that leads to satisfaction is necessarily mediated by the psyche (or, some might say, the central nervous system), whether this concerns animals or humans. In order to begin to act, the psyche must be affected by a somatic impulse, what we call instinct in animals and drive in humans. These two domains, the somatic and the psychic—and on this, Freud is uncompromising, and justly, in my opinion—are perfectly heterogeneous. In one domain, the body, we have masses and movements, as he says in the 1895 text *Project for a Scientific Psychology*; in the other, the domain of the psyche, we have qualities and representations—let us say, images. The impulse that corresponds to the drive or the instinct cannot jump start the psychical universe, except by producing within the psychical universe, by induction as they say in electricity theory, the appropriate and analogous image. This image is what Freud calls the ideational representative of the drive (*Vorstellungsrepräsentanz der Trieb*). What this means should become clear from the difference I will draw between humans and animals. In animals, the ideational representative of instinct is determined, canonical, and biologically operative. For example, the ideational representative of a male dog's sexual instinct, which mobilizes his energy in this direction, is the view and smell of a female dog, and it is only and always this. The same goes for food, shelter, and the like. In other words, there is a solid once-and-for-all connection between what is a somatic impulse, the source of the drive, and the representation that, coming from within the animal psyche, will lead the animal to act accordingly, to chase the rabbit if he wants to eat.

What happens with humans is that this correspondence is disrupted. Why? Because in the human psyche we have an enormous and monstrous neoplasia, a carcinoma of the human psyche, which is the radical imagination. I call it a carcinoma because its development is uncontrollable and because it does not correspond to any biological operation—to the contrary, if looked at in isolation, it is rather destructive biologically, whatever might be its positive results from other standpoints. For this reason, and because of the radical imagination, the ideational representative of a drive may differ enormously among human beings, or within even the same human being in different periods of his or her life. In the sexual domain, for example, we have so-called normal relations, but we also have homosexual relations in both sexes, we have bisexuals, fetishists, sadomasochists, voyeurs, exhibitionists—we have whatever you like. And even in the case of people in so-called normal relations, if you scratch a little the phantasms that escort their sexual arousal and the possibly subsequent sexual act and satisfaction, you will find that these phantasms are anything but (or have anything to do with but) the biological instrumental satisfaction of a sexual drive and a biological purpose, that is, the fertilization of the female by the male.

We thus distinguish human beings fundamentally by the radical imagination, which consists of, briefly, the following basic characteristics: not causally determined flux of representations, desires, and affects; the substitution of organic pleasure with phantasmatic pleasure; the noninstrumentality or even anti-instrumentality of pleasure; the unlimited and unsurpassable egocentrism; the capacity for sublimation, that is, investment in "invisible" objects of social significance; the capacity for symbolism; and, as we will see in a minute, the ineffaceable demand for significance or meaning. Therefore, human beings are animals that are perfectly abnormal, insane, and essentially and fundamentally inept at living, if left to their own devices. They are inept at living *not* because they would abandon themselves—this is what Freud allows us to suggest—to the limitless satisfaction of their sexual drives or other such drives, but because they would remain caged within this primary form of their existence, that is, a self-sufficient psychic monad, which is self-enclosed in its own representations and is thus abandoned to the limitless pleasure produced by these representations—and which, for it, cannot be distinguished from real perceptions and can thus be considered, as Freud says of infants, to consist of hallucinations. And we positively know that this is the primary psychic condition of newborn infants, but also of adults, who are perfectly capable of abandoning themselves as much to daydreaming as to their nightly dreams.

This is a condition wholly antithetical to the survival demands of the human as a biological being. On one hand, you cannot be nourished with hallucinations or phantasms, and on the other, let us not kid ourselves, we are not born or we do not come into this world as separate individuals; we are born among others and specifically very close others. The combination of somatic need and the presence/interference of the other, more generally the mother, leads to a more or less violent rupture of this singular or monadic condition, compelling the infant to enter a process of socialization—that is, humanization, in a secondary and more powerful sense. Of course, a mother cannot socialize her child if she is not herself socialized. For example, she must speak and listen—I do not say *hear*, in the neurophysiological sense, because the infant does not speak; it cries. Yes, a mother can hear her baby crying, but so can a cat hear her kitten crying. The issue is that the mother *speaks*, and at one point the infant responds and the mother listens, in more than one sense, that is to say, understands even when the infant does not speak, what it is that it wants, what it desires. The mother speaks; she is present within language. Can we produce or deduce language psychoanalytically? Surely not. When all is said and done, there is not, there cannot be, a psychoanalytic answer to the question of the genesis of society, because society must already exist in order for human beings to live. Again, human beings as such are incapable of survival. You can abandon a weaned kitten or a weaned gorilla, and they will survive. A human infant will not, or if it does, it will not be human—we know this from infants raised among wolves and other animals.

Thus, there must be a society in existence, so that these inept and insane beings can survive and become human, and there is nothing in the human unconscious capable of producing the basic characteristics of every society, that is, institutions and imaginary significations. The psyche cannot be reduced to society, even if the socialized subject is almost nothing but successive layers of socialization, but the psyche as such, in its depth, cannot be reduced or confined to society and society cannot be confined to the psyche because, yet again, there is nothing within the human unconscious that can produce institutions. Freud's scientific myth is the unproductive effort to *extricate*, in some manner, institutions out of drives or instincts. The only thing one can say is that there must be some sort of correspondence between the demands of the psyche and the demands of society. This correspondence is reduced to the fact that institutions and social imaginary significations must offer meaning to the socializable psyche; that is, they must create for the psyche a daily world where distinctive things and distinctive human beings exist, where all these are combined and intertwined, and where, for the socializable subject itself, life and even death have a meaning.

Consequently, we cannot respond to the question "Where does society come from?" except by saying that society is a creation, a collective creation, a creation of anonymous collectivity or, in other words, of the radical instituting social imaginary. When it creates institutions, this imaginary must surely take into account, up to a point, the surrounding natural and biological reality—and it does so every time, which is why all theories deriving from the production and reproduction of material life tell us nothing, and are mere tautologies. Every society must account for the biological needs of the human being, and therefore it must organize production and reproduction, and every society must account for its need to reproduce itself as human collectivity and thereby regulate, in some fashion, the reproduction of human beings as human social beings—to regulate, in other words, an elementary family life and education of individuals via the familial and more generally social life. And this education exists as well in the most primitive societies we know, not of course in the form of schooling. When we take into account the amazing heterogeneity of social forms we observe in history, we discover, yet again, the creativity of this radical instituting social imaginary. It is not, in other words, that a type of society was formed once and for all and we remained there, nor is it that we can explain the difference between societies by virtue of a historical development that would signify some sort of "progress." The imaginary significations that, for example, distinguish the modern West from ancient Greece and ancient Greece from Egypt or China or India cannot be compared between them along the line of progress in the strict sense of the word.

Why, then, do Freud's two attempts to produce society out of the unconscious fail? Because they both presuppose, in one form or another, the very thing they want to prove or to produce: the institution. The attempt to begin this formation of the social out of psychic elements ignores that such psychic elements—ambivalence, for example—presuppose a human psyche that has been radically altered relative to any biological psyche of the animal, bearing with it clear signs of a certain socialization, of language, of relations that are not simply sexual but also conventional. On the other hand, Freud sees clearly something central in the psyche, its asocial or antisocial character—something he especially emphasizes in "Thoughts on the Times of War and Death" and *The Future of an Illusion*, and no doubt in *Civilization and Its Discontents*. He sees that society presupposes, and will always presuppose, the denial or repression of certain psychic tendencies. But because he sees these tendencies only as biologically

rooted and characterized—the sexual instinct and the instinct of self-preservation, even if he correctly does not call them instincts but drives—he
finds incomprehensible, for example, the unbridled and, from a biological
perspective, inoperative element of these drives. In other words, if we
spoke of a canine or a bovine society, we would not have to face, even on
sexual matters, what we face with the human, namely that, on the one
hand, these drives are inoperative or dysfunctional and, on the other hand,
unbridled and forever insatiable.

In the end, then, this effort to present this huge edifice of the institution
of society as an outcome of psychic tendencies fails. The genesis of society
is not "explained" by the instinct for self-preservation, the sexual drive,
the need for love, which once again already presupposes an enormous sublimation of the sexual drive, or the role of reward and punishment, where
also what is sought is already granted, because the sexual drive does not
seek love but sexual satisfaction, reward and punishment presuppose the
existence of society, and reward presupposes additionally an important and
foundational sublimation of narcissism: self-love must have been transformed to the need for positive appreciation of the other or others.

We can also say something more, not in the sense of a psychoanalytic
production or procurement of society, but in terms of the contribution
psychoanalysis makes to the elucidation of the decisive dimensions of this
institution. First of all, there is something elemental in the psyche that
responds to the institution of society as an imaginary, not instrumental or
functional, institution. This is the very thing that consistently escapes
Freud. The psyche has a need for *meaning*, and the imaginary institution
of society always offers it meaning. To put it in other words, society encounters a nearly limitless plasticity and flexibility of the psyche and, as
the history of humanity demonstrates, it makes out of the psyche almost
whatever it wants. Society can make the psyche Muslim, Christian, Hindu,
Buddhist, idolatrous, communist; it can make it polygamous, monoga-
mous, whatever you want. There is but one thing it cannot do: It cannot
not give it meaning. And we see in the crisis of contemporary society what
happens when, in a certain social condition, the instituted meanings begin
to fray and human beings are no longer able to find meaning in social or
political life. But, of course, this meaning that society gives to the psyche
is, from a certain standpoint, the exact opposite of the primary meaning
that the psyche seeks, namely to remain self-enclosed and enjoy the flux
of its phantasms. The meaning that society presents and imposes on the
psyche is the world of things, of others, reality, work, means, ends, and so
on. From another standpoint, however, one finds many correspondences

between these two categories of meaning, not strictly or singularly signi-
fied, but characteristic nonetheless.

Therefore, to sum up a bit what I have been saying, we have first of all
the rupture between the human and the biological, with the emergence of
the psychic monad and the radical imagination with its various characteristics—limitless egocentrism, omnipotence of the unconscious, substitution
of organ pleasure with pleasure of the phantasm, ability for sublimation,
ability for symbolism, need for meaning; second, the simultaneous emergence of the radical social imaginary as instituting imaginary; and third,
the leaning of the institution of society on certain of the psyche's characters, with repression or sublimation of other characters. This leaning or
support, for example, we find in all religions, whether they are animistic,
monotheistic, or polytheistic, and we also find it, to a powerful extent, in
the identification of every individual with the given social world, as world
of meaning and signification, which, if we had ample time, we would have
explored a lot further.

But there is something to say about the structure and content of social
and political institutions. First of all, there is the matter of religion. On
this, Freud is clear and, to my mind, situated entirely within the truth of
the matter, even though one could add certain things. Freud sees the essential role of religion in relation to the denial and repression of drives,
but he also sees, and this is the only time he really sees it, that the role of
the institution, and especially of religion, is to grant meaning. He names
religion illusion, gives a definition of illusion, and correctly states that
illusion is not merely false trust, but a false trust supported by desire—
here, desire being the desire to know. This is what Freud means when he
says that religion substitutes psychology for natural science, meaning by it
that all divine forms, whether monotheistic or polytheistic, are animist
projections of the human psyche upon the universe. He also says correctly
that religion attempts to protect one's sense of self from being threatened
by the bottomless expanse of the world, that religion plays a palliative role
and presents a so-called solution to the most horrific enigma of all, the
enigma of death. For this reason, he goes on, religion humanizes the
world, with an anthropomorphic representation of the universe, which, of
course, leans on infantile projections—here he specifically has in mind the
father image, but one could equally consider, without changing his text at
all, the mother image.

Freud believes that religion can be overcome because, as he says, humanity cannot remain forever at an infantile stage; it must venture out
into the big world, the stranger world. But he is rather economical or

stingy, if one could put it this way, and perhaps rightly so, as to how this overcoming is to take place, and I think this difficulty still lies before us, not only because religious beliefs continue to exist or because certain of the political beliefs of the twentieth century took on a kind of religious character (as communism, for example), but also because beyond this over-coming of religion lies an enormous unknown: Can human beings in their totality, and not just a few, encounter their mortality with total clarity? Theory alone cannot possibly respond to this question. Historical experi-ence gives us one or two examples, or half-examples: one is the Greek example, until about 400 BCE, where religion plays neither a political role nor is there an affirmative sense of immortality. The half-examples include early Buddhism—which, however, went together with a certain unworldli-ness, a withdrawal from the world, but this too soon became an instituted religion like all others—and the contemporary era, in which, however, we saw a nonreligious religion of progress, let us say, take the place of religion in both capitalism and Marxism with the well-known destructive results, or on the other hand, what I mentioned earlier, namely, the insignificance of life for the typical subjectivity in today's society and the compensation sought in consumption and televisual masturbation and what I think in the end is the incapacity of such compensation.

Now, regarding the domination of one sex by another, it is common knowledge that efforts have been made to give a psychoanalytic explana-tion to the question of the inequality of the sexes and to what produces a sex beyond anatomy. Such efforts were made in order to justify existing male domination—naturally, the initial guilt belongs to Freud, but this was continued by other psychoanalysts and extended by Lacan with all these stories about the phallus—or, in a more paradoxical way, in most recent years, by certain feminists who tried to reverse the Freudian schema.

I do not think there is any reason to expect that psychoanalysis will explain the domination of one sex by another or the patriarchal organiza-tion of society any more than it could possibly—and it cannot—explain the antagonistic and asymmetrical division of society in dominant and sub-ordinate parts.

Freud used to paraphrase Napoleon, who said that geography is fate, while Freud said that anatomy is fate. But this anatomical fate could at the very most give ground to an instituted sexual difference, not an instituted sexual inequality. The slippage from the first category to the second is mere sophism. The explanation that Freud gives to the inequality of the sexes is also a case of having already granted what is sought. As you know from popularized versions of psychoanalysis, the little boy represses the incestual love he feels for his mother and retreats before his father, terrified of his castration but in the hope that one day he will succeed in taking his place. The little girl discovers, says Freud, her castration—paradoxical notion, because the little girl is not castrated at all; this is but a phantasm, as the castration of a woman would consist of the destruction of her genitals, the uterus, the ovaries, and so forth—and she consoles herself, hoping that the father or the future father-substitute will give her a child as a substitute for a penis.

If we are not going to speak of psychic phenomena we encounter on the couch but of social conditions, this entire construction presupposes, of course, the existence already of an instituted position of the dominant father and, moreover, the quasi instituted exceptional value of the penis or phallus instead of, let us say, the extended belly of the pregnant mother, which could also be utilized, as it has been utilized in many religious beliefs.

In a manner rather inconsistent with what we have been saying (but contradictions and inconsistencies are fertile in a great author), Freud justly insists on what he calls the intrinsically psychic bisexuality of humans. Psychic certainly because it cannot be biological; no one can support such an argument by reference to hormones and the like. And he wonders in a passage from "Analysis Terminable and Interminable," if I remember correctly, why it is so difficult for a person to be bisexual, to go both with women and with men. Gaius Suetonius used to say of Julius Caesar *"omnium mulierum vir, omnium virorum mulier,"* that he was "the man of all the women and the woman of all the men" in Rome. This did not obstruct Caesar from being a great warrior, dictator, genius, and such. So, Freud wonders at a certain moment, even though he was strictly monosexual, why the hell it is so difficult for humans to be bisexual—and he gives no answer.

I think, without necessarily insisting on the matter, that the answer is in part a social issue, that, in other words, it is due precisely to a particular social institution. In any case, we know all about bisexuality in the human psyche; we see it in the polymorphous perversion of children and the bisexuality, or if one can say pansexuality, of sexual fantasies. Therefore, active and passive positions exist from the outset in both anatomical sexes and gradually become, not only differentiated, but also even antithetical, so that they almost become—or had become until recently—antinomian and incompatible characteristics between both sexes. I mean this in the social sense: in reference to the identification of passivity in women and activity in men, which, to my mind, is clearly a product of socialization and societal institution. Thus, we find no structurally psychoanalytic need for a patriarchal organization of society. The only structural need we find is, of course, that this double relation, exclusive and face to face, between the mother and her infant must be broken at a certain point, a third must intervene, a qualitatively different third, but not necessarily a dominant third, as is the father in the patriarchal family.

The same goes for social domination, about which I will say little. Freud speaks of civilizing minorities. This rests on nothing, and we cannot see why it would have to be psychoanalytically inevitable that society must continue to have a social hierarchy and, in a sense, a relation between master and slave, dominator and dominated. What we do know simply is that in contemporary societies these relations are surely internalized, but they are so because they are thus instituted and because they prevail in the imaginary.

I must come to a conclusion, and I will only say a couple of things about whether psychoanalysis has anything to say about a possible radical transformation of society. I will say that here open two paths, one darker, which perhaps (or rather, surely) is closer to Freud, and another more lucid, which, though not contradicting what Freud has written, does go in a different direction.

The darker path, evident in the thoughts about death and war and in the book about civilization's discontents, leads to the idea that not only is civilization tantamount to denial and repression of drives—which is correct, yet, in my opinion, not irreconcilable with a transformation of society, a point to which I return shortly—but also there can never be, as Freud says, an overcoming of the death drive, the catastrophic drive that destroys both self and other. Without insisting on the death drive as such, there is at least an interpretation of the drive toward destruction that suffices to support pessimistic conclusions. This is the repetition-compulsion, or simply what Freud called conditions of indolence and inertia, when speaking of his patients, though this is surely the case in the totality of human peoples.

There is, moreover, another element, which is more characteristic and significant: the mutual enmity of human society, which relates, according to Freud, to the necessity of narcissistic identification, or the identification with dominant culture, the culture of the dominant minorities. He makes this point explicitly in *Civilization and Its Discontents*. But this opens up an enormous catalogue of questions that I cannot now address. When I do say, however, that he is correct to speak of the denial and repression of drives, I agree in the sense that there exists, and there must always exist, an unassailable enmity of the psychic core against the processes of socialization it must necessarily undergo, as well as an outmaneuverable obsession formed by this constellation of primary narcissism, egocentrism, omnipotence of thought, hatred of the other and the tendency toward the destruction of the other (to the extent the other stands opposed to our desires or is simply just other), and the tendency to recede into an imaginary universe.

From this standpoint, certain limits enter into the potential conditions of human society, but these limits do not really concern us much. They refer to the idea that the nature of the human psyche precludes the possibility that a perfect society can ever be realized—and the phrase "perfect society" is void of meaning—or that the nature of the human psyche, and this is more significant, will always impose a psychic rupture in human beings. In other words, to the idea that Marx's utopia, for example—the reconciliation of all and every one with oneself—is utopia in the bad sense of the term.

Yet, I do not think the real question lies there. If we can overcome messianisms, whether religious or secular, and if we can overcome the ideas of an idyllic Arcadia, which we find sometimes in Marcuse, the problem at hand is the possible access of large masses of people to a condition of lucid thought, self-reflexive and self-critical thought, which would permit a collaboration between brothers and sisters without the totemization of institutions, in addition with a willful guidance of the polymorphous impulses of the psychic chaos toward paths that make life possible and enable the working of autonomous individuals and societies. And, even more, the capacity to transfer the narcissistic identifications of the horde, tribe, or nation to more generalized identifications—let us say, along the lines of the fact the human belongs to humanity. This is a difficult matter because it does not merely pertain to the narcissism of petty differences, as Freud used to say—even if this is hardly easy, as we often see in the case of the fan of one football team breaking the head of a fan of another team, for just that mere fact. Of course, this has much graver dimensions, religious, for example: the antagonism between Christianity and Islam or Islam and Hinduism in South Asia, so as not mention the indelible hatred that divides Eastern Orthodox from Catholic Christians for more than one thousand years, which led to our ancestors' claim that they would rather see a Turkish turban in Constantinople around 1450 than a Latin crown and that today makes Serbians and Croatians massacre each other, and so on.

I am not trying to respond to all those very difficult questions that pertain to the darker path. I will merely add just a couple of words about the lucid path, which also springs from psychoanalysis because, when it comes down to it, to speak of the capacity to transform society presupposes that we can simultaneously respond to the question of the transformation of the human individual. In other words, there is at some level a kind of nonsense to the extreme social pessimism of Freud and even more—dare I say?—of the more frayed psychoanalysts of the day, when, by definition, by virtue of their mission, they necessarily presuppose and support the claim that a substantial transformation of human individuals is possible—otherwise, what sort of justification is there to assume them as patients in analysis?—yet, simultaneously, also claim that the very nature of the human psyche makes a radical transformation of human societies perfectly impossible.

The problem we encounter here is, in other words, the problem of *telos* in psychoanalysis in the ancient double sense of the word, meaning the chronological end and the end as aim. From that point on, we can run with the ball, as the kids would say. What is the aim of psychoanalysis and how can one determine it? I will not return to the vast range of discussions that have been conducted on this point; I will merely summarize what I have elaborated in a piece called "The State of the Subject Today."[2]

There is no way to determine the aim of psychoanalysis other than the autonomy of the analysand. The notion autonomy hinges neither on the ostracism or total repression of the unconscious, something in any case monstrous and impossible, nor on the domination of the unconscious by consciousness, but on the establishment of a different relation between the conscious and the unconscious. This different relation can be determined as a relation where the subject, to the greatest degree possible, has an understanding of its unconscious drives and does not repel them, in the strictest sense, but can contemplate them, so by virtue of this meditation can decide, with willfulness and multiple consideration, if he or she wants or does not want to act according to such desires. In other words, I think that the motto of psychoanalysis should be, "I know what my desire is, but after a fully nurtured set of thoughts I will not realize it." This means, if such an aim is not utopian, that the subject is capable of positing, in a certain way, its own rules of thought and behavior.

Now, the subject is not an island; it is a social being—therefore, his or her autonomy is necessarily limited and can even become a simple delusion, if the subject ignores the enormous significance of his or her social dimension. And this takes place today, in comic ways, in theories of liberal individualism. Never have we heard more rhetorical talk about individual freedom, which contemporary capitalism allegedly secures, and never had we had a society with such few free and autonomous individuals, with such conformist individuals, a society in which at exactly the same moment all of the country's households push the same buttons and turn to the same channels to watch the same stupidities on a television screen. This is the freedom of choice. To the degree the subject participates in a society, it is necessarily subjected to social laws, rhythms, and modes of social influence. And this would have been an entirely heteronomous condition, except for one thing: the instance when the subject can say, justifiably, that these laws are also my own laws, not because they have been imposed on me, but because I have participated, on equal terms with all others, in their institution. This instance, of course, does not exist today.

In other words, autonomous individuals can only exist in an autonomous society, that is, a fully democratic society, and vice versa. From this standpoint then, the ultimate aims of psychoanalysis are the same with the aims of a truly democratic, political, and self-instituting society. And I think that, in order for one to be honest before the many deeper currents in Freud's thinking and his positions, and despite his frequent pessimism, one must accept that this is the meaning that Freud expresses when he speaks of Reason our God and the necessity for humanity to emerge from its infantile condition; and that this is the meaning of half of the scientific myth in *Totem and Taboo*, which psychoanalysts usually neglect, that is, the oath of the brothers (we would add, also of the sisters), after the supposed murder of the father, according to which no one will henceforth demand the totality of power for himself alone. What is missing from this side of the myth, in the form Freud gives it, is that the brothers and sisters cannot make this agreement, but only simultaneously with the totemization of the killed father, that is, the totemization of the institution or institutions.

What we have before us, what in their own way the ancient Athenians and, to an extent, the West attempted without fully succeeding, is—please excuse the barbarous phrase—the full detotemization of institutions: the recognition that, of course, there can be no human society without institutions, but also that institutions have always been and always are our own creation, under certain specific limitations. We must recognize this fact and cease asking for transcendental or extrasocial guarantees of our life's meaning, knowing that meaning can only discovered and created within and by means of our own free and conscious action.

Translated by Stathis Gourgouris

The Hermeneutics of Suspicion Reconsidered

Joel Whitebook

I

Somewhere around 1980, the hermeneutics of suspicion more or less disappeared from the field of philosophical discourse. It was a casualty of postmodernism and the linguistic turns—which overlap but are not identical—in philosophy and the social sciences. We can, following Dreyfus, understand the hermeneutics of suspicion as a theory of a "motivated cover-up."[1] It holds that many of the most important contents of individual and collective consciousness are distorted facades that mask deep underlying and potentially emancipatory truths—whether they be economic, as they were with Marx; psychosexual, as they were with Freud; or ethico-aesthetic, as they were with Nietzsche. Because the cover-up—which is motivated by power's attempt to maintain its interested position—is systematic and self-reinforcing, it is cunning and difficult to unmask. The practitioner of suspicion therefore needs a privileged theory that stands outside the ideological fray and is commensurate with the task—that is, a theory that is itself cunning enough to apprehend and expose the cover-up, thereby emancipating the deeply repressed truth.[2] Needless to say, the three masters of suspicion believed they possessed such a theory: the critique of political economy with Marx, psychosexuality with Freud, and the will-to-power with Nietzsche. Indeed, the first two believed they possessed a theory that was strictly scientific. It is important to stress that the hermeneutics of suspicion is not skepticism. It criticizes a given form of consciousness in order to achieve a fuller form of consciousness.

The problem is that postmodernism grew suspicious of such privileged theories. Indeed, Rorty believed that "suspicion about the masters of suspicion" was the hallmark of postmodernism.[3] In a curious development, the Left's belated disillusionment with Marxism—which was helped along by the killing fields of Cambodia, the "Solzhenitsyn shock" in the West, and the rise of Solidarity in Poland—dovetailed with a heated debate in the philosophy of science to produce what Lyotard called incredulity toward about all grand "metanarratives."[4] It was believed that—because they did not realize that all theories are bounded by paradigms, as Thomas Kuhn had demonstrated—general theories were not only epistemologically suspect but also led to totalitarian politics. (In aesthetics, postmodernists sometimes identified the notion of the avant-garde with the idea of a vanguard party in an attempt to discredit the modernists politically as well as artistically.) In an attempt to affect the modesty that was believed to be appropriate to the new insights in politics and the philosophy of science, it was argued that, to avoid the totalitarian temptation, all politics and theory had to be local—or even "weak," as the Italian philosopher Gianni Vattimo has called it. I would like to point out that even the resurgence of liberal thinking—which accelerated after the collapse of communism—purports to partake in this self-limiting attitude toward politics and theory. Its proponents claim to restrict themselves to formal questions of justice and to abstain from addressing ethical questions of the good, arguing that opening substantive questions of the good always carried with it the potential for antidemocratic excesses. This claim, however, is a sham, for liberalism has a whole way of life, and therefore a concept of the good, embedded in its supposedly transhistorical principles.

It follows that, if the postmodern/linguistic turn undermined the legitimacy of privileged theories, and if the paradigm of suspicion requires precisely this type of theory to carry out its unmasking critique, then the hermeneutics of suspicion is discredited as well. But this raises another question. The hermeneutics of suspicion had for years provided the central model of critique, and, once discredited, a question arose as to what model of critique would be there to replace it. This is the question that postmodernists—especially Foucault—have been circling for years, unable to answer it. The problem is, in a nutshell, that the very notion of critique requires a privileged standpoint—however it is conceived—from which it can be made. And the strong paradigm-relativism of the postmodernists has deprived them of such a standpoint, and therefore of the possibility of critique.

II

No one who came of age philosophically during the 1960s can underestimate the significance of the linguistic turn. The hermeneutical critique of positivism removed a conceptual logjam, which had blocked philosophical creativity for nearly two decades. At the same time, however, the linguistic turn—which appears to be running its course—has often assumed a radicalized form that created an impasse of its own. That is, the critique of scientism and objectivism often slipped into the rejection of science and objectivity as such. It was argued that the human sciences are not only distinct from the natural sciences but also must include an interpretive dimension because of the self-interpreting nature of the human animal. At times, it was also argued that, because scientific theory and practice are embedded in the linguistically mediated lifeworld, which constitutes an unavoidable background of prescientific understanding, no privileged status can be claimed for science. Science, so the argument goes, is simply one language game among many—on a par with poetry or religion—and no special status can be claimed for it.[5] But this argument is based on the mistaken view of science that was assumed by the critics of positivism.

Let me preface my remarks by saying that the positivists' concern that scientific theories be intersubjectively communicable has a good deal of merit and should be respected. Having said that, however, I need to point out that the self-understanding of the actual working scientist was not the primary target of the critique of positivism. It was rather the *prescriptive* picture of science promulgated by the logical empiricists—a picture most scientists were not particularly interested in. One of the central assumptions of the positivists was that mathematical physics provided the paradigm for true science and that all other candidates, aspiring to scientific legitimacy must be measured against it. Following a tradition stretching back to Plato, they believed that mathematical physics constituted the highest embodiment of strict *epistemé* because of the transparent demonstrability of its theories.

This assumption, however, does not have to be accepted. Just as feminists have rid themselves of penis envy, we can, as Rorty suggests somewhere, rid ourselves of our "physics envy." It must immediately be stressed, however, that working through our "physics envy" does not mean that we must give up our preference for science. It only means that we have to give up the *hypostatization and idealization of mathematical physics:* The answer to the positivists, who called for a unified science, is that there are many successful sciences—evolutionary biology, paleontology, cognitive psychology, and primate research, to name a few—that do not approximate the method or achieve the rigor of Galilean physics.[6] Likewise, there are many valid forms of scientific methodology that are apposite to the various sciences. Indeed, there may be a methodology appropriate to psychoanalysis that is valid, while bearing little resemblance to mathematical physics. Today's postmodern philosophy of science at its best examines the actual history as well as theory and practices of various successful sciences in order to understand *in concreto* how they work, what norms inform them, and how internal logic interacts with experience in their development.

III

The upheavals in epistemology and the philosophy of science in the 1960s had consequences for the social sphere, especially with respect to religion. When postmodernism first appeared, it presented itself as a radicalization of modernism. The postmodernists promised to complete the program that began when Nietzsche declared the death of God.[7] This radicalization often involved turning the Enlightenment's critique of metaphysics and theology back against the Enlightenment. Postmodernists argued, for example, that basic concepts of the Enlightenment—the centered subject and self-grounding reason—had not sufficiently freed themselves from the ontotheological tradition and should therefore be displaced. Their displacement, however, threatened to jeopardize the critical project.

As I have already mentioned, insofar as the Enlightenment's hermeneutics of suspicion presupposed the legitimacy of science and reason, it was not clear how critique remained possible after they were delegitimated. The typical postmodernist response was to claim deployment of a radicalized form of critique that no longer relied on the validity of science. However, the nature of that hyperradical critique has yet to be satisfactorily elucidated.

Furthermore, social developments in the real world showed that this hyperradical critique did not have enough traction to sustain its commitment to the death of God—the touchstone of the radical Enlightenment.

Recent years have witnessed a remarkable religious turn among the former disciples of the uncompromising Nietzsche. With regard to religion, their hyperradicalism turned out to be pseudoradicalism.

In retrospect, the convergence between postmodernism and the new religiosity should not have surprised us. Indeed, it is perfectly logical. The fate of modern reason and the fate of modern secularism are bound up with each other, so that the decline in the standing of the first should result in the decline in the status of the latter. Once science had been dislodged from its privileged position and relegated to the rank of one language game among many—on the same level as all others—it was only a short step to the rehabilitation of religion. It could then be claimed that, as a form of interpretation, the religious worldview is as good as the scientific, and that one is free to choose between them. The antisecularists quickly realized how congenial this argument was to their position and seized on it, maintaining that secularism is just one life form among many, with no special privilege over religion. Indeed, things have become so topsy-turvy that antisecularists even argue that the secularists, not the believers, are the intolerant dogmatists, who have imposed their position on everyone else.

Given the tenor of these remarks, I must guard against the wrong impression. I do not mean to say that the postmodern critique of positivism was not enormously important. I want only to say that it is often carried too far, causing the critique of objectivism to slide off into the rejection of objectivity, the critique of scientism into the rejection of science. Nor do I want to deny that the Enlightenment theory of religion—especially Freud's in *Future of Illusion*—has often been insensitive to the apparently ineradicable religious needs of human beings, and that it is thereby seriously flawed. I do want to insist, however, that the criticism of the Enlightenment position on religion does not ipso facto reinstate the validity of the religious position—in other words, that the critique of the critique of religion does not automatically validate religion, as many antisecularists want us to believe.

Now that early phases of postmodernism are over and the dust has settled, we can see that the really hard questions are still with us—indeed, are perhaps even harder—after the critique of the Enlightenment. Positivism and foundationalism have been discredited, but it has become apparent that we cannot function without such basic notions as objectivity and truth—or their functional equivalents. A task therefore that confronts us is to reconceptualize objectivity after the critique of objectivism. Likewise, the resurgence of religion over the last forty years as well as the arguments of the antisecularists have forced us to recognize the substantial deficiencies in secularism as it has been traditionally conceived. Under the weight of this historical onslaught, there is a widespread temptation to simply give up on the secularist project and accept the validity of the religious standpoint. I would argue, however, that the proper response would be rather to try to rethink secularism after its supposed demise. And, most crucially, I am concerned that an overzealous attempt to correct the Enlightenment's rather shallow treatment of religion may trump one of its most cherished accomplishments—namely, the establishment of the right of critique.

IV

By 1980, the critique of the myth of the given, of transcendental philosophy, and of foundationalism should have been old hat. After Hegel's critique of firstness, indeed, after Kant's transcendental aesthetic—not to mention the work of Marx, Nietzsche, Freud, Dewey, Merleau-Ponty, Heidegger, Adorno, and the late Wittgenstein—philosophers should have largely worked through the demise of first philosophy. Yet, a significant number of them remained scandalized by the death of the Absolute in its various forms—much in the way children are shocked when they find out their parents have sex. The attack on first philosophy at the time only appeared scandalous, however, against the rigorist and logicist, that is, absolutist, assumptions of philosophers such as Frege, Husserl, and Carnap—with their antipsychologistic and antisociologistic corollaries. These philosophical projects, moreover, were themselves the latest instantiations of the philosophical program defined by Parmenides and Plato—a program that equated true being with immutability, timelessness, and intelligibility. What was really at stake was the two-thousand-year-old tradition of, *philosophia prima*, first philosophy itself.

A whole slew of postmodern philosophers have got a lot of mileage out of repeatedly demonstrating that one theory or another—and the examples are plentiful—fails to live up to the absolutist demands of the Parmenidean-Platonic tradition. Psychologically, their repetitive and sometimes hypermanic celebration of the death of the Absolute suggests something like a failure of mourning. They have not, that is, mourned its death and internalized the loss of the Absolute, but are traumatically arrested at the moment of the loss itself, which they try to master with repetitious theoretical rituals. The hyperradicalism of these philosophers, however, is really pseudoradicalism. Indeed, it is in fact conservative in the strict sense in that *it tacitly accepts the demand for the Absolute as legitimate*, only to triumphantly and repeatedly demonstrate that it cannot be fulfilled.

The really radical move—the truly postmetaphysical move—is to contest the demands of first philosophy itself.[8] This is what the late Wittgenstein thought he was doing with his therapeutic approach to philosophy. And despite its possible reductionist potential—which I believe can be avoided—Freud had something like this in mind when he proposed translating metaphysics into metapsychology.[9]

Often, the critique of first philosophy is only done by half. What we get then is either the "cheap defeat" of the given, one the one had, or the "cheap defeat" of transcendental philosophy, on the other.[10] In the first case, the realization that a neutral observation language—which was supposed to have provided the foundation for scientific realism—was not to remain in place unleashed an orgy of holism. Whether they were conceived as paradigms, epistemés, language games, conceptual schemes, or what have you, coherentist and holistic theories of truth—and the framework-relativism that goes along with them—became the order of the day across a large swath of the philosophical landscape.

But the proposition that all facts are conceptually mediated—that we only have oblique access to our objects—should not be taken as a *terminus a quo*, as it often was during the headiest days of the linguistic turn. If that were where our reflection came to a halt, what we would be left with is a multitude of conceptual schemes frictionlessly "spinning in a void,"[11] without any constraint from extraconceptual reality. The defeat of the given should, rather, be taken as a *terminus ad quem*—as a point of departure for the investigation of how our conceptual schemes rub up against reality so that experience can, in some important way, act as a tribunal for our theories.[12] The task—which requires considerable heavy lifting—is, as John McDowell puts it, to "avoid the Myth of the Given without renouncing the claim that experience is a rational constraint on thinking."[13]

In the second case, what transcendental philosophy seems to have going for it—whether it is formulated in terms of the philosophy of mind or the philosophy of language—is its apparent "ontological supremacy," as Adorno put it.[14] The transcendental philosopher argues that, because consciousness (Husserl) or language (Gadamer) provides us with the *only means of access* to the world, the transcendental elucidation of consciousness or language—which can supposedly provide the a priori structures of the world[15]—must precede the attempt to acquire first-level knowledge in the extramental or extralinguistic world. Only transcendental reflection, it is argued, can "found" the validity of an empirical science, and it must therefore precede the "founded" sciences. An implication of this proposition, according to strict transcendentalism, is that the founded sciences— "merely" empirical sciences such as biology or psychology—cannot be used to elucidate transcendental reflection.

Against these claims, the typical antitranscendentalist argues that the putatively universal and invariant structures, which the transcendental philosopher purports to have discovered, are, in one way or another, empirical structures that have been hypostatized into transcendentals. The critic, as Adorno puts it, typically argues that the putative "*prius*" of transcendental philosophy is in fact an a posteriori[16]—that, for example, transcendental psychology is simply empirical psychology writ large.

If the cheap defeat of transcendental philosophy is to be avoided, its refutation must, again, not be taken as a *terminus a quo*. To do so leads to two equally unacceptable possibilities. First, the fact that the transcendental path proves impassable can lead to a return to objectivism. But, as Adorno argues, the metacritique of transcendental reflection "does not mean that objectivity is something immediate" and "that we might forget our critique of naïve realism."[17] Whatever solution we arrive at *must preserve the truth content of the reflective turn after the critique of transcendental philosophy*. Second, the fact that a transcendental program, in its strict Kantian or Husserlian variation, cannot be executed in its entirety can lead to the proliferation of hermetically sealed conceptual frameworks—of merely local transcendental schemes.

V

If Adorno takes meta-reflection on transcendental philosophy as his point of departure, where does he go from there? Significantly for my purposes, in passages that have not received the attention they deserve—indeed, passages in which Adorno uncharacteristically verges on putting forth a positive program—he argues that some of the central antinomies of modern philosophy, manifested most perspicuously in Kant, can be traced to *his separation of empirical and transcendental psychology*.[18] Adorno's doctrine of "the preponderance of the object" is intended to solve the problem.[19] While the doctrine is meant to preserve the truth content materialism, it does not constitute a return to naïve materialism, which is to say, to objectivism. Rather, it represents an attempt—against both idealism and materialism—to elucidate dialectically the entwinement of subject and object—of *constituens* and *constitutum*. Against idealism, Adorno denies the central argument of the transcendental philosopher, that is, the argument from access. The "ontological supremacy of consciousness [or language]" does not, Adorno maintains, follow from the argument "that without a knowing [or speaking] subject nothing can be known about the object."[20] In other words, the priority of consciousness or language *in the order of knowing* does not entail their priority *in the order of being*. We know that, in the order of being, the object always precedes the subject, and that all subjectivity is embodied subjectivity. Consciousness and language are, Adorno argues, always functions "of the living subject, and no exorcism will expel this from the concept's meaning."[21]

But the transcendental philosophers have a reply to Adorno's objections. Granted, they argue, we know that, *factually*, consciousness and language are always embodied, but the manner in which we "know" this "fact" does not meet the requirements of rigorous philosophy; it is precritical, naïve. Either we know it through common sense, in which case the knowledge is subtheoretical; or we know it through an empirical science like biology, in which case the science must be transcendentally founded in order to possess legitimacy. Both these points, so it is argued, establish the continuing priority of transcendental reflection.

And, not unexpectedly, Adorno has his own response to these objections. He argues that the idea of a "transcendental subject" that can function as an "Archimedean fixed point from which the world can be lifted out of its hinges" is a "delusion."[22] It is delusional, that is, to think that the circularity, which characterizes all foundational questions concerning finite beings[23]—where the (naturally) constituted subject (transcendentally) constitutes nature—can be eliminated. It is a sign of philosophical maturity to recognize that the circularity that characterizes the relation between *constituens* and *constitutum*—the doubling, as Foucault called it—is intrinsic to the condition of finitude, and the demand that it be removed still presupposes that the Absolute can be attained. To dismiss this circularity as vicious, as Foucault does, is to tacitly treat finitude as defective—as "mere 'finitude'"[24]—not as our unsurpassable condition, and to continue to yearn for the fullness the ontotheological tradition had promised. But if the circularity of *constituens* and *constitutum* cannot be eliminated, it can be dialectically elucidated from within.

Thus, in yet another turn of the dialectic, Adorno seeks to preserve the truth content of reflective philosophy. Indeed, he tells us "the preponderance of the object which maintains the object's precedence over the subject is solely attainable [that is, accessible] for subjective reflection, and for reflection on the subject."[25] "Subjective reflection" and "reflection on the subject": what do they mean? Reflection on itself, on its own nature, leads the subject to the point where it must reflect on nature *in* the subject. It is led, in other words, to the insight that "genetically, the consciousness that has achieved independence"—that is, reflecting consciousness—"has branched off from libidinous energy of the species."[26] For Adorno, this is the point where Kantian philosophy meets Freudian psychoanalysis. Only the right kind of genealogy of the subject—Adorno offers the *Urgeschichte* of subjectivity that he and Horkheimer presented in *Dialectic of Enlightenment* as a model—can resolve the antinomies concerning freedom and nature we have been considering. Only the right kind of genealogy, that is, can show how the subject, having emerged from nature, is natural *and more than baldly natural* at the same time. My claim is that psychoanalysis, properly understood, presents the right kind of genealogy of the subject.

Before Nietzsche and Freud—who, we should point out, both chose to remain outside the academy—the intellectual division of labor, which began with Kant, prevented the right kind of genealogy of the subject from being written. In a well-intentioned attempt to defend the dignity and autonomy of the subject, Kant banned the inclusion of any genetic factors—which, for him, belong to the realm of empirical reality and hence of heteronomy—into the account of the subject.[27] The result was a transcendentally purified and free-floating subject, that is to say, a desiccated subject, which was, by its very nature, disconnected from empirical freedom and practice. As a result, Adorno observes that Kant's pronouncements on freedom, deteriorated into the sort of "jejune edification" that Hegel found so distasteful."[28]

From the other side, the psychological element that Kant's transcendental philosophy discarded was taken over by empirical psychology, which meant that the question of the genesis of the subject came within its purview. The problem, however, is that the psychological sciences—with their scientistic self-understanding and lack of philosophical sophistication—are not equipped to handle the topic adequately, that is, in a way that would elucidate the relation between the genesis of the subject and autonomy. As a result of this theoretical arrangement, both sides suffered: not only did "the sciences pay the price in narrowmindedness, and philosophy, in noncommittal vacuity,"[29] but the right kind of genealogy of the subject also fell between the cracks.

VI

Before turning to the right kind of genealogy of the subject, there are two preliminary and interrelated topics that we must take up: namely, naturalism and reductionism. It is my claim that, given the current state of scientific knowledge and philosophical reflection, naturalism is the most compelling position available to us.[30] Naturalism, as I understand it, involves two things. The first is the principle of "immanentism,"[31] as Yirmiyahu Yovel calls it, which holds that our theories must explain all phenomena, in all realms, immanently—from within nature—and make no appeal to transcendent or supernatural entities or principles such as deities, *entelechies* or vital forces that lie beyond it. Second, naturalism requires us to adopt the concept of nature that best fits with the most highly developed state of scientific knowledge.[32]

The way I have characterized naturalism thus far, however, is completely compatible with "bald naturalism,"[33] that is, with the physicalist position that equates nature with the world presupposed by chemistry and physics and tries to reduce all putatively higher level phenomena—biological, sociological, or psychological—to it. At its most ambitious, the goal of reductive physicalism is to *eliminate* all putatively higher order phenomena as only apparent. But again, this interpretation of naturalism holds only if one has not worked through one's physics envy and still believes in scientific monism and an ontology of *res extensa*. But, as we have seen, there exists a plurality of serious sciences, and each places different demands on us with respect to how we formulate our concept of nature. Furthermore, if our concept of nature must be congruent with the current state of scientific knowledge, and if the sciences are themselves constantly evolving, our concept of nature must be evolving as well. At this point, for example, I would argue that it not only contains consciousness but also the unconscious—yet, it does not contain angels.

Under Foucault's impact—who may or may not have been following Nietzsche in these matters[34]—a tendency has developed to equate genealogy with *reductive delegitimizing critique*. Genealogy's aims, so it is assumed, are destructive: to efface the value or legitimacy of whatever cultural object is brought into its crosshairs by tracing—which means reducing—its current valorized state to its lowly *Pudenda origio* (shameful origins).[35] It should be obvious that delegitimizing genealogy and bald naturalism tend to go together.

We have Raymond Geuss and Bernard Williams to thank, however, for shaking us from what has become a habitual way of thinking in these matters and reminding us that genealogy need not necessarily be deflationary and reductive. Indeed, according to them, genealogy can even be *legitimiz-ing* or "vindicatory."[36] Rather than trying to eliminate the object's value through reductive analysis, vindicatory genealogy can seek *to elucidate the genetic process by which the object came to acquire the value that can legitimately be ascribed to it.* To take a hackneyed example from psychoanalysis: whereas a reductive or pathologizing account tries diminish the value of a surgeon's skill and competence by tracing them back to the physician's sadism, vindicatory genealogy attempts to elucidate the genetic process by which that sadism underwent a change of function and was transformed into those abilities that allow a surgeon to save lives and perform many marvelous feats.

To get the right kind of genealogy that Adorno's analysis was pointing toward, we need a theory that is *genetic and nonreductive at the same time.* And only a theory of emergent properties will enable us to formulate this *nonreductive genealogy.* Such a theory would account for how a new stratum of nature—for example, life, society, or the psyche[37]—emerges out of the stratum below it. And it would also elucidate how the new stratum—once it has emerged—has achieved a sufficient degree of freedom vis-à-vis the genetic conditions from which it emerged that it cannot be reduced to them.[38]

VII

Psychoanalysis, then, should be understood as a nonreductive genealogy— which is, at the same time, a nonreductive naturalism. Freud's theory, like Darwin's, is naturalistic in that it seeks to situate the human species en-tirely into the natural world.[39] But it is not baldly naturalistic because it deploys a theory of emergent properties to explain how the genetic en-dowment of humans allows them to become more than merely natural beings through their socialization and entry into culture. Somewhere in the history of nature, evolution reached a point where it could give rise to a species with specifically hominoid characteristics, however they are delineated. The opposition between biology and culture is, as Heinz Hart-mann recognized,[40] a false one, for at that point in prehominoid evolution, our particular biological makeup—having to do with our enlarged brains, premature birth, and helplessness—made it both necessary and possible for us to acquire culture, which is our main organ of adaptation. One can argue over what characteristics should be counted as essentially human—

language, virtual thinking, nongenetic learning, the human psychism, self-reflection, or the ability to cooperate and so on. And one can debate the various accounts of when and how that point was reached in the course of evolution. All that is required for my argument at this point is that one accepts the proposition that, *in principle*, such a point was reached.

It must be stressed that psychoanalysis has a highly delimited topos: its subject matter is neither biology nor society—neither first nor second nature—per se. It is, rather, *the emergence of second nature out of first nature*—what Castoriadis has charted, in various ways, as the transformation of the little animal into the citizen of the *polis*. This means, methodologically, that psychoanalysis must avoid the Scylla of sociologism and the Charybdis of biologism.[41] Whereas the "linguistic reformulators"[42] of psychoanalysis—Habermas, Schafer, and Marcia Cavell—had trouble steering clear of the first danger, today the more exuberant champions of neuroscience are in danger of falling into the second. This also means that a theory of sublimation—*which elucidates that transformation of first nature into second nature*—is essential to the entire psychoanalytic project. As Laplanche and Pontalis observed forty years ago, the idea of sublimation "answers a basic need of the Freudian doctrine and it is hard to see how it could be dispensed with." But, unfortunately, what they said about the "lack of a coherent theory of sublimation" in psychoanalysis—namely, that it "remains one of the lacunae in psycho-analytic thought"—remains as true today as it was then.[43]

It is significant that McDowell, like Adorno—but basically as a result of the immanent development of analytic philosophy—has seen that the idea of second nature might supply a solution to major antinomies in contemporary philosophy.[44] It would do so, in his language, by supplying mediation between the logical space of causes and the logical space of reasons. The problem is, however, that McDowell simply mentions the concept but never develops it in a sufficiently robust way. The situation is different with Adorno. As I have argued elsewhere, he recognized that a theory of second nature can provide a solution to central antinomies of the critique of practical reason.[45] By explaining how we are in nature, yet also possess a degree of freedom from it, such a theory supply the mediation between nature and freedom that is missing in Kant's philosophy. Moreover, Adorno in fact spells out why a theory with the conceptual structure of sublimation is required to elucidate the movement from first to second nature. But because the concept of sublimation seemed too ameliorist—too "affirmative"—for the negative dialectician, he never calls by its rightful name.

One of the reasons that psychoanalytic studies of artists, writers, and historical individuals have acquired such a bad name is that they are often crude and reductionist. They try to account for the lives and accomplishments of their subjects in terms of their psychopathology. While Freud was not always innocent of this type of vulgar Freudianism, he was *in principle* opposed to it, and he saw psychoanalysis as a vindicatory genealogy. Thus, at the beginning of the Leonardo monograph, he tells us that laymen—projecting their own malicious wishes onto the researcher— often assume that the aim of the biographer is to cut the great person down to size:

> When psychiatric research, normally content to draw on frailer men for its material, approaches one is among the greatest of the human race, it is not doing so for the reasons frequently attributed to it by the layman. 'To blacken the radiant and drag the sublime into the dust' (Schiller) "is no part of its purpose."[46]

If psychoanalytic biography tries to assimilate elements of the personality of the genius to the average person's, it is not to discredit the genius. It is rather to understand the general "laws which govern both normal and pathological activity with equal cogency." For Freud, the realization that a great individual's development, like ours, unfolds in "the slime of history" should not diminish their accomplishments. On the contrary, the fact that such individuals go on to create something of public value, which transforms and transcends that same genetic material, should fill us with wonder. The point is not to invalidate the accomplishments of the genius, but to accept them *as actual accomplishments* and elucidate their genesis out of the stuff that forms all of us. But because the pathographers cannot "tolerate" any "vestige of human weakness or imperfection," they deprive themselves of the opportunity of exploring how this process of sublimation works. They deprive themselves, that is, "of penetrating," as Freud puts it, "the most fascinating secrets of human nature."[47]

VIII

My thesis, then, is that understood as a nonreductive genealogy, psychoanalysis can provide the general theory that is required for a hermeneutics of suspicion. Psychoanalysis should be seen as a reflective human science, which combines clinical experience, empirical research, and metatheoretical reflection. It seeks to explain how, phylogenetically and ontogenetically, the specifically human capacities for autonomy and individuation arose from nature. The argument is this: at some point in the history of the species, a concatenation of specific biological developments—for example, the advent of language, greater impulse control and self-reflection—coalesced to make it possible for humans to achieve a relatively individuated identity vis-à-vis the group and self-consciously give themselves the norms that governed the behavior. Needless to say, the achievements are always relative and not absolute.

Likewise, the claim is that, in the course of human history, certain modes of childrearing and socialization—of transforming first nature into second—were created, which facilitate the emergence of a relatively individuated and autonomous self. Today—because of the combined contribution of psychoanalysis, developmental psychology, attachment theory, infant research, and even neuropsychology—we are in a position to more or less specify what sort of "facilitating environment"[48] is required for the formation of an autonomous individual. And we know that love's got a lot to do with it.

I must stress that I am not proposing a teleological philosophy of nature, which sees human consciousness as the culmination of evolution. There is nothing necessary about the process I am describing; it is shot through with contingency. My argument is that, at some point in evolution, the contingent coming together of certain phenomena resulted in the emergence of autonomy and individuation as human *potentialities*. The whole process, moreover, took place according to the operative laws of nature. The point is that this coalescence did not have to happen. Furthermore, this potentiality for autonomy and individuation, once it has emerged, does have to be realized. Be that as it may, for equally contingent factors in the course of human history, certain societies did in fact emerge that took individuation and autonomy as their values, and, as Hegel recognized,[49] created family structures and forms of socialization that could promote the realization of such values. It must be stressed that, at this point, I am not saying that we *should* take autonomy and individuation as our basic values. My claim is hypothetical. I am saying that *if* we want to promote them as basic values, then psychoanalysis can tell us something about the childrearing practices we must adopt.

This brings me to the two really hard questions that confront my position. They were in fact posed by Cornelius Castoriadis, who formulated the idea of "the project of autonomy," and who had enough honesty to raise them against himself.[50] The first is the problem of ethnocentrism. It is true that autonomy and individuation arose in the West and have largely been promoted only there. Does this mean that they are reduced to Euro-centric prejudice, applicable only to our ethnos, which can claim no value beyond the Occident? Or can we justify promoting them in the broader world? The second question is even more difficult. Castoriadis admits that most societies that have existed historically have been heteronomous, and that the breakthrough to autonomy, which happened in the West, is in fact an anomaly. He admits, moreover, that this breakthrough goes "against the grain" of human nature—both collectively and individually. (With regard to the latter, we know from psychoanalysis about the enor-mous resistances individuals encounter when they try to realize their au-tonomy.) The question becomes this: Does it make sense to pursue "the project of autonomy" when it seems to run so counter to certain deep-seated conservative trends in human nature? Or should we continue to pursue it in the name of human dignity and creativity, despite the fact that it goes against the grain?

On the Epistemological
Status of Psychoanalysis

Aristides Baltas

The following conversation between philosopher Aristides Baltas and analysts Réginald Blanchet and Nasia Linardou was held for the benefit of
the Greek review *Psychoanalysis*, of whose board both these analysts are
members. It was published in issue 5 (Spring 2002), at pages 53–70. The
same conversation was reprinted as a conclusion to Thanassis Tzavaras
and George Papadopoulos's edited volume *Aristides Baltas: Newton's Unconscious and Freud's Apple* (Athens: Exantas, 2004). Here mistakes have
been corrected and references have been updated, while some minor
changes have been made, for reasons of clarification. Aristides Baltas
wishes to thank Spyros Petrounakos for the translation of the text from
the original Greek.

The Model of Physics

Réginald Blanchet: As a philosopher, your concern with the epistemological status of psychoanalysis revolves around two questions. The first is
a time-honored one: is psychoanalysis a science? The second is provocative: is there a possible philosophy of science that would consider the kind
of rationality exhibited in psychoanalytic knowledge as a form of scientific

rationality, if we could talk at all of science in this context? You approach the first question from a negative starting point, by placing natural science at the opposite extreme of psychoanalytic knowledge. What are the reasons behind this detour, and in what way is it instructive?

Aristides Baltas: What you are asking is why I choose to examine the epistemological status of psychoanalysis via a detour through physics. This is indeed what I am doing, and this forms part of a strategy. Today almost everyone accepts that physics is the science par excellence. So if we use physics as a point of departure for building a philosophically satisfactory picture of what a science can amount to—that is, a picture that would be more or less acceptable to those working within present day philosophy of science—we will have carved out a common ground on which we can begin investigating the epistemological status of psychoanalysis. I feel that such an approach would be particularly productive even from a rhetorical perspective, especially since it wasn't always the case that physics was considered the science par excellence. Here is a historical issue we ought to consider.

Physics achieved the status it enjoys today in the seventeenth century. Before that time, almost everyone believed, or has been taken to believe, that the science par excellence was mathematics. This is to say, physics came to occupy its present hegemonic position by ousting mathematics, and it is only recently that this position has begun to be questioned, albeit very tentatively and in hushed tones. By understanding the mechanisms that led to this change of "regime," we might begin to discern at the same time some of the inherent limitations of physics. This, in turn, may make us realize that the hegemony of physics does not lie, as it were, in its genes. It is in such terms, I believe, that we can open some ground for an unprejudiced examination of the epistemological status of psychoanalysis. I should add that my position springs from a particular philosophical perspective, about which I cannot go into detail here, but that is nonetheless informed by the thesis that valid human thought can be expressed within different forms of rationality. Simply put, the form of rationality governing and permeating physics need not be the only one.

If we see things on such a basis, if we come to realize that no unique form of rationality can pronounce upon the whole of reality, we may begin to appreciate that physics, as an endeavor dealing with the world solely from its own particular perspective, is unable to address, is constitutively blind to, the facets of reality that are within the purview of other forms of rationality. Thus psychoanalysis might constitute a form of rationality radically different from that of physics, dealing with things that are inherently inaccessible to natural science and hence irreducible to it.

Réginald Blanchet: In your work, you draw a sharp distinction between the object of psychoanalysis and the object of natural science. All particular objects of natural science possess neither singularity nor history: the fall of Newton's apple has always been nothing but an instance of the law of universal gravitation and, for physics, that apple is no different from any other apple. In contrast, the object of psychoanalysis (the subject of the unconscious) possesses, as you have put it, absolute singularity and is fundamentally historical in its own way. And here we encounter the first difficulty: if science cannot be thought of otherwise than as universal and if, further, the subject of the unconscious, that is, the object of psychoanalytic knowledge, must be thought of as necessarily singular, how can psychoanalysis make the transition from the singular to the universal and vice versa? Would it be true to say that this is a structural limitation to our trying to conceive psychoanalytic knowledge as scientific?

Aristides Baltas: Physics deals with singularity on such a minimal basis that, within its perspective, not only every apple but also all oranges, all stones, or all bricks are considered as essentially the same (once they have, say, the same mass). It can formulate the kind of universal laws we know precisely because it blots out the singularity of all objects it engages. And from its own perspective, this is exactly what it ought to be doing. Yet, although it is true that psychoanalysis ought to exhibit some kind of universal "laws" if it is to merit the title of science, it is constitutively incapable of blotting out the singularity of the objects belonging to its domain. Hence these universal "laws" should be substantially different while psychoanalysis should adopt the corresponding substantially different strategy to gain knowledge of these objects.

To go a step farther, I maintain that the main source of psychoanalytic knowledge is the psychoanalytic session. (It can be said as well that it is the "laboratory" wherein the claims of psychoanalysis are tested.) Take the example of agoraphobia. Your agoraphobia, on one hand, and mine, on the other, if they are indeed agoraphobias, should be instances of the general concept of agoraphobia and should be "subsumed" under the corresponding universal "laws." Yet, this doesn't tell us much and is not at all effective unless our two agoraphobias are considered as absolutely singular and are treated separately in the radically different psychoanalytic sessions we separately follow, while it is in such sessions that the "laws" of agoraphobia themselves can be tested.

Anyway, the general issue of how to combine universal laws with singularity is very difficult. And, among many other reasons, it is difficult, I maintain, because this connection may exhibit different forms. We have difficulties in even recognizing such diversity because we remain trapped within the form of rationality proper to physics and hence by the type of thinking that physics has imposed. What I mean is that general philosophical categories such as "rationality," "science," or "scientific law" tend to be inseparably linked with the form of rationality proper to natural science and that we are inclined thereby to see the relation between universal laws and singularity as simply the relation between such laws and their applications or instances. What I am proposing is to start by reversing the perspective: instead of trying to see how and what psychoanalysis is doing may or may not conform to the relation between the universal and the singular that physics dictates, we simply *acknowledge the fact* that, within its own practice and through its own means, psychoanalysis has already provided its own solution to the issue. De facto, *à l'état pratique*, as Althusser would have put it, psychoanalysis works at both the levels of singularity and of universal law and is indeed capable of dealing effectively with the former by using the latter. We can readily ascertain not only that psychoanalytic therapy often works but also that there exists an articulated theoretical space explaining such successes (as well as some telling failures), while, within it, various approaches cross intelligibly their arms, various proposals on which concepts or partial theories should be developed or modified emerge, while various case studies or particular episodes are adduced as the corresponding evidence. My main philosophical question is how psychoanalysis can do all this while not conforming to the model of physics. To answer this, we should come to understand the form of rationality that psychoanalysis embodies.

Réginald Blanchet: The issue of universalizing psychoanalytic knowledge can be expressed in more than one ways. Let us stick to this one: it is not easy to establish an analogy between therapy and a scientist's experimentation in the laboratory and regard psychoanalytic practice as an experiment or as an application of the corresponding theory, the way we can regard the practice of the engineer or the surgeon. In psychoanalytic practice, the desire of the "experimenter" (the analyst) forms an integral part of the process, while this is not the case for what the engineer or the surgeon does. In psychoanalysis, then, we have an idiosyncratic relationship between theoretical knowledge and "application" or "experimentation," a relationship that is not "mechanical" or "algorithmic" in the sense of excluding the subject and his or her desire. Therefore, psycho-analysis does not seem to comply with scientific protocol. What do you say about this?

Aristides Baltas: I start my answer by agreeing with your formulations. Yes, the desire of the analyst does have a decisive role in psychoanalytic therapy, and it is only natural that it does, since desire forms an intrinsic part of the object of psychoanalysis. Elaborating on the motif of my previous answer, I would say that what we ought to be considering is indeed how psychoanalysis manages to deal precisely with this "invasion" of desire in its object at both the levels of knowledge and of practical effectiveness. The strategic, so to speak, aim of my work is precisely to pinpoint the form of rationality that can allow and vindicate such "invasion." Roughly speaking, I take psychoanalysis to be the science of human subjectivity. Therefore, if something belongs to human subjectivity, it necessarily belongs to the object of psychoanalysis. The desire of the analyst as well as of the analysand, the transference relation and so forth are parts of this object. Among other things, this is precisely what psychoanalytic theory wants to understand and to explain through the particular methods it employs. In addition, and as you certainly know much better than I do, human subjectivity is constituted through a relation to the Other and to the desire of the Other, and hence the science of subjectivity cannot but allocate a strategic role to this Other. Therefore, the fact that psychoanalysis takes the desire of the analyst as part and parcel of its object should not be held against it. On the contrary, if it is what I take it to be, it cannot do otherwise. I would add that there is no overarching law, no inescapable metaphysical system, no inexorable epistemological principle imposing that we exclude desire from any possibility of scientific investigation, that we conceive science in general, all forms of rationality, as inherently incapable of understanding and explaining human desire. No law, system, or principle binding us in this way exists.

The Nature of Scientific Rationality

Réginald Blanchet: If what you say about different forms of rationality is true, what is the difference between psychoanalysis and other forms of knowledge that are undeniably genuine, without nevertheless being scientific? Not every form of rationality is scientific.

Aristides Baltas: I take science to be an endeavor constituted by three "elements" that define one another and complement or support each other. First, each science is characterized by its conceptual system. A scientific concept is not alone; it is defined and it functions only through the strict relations it entertains with the other concepts within the system they all form together. Second, each science is characterized by its particular object, its own scientific object. The scientific object is delimited, structured, and organized by the concepts of the corresponding conceptual system, while simultaneously the concepts themselves acquire their meaning and their particular epistemic function by being constitutively thus "attached" to that object. Third, each science is characterized by appropriate test procedures, by the experimental transactions proper to it. Hypotheses or laws regarding the scientific object are formulated in terms of the corresponding conceptual system. However, these hypotheses or laws cannot be accepted unless they pass the test of the corresponding experimental transactions, unless we can assess thereby, however provisionally, their adequacy. For me, science always involves these three elements in their interconstitutive relations. This is its definition, if you like.

On the other hand, religion, astrology, a given ideology, or even the empirical knowledge we glean from our everyday contact with the world, do not fit into this picture. In these cases, the various notions involved are not rigorously connected, no specific object is carved out or is delimited only very hazily, while the possibility of error is often not entertained. Even if it is, no disciplined way for pinpointing its source and for correcting it is available. Let me elaborate a little on this. In physics, in psychoanalysis or in any other endeavor that merits the title of science, each concept is systematically linked to the other concepts of the corresponding conceptual system. If, for instance, we take a look at Laplanche's and Pontalis's dictionary of psychoanalysis, we will ascertain that every entry refers to other entries; there is no way to understand a single entry in isolation, without taking into account its relations to the others. This to say that the concepts these entries name form a system that demarcates, structures, and organizes the object of psychoanalysis—human subjectivity—while the concepts themselves are bound by this object. At the same time, the psychoanalytic sessions are carried out within the framework of relations connecting this object to that conceptual system. On the present view, this is why these sessions, in addition to their therapeutic effects, also yield epistemic results, psychoanalytic knowledge. We already know from Freud that a series of psychoanalytic sessions—an experimental transaction proper to psychoanalysis, as we have said—might not lead to the anticipated results. When this happens, we are led to an extension, a correction, or a modification of the relevant part of the conceptual system. Or, alternatively, we might be led to isolate (always fallibly) what went wrong with the analysis itself. Most of Freud's famous case studies show this very clearly. This is very similar to what happens in physics: the unanticipated result of an experiment may mean either that the corresponding theory is inadequate or that the experiment itself had not been performed correctly. This kind of internal relationships, this kind of internal mutual control, and hence the capacity to deal with failure in the corresponding disciplined way, is absent in ideology, religion, astrology, or everyday knowledge. Therefore I take these three elements in their interconstitutive relations as offering a definition of science at the minimal degree of generality we seen to require if the category "science" is to refer to endeavors as different as physics, chemistry, biology, psychoanalysis, or mathematics.

Réginald Blanchet: Does mathematics belong in this picture?

Aristides Baltas: Yes, I think it does. I rely here on the work of Pierre Raymond, a student of Althusser's, who considered mathematics in exactly this way. His basic idea, which I try to develop in my essay "Do Mathematics Constitute a Scientific Continent?"[1] is that every mathematical text can be divided into two levels, a level functioning as a conceptual system and the other functioning as its corresponding object. In analytic geometry, for example, we use algebra to solve problems of Euclidean geometry. Hence, algebra is here the conceptual system and Euclidean geometry the object. We can also envisage in this context what would be analogous to the relevant experimental transactions: within the very process of mathematical demonstration, we can distinguish, I maintain, an aspect that pertains to the "game" of the concepts of the conceptual system narrowly conceived and an aspect that can be assimilated to experimental testing. From the same point of view, we can also talk about the Real (Lacan's "*le Réel*") as that which resists the "Symbolic" of the conceptual system and hence talk of mathematical discovery as the process managing to appease such resistance. We know well that there exist mathematical conjectures that resist "classical" proving procedures and that, if proved, may alter radically our notion of what the corresponding mathematical entities amount to. A good example here might be the evolution of the concept of number.

It is important, I believe, to see mathematics from this perspective, given especially the fact that, as I have already indicated, mathematics was considered the science par excellence until the seventeenth century. The hegemonic position acquired by physics since then relegated mathematics to the rank of a formal content-less system, a bare symbolic language, if not to a mere tool simply helping us come to grips with "real" objects of the "real" world. Expanding the concept of science to include psychoanalysis along with physics, chemistry, biology, and so on thus gives us an additional benefit: it allows us to look at mathematics afresh and reattribute to it the epistemological dignity it seemed to have lost for good.

Réginald Blanchet: However, it is perhaps no coincidence that your example was geometry, which does have an intuitive dimension.

Aristides Baltas: I think we can do the same with any mathematical text. Mathematicians would say that a mathematical text brings together certain mathematical concepts for the purpose of solving a mathematical problem. For my part, I would change slightly the formulation and say that a mathematical text brings together certain mathematical concepts for the purpose of knowing a mathematical object. Both concepts and object are "parts" of mathematics, although they perform different functions within any given mathematical text. However, they should not be conceived as ontologically distinct per se: a "part" functioning as object in a given mathematical text may function as conceptual system in another mathematical text. In a nutshell, it is each mathematical text that determines which "part" of it functions as the object under investigation and which "part" functions as the conceptual system through which this object becomes known. Seen under this light, mathematics both possesses its own scientific object and provides the means for knowing that object. Along the same lines, a mathematical demonstration or proof, on one hand, unfurls the properties of the corresponding conceptual system and, on the other, connects this conceptual system with the corresponding object.

Réginald Blanchet: What exactly is the experimental dimension here?

Aristides Baltas: The mathematical demonstration itself is the experimental transaction, but seen from the perspective connecting the conceptual system with the object. In other words, a mathematical demonstration has two distinct functions that, to repeat, work simultaneously: one involves narrowly the part of the mathematical text functioning as conceptual system while the other involves the relations of this system to the corresponding mathematical object, functioning as the corresponding experimental transaction. Traditionally, the mathematical text has been considered as one-dimensional because the second function has been collapsed onto the first.

Réginald Blanchet: Would you then say that an experiment might be merely a thought experiment?

Aristides Baltas: I wouldn't say that. The functions I have just delineated seem to be confined strictly within the mind, but I don't think they are merely that. Most mathematicians have witnessed in their practice what Lacan calls *"l'irruption du réel."* I take this as implying that, if we define "matter" precisely as that which resists symbolization, and as scientific discovery that which manages to appease such resistance, there is then indeed matter in mathematics. I believe that there is an urgent need to reconsider the distinctions between real and ideational, world and mind, matter and spirit, the extended thing and the thing that thinks, from Plato to Descartes and beyond.

In a recently published essay, I try to examine what a radical scientific discovery can amount to and consider some examples from physics and from mathematics.[2] One of my claims is that a radical scientific discovery consists in taming the resistance of the Real. Let me explain briefly. The conceptual system of physics, say, is a symbolic system allowing us to explain a number of things. Now, while this system is doing perfectly its job, at a certain moment and while nobody is expecting it, it becomes incapable of explaining certain phenomena whereas we remain unable to understand why these remain thus recalcitrant. These phenomena mess up the conceptual system; they show its inadequacy; they open a hole in it. The invasion of the Real consists precisely in the opening of such a hole. Radical scientific discovery amounts then to our succeeding in absorbing or mending this hole through the constitution of a radically novel conceptual system, a system that can explain in its own terms the phenomena that caused the problem. Needless to say, this picture is oversimplified, while there would be a lot to say on the relations—or lack thereof—between the new conceptual system and the old as well as between these systems and the Real.

Réginald Blanchet: Can a psychoanalytic session be compared to medical treatment? Could a psychoanalytic session be seen as theory application?

Aristides Baltas: I don't think so. There is a whole school of thought that views medicine, or engineering for that matter, as applications of scientific knowledge, but I would be hesitant to call them applications. In fact, I am not at all happy with the notion of "application" in such a context. Going back to psychoanalysis and science in general, the idea I am working on is this: Take any object that we come across in our daily dealings, say this glass in front of me. I believe that a science forms a particular point of view that carves out a certain slice of this empirical object. It carries out a projection, as Heidegger would say, or constructs a perspective, as Nietzsche would say. This projection, this perspective, is narrowly circumscribed in a specific sense. Physics, for instance, sees this glass only as mass that is subject to gravity, ignoring its other empirical characteristics. Chemistry, for its part, tells us that the glass is made up of certain chemical compounds, that it is the result of specific chemical reactions, and so on. Political economy will characterize this glass as a commodity, sold at a certain price, produced in factories within which certain relations prevail, and so on. Psychoanalysis might say that this glass is invested with a psychoanalytically telling affective value because it brings to mind my drinking milk as a child. This single empirical object is viewed differently from the perspective of each science. But because the corresponding facets are radically incommensurable, they cannot either be reduced to one another or become articulated within a hypothetical hyperperspective or superscience.

Although physicians as well as engineers learn the basics of such scientific perspectives and incorporate some of their results in their own work, they always refer back to the corresponding empirical objects because it is precisely such objects they have to deal with in their specific practices. This is to say that the work of the physician or the engineer is not, strictly speaking, scientific; in the present context at least, I would call it *interdisciplinary*. What this term can refer to might be assessed by looking at both the academic programs of the corresponding schools and at the relevant practices. For example, to make our house earthquake-proof, the engineer has to combine knowledge coming from geology, from seismology, from mechanics, from material science, and so on. Or a physician has to combine knowledge coming from chemistry, biology, physiology, and so on, in learning how the heart, the liver, and all our organs work and proceed with our treatment on this basis.

Philosophy of Science Today and the Epistemology of Psychoanalysis

Réginald Blanchet: What is the attitude of philosophy in respect to science in the present conjuncture? Is there an epistemology that would lend credence to the idea of a science of psychoanalysis?

Aristides Baltas: I will start answering by referring mainly to the situation in the United States, with which I am more familiar. I note first that Bachelard and Canguilhem—important names for you and me—are just barely starting to be discovered within philosophy of science. Nevertheless, most of the interesting work is not concentrated in philosophy of science proper but in the philosophy of mind and in cognitive science.

Cognitive science, in particular, aims at approaching the issue of knowledge from many points of view simultaneously, both scientific and philosophical. Biology, psychology, neuroscience, and computer science, on one hand, and the philosophy of mind, the philosophy of language, and the philosophy of science on the other hand, are brought to bear on the question of what knowledge is and on how it is acquired. A lot of money goes into this research, mainly driven by computer science, with the creation of artificial intelligence as its main target. At least in its initial stages and for quite a while, the entire project was based on radically reductive and ultimately Cartesian premises, with its protagonists holding the view that the mind is one thing and the body another. They left the body more or less alone and concentrated on the physical basis of mental phenomena, attempting to reduce them to the physiology of the brain. On this view, mind and brain form the two facets of a computational machine, more or less along the lines of the relation between software and hardware. Such efforts, however, stumbled upon a number of insurmountable obstacles, and thus many in the field have begun looking elsewhere for inspiration and basic concepts. This led to an influx of ideas coming from Heidegger, from Merleau-Ponty, and from Canguilhem, among others. For instance, the idea that the subject always acts within a certain framework, that such action is based on trivial knowledge that cannot be given exhaustively propositional form and hence cannot be processed by a computer, that knowledge is irreducibly anchored in the human body, that the human body itself has a quasi-mental dimension, are ideas that are becoming increasingly popular. The entire field is in upheaval while novel approaches, disagreements, and animated discussions of all sorts and kinds seem to change the whole philosophical terrain, at least in the United States. However, philosophy of science has a very small part in these developments.

Philosophy of science itself has evolved along three main directions. The first is the philosophy of individual sciences, mainly physics and biology. Those who work in this direction try to investigate the philosophical dimensions of the corresponding advanced theories: quantum mechanics, relativity theory, quantum field theory, molecular biology, the neo-Darwinian synthesis. They try to analyze the concepts implicated, to locate the philosophical issues involved and promote deeper understanding while mustering for the purpose all the highly sophisticated technical tools employed by the corresponding scientists. For this reason, such work is very similar to scientific work. I consider it very interesting, although relatively cut off from the rest of philosophy. A philosophy of psychoanalysis could perhaps find a niche in such a context.

The second direction has a strong technical, as opposed to philosophical, dimension. Issues related to the confirmation of scientific theories are examined through the use of probability theory, statistics, game theory, and decision theory. Of central importance here is a theorem on conditional probabilities, that of Bayes, that talks about the probabilities connecting the validity of a scientific hypothesis with its evidential support.

The third direction focuses more on the history rather than the philosophy of science. A typical question here might be: what relations existed between Boyle's experiments on the existence of the vacuum and the conception of the state that Hobbes was developing during the same period and how, on the basis of such relations, could a "scientific community"—or what we call that today—be formed? The work that goes on here consists in the examination of science in the material, social, historical, and anthropological conditions of its practice and therefore appeals to sociological, historical, sociological, or anthropological methods. The interests of people working in this direction have little to do with philosophy.

All the above imply that today very few people work in philosophy of science, as we used to know it from the time of the Vienna Circle and the constitution of logical empiricism, or as Kuhn and those who came after him transformed it. Stating it hyperbolically, I would say that it is almost dead.

Réginald Blanchet: This is very interesting.

Aristides Baltas: Yes, it is. And it would perhaps be instructive if we try to put together a rough picture of how we got there. At the beginning of the twentieth century, more or less, a deep crisis shook the foundations of both mathematics and physics. A new terrain of philosophical questions thus opened up, going together with the need to understand how we could have been so certain about mathematics and physics when things proved to be so very different. In other words, it became compelling that we come to a philosophical understanding of what science finally amounts to and of how it can change so dramatically. This catalytic question spawned the new logic of Frege and of Russell as well as the ambitious program of logical empiricism that undertook to make clear once and for all the logical structure of science. Relatively soon, however, this program foundered on a number of serious internal difficulties and began to degenerate. Kuhn, along with a number of philosophers of science, then came in the 1960s to claim that the very basis of logical empiricism was defective because it did not take into account the history of science. Accordingly, a second, equally ambitious, philosophical program gained center stage, which, on one hand, shifted the terrain of questions introducing new ideas and new tools while, on the other, it retained the same fundamental question: what, after all, is science and how it evolves.

This second program reached its limitations in the 1980s, as it started becoming clear that science and scientific activity were too multifaceted and hence too elusive to be made sense of by means of this or that overarching philosophical scheme. New ideas, new tools, and new areas of interest thus entered the arena. For example, associated with the work of Ian Hacking, among others, comes the realization that experiment is relatively independent from theory and carries its own specific tradition. From another angle, the importance of social factors in the development of science is highlighted and a whole body of work concerning science in the actual conditions of its practice sees the light of day. We have to underline, though, that the driving force behind this turn toward the social was the movement of ideas named "social constructivism." This became immediately notorious because it drove things to the limits, claiming that science had nothing to do with truth but everything to do with power relations: a given theory does not win the battle because it is true but, conversely, it is taken to be true once it has won the battle. If you take the comparison with the necessary pinch of salt, this is not too different from what Zdanov used to claim in the Soviet Union of the 1930s.

Réginald Blanchet: This seems dangerous.

Aristides Baltas: Yes, it is. Yet, the idea acted as a springboard to the historical, social and anthropological studies in science that I have already noted while many philosophers historians and sociologists of science joined the debate by trying to support, temper, modify, or straightforwardly reject the main ideas of that movement, employing for the purpose arguments, detailed case studies, and a variety of methodological tools. The net result is that such social and historical approaches to science have more or less imposed themselves on the whole field, and the place previously occupied by logical empiricism, Popper, Kuhn, and other "generalist" philosophers of science, seems to have been almost emptied. Those whose concerns remain mainly philosophical have mostly turned to the individual sciences, as I tried to explain a moment ago. "Traditional" philosophy of science has been broken down into fragments. My own work, if you permit me to talk so directly about it, is out of fashion because I am sticking to general philosophy of science by trying to argue that many interesting issues still remain open. To deal with these we can neither simply do history or sociology of science, nor get caught up in this or that advanced theory of physics or of biology.

Kuhn and Popper: Is Psychoanalysis a Pseudoscience?

Réginald Blanchet: Regarding your own work, if I am not mistaken, you subscribe to historical relativism, which, after Gaston Bachelard, Alexandre Koyré, and Louis Althusser, crystallized in Thomas Kuhn's important work. But, in what is almost a paradox for the view to which you subscribe, Kuhn, as well as a number of philosophers of the same orientation, denies psychoanalysis the status of science. How do you explain this?

Aristides Baltas: To begin with, I would like to categorically reject the label "historical relativism." I don't think that the work of any of the thinkers you just mentioned promotes relativism. This is exactly the accusation—a type of mudslinging—advanced by those who unthinkingly stuck to the dogmas of logical empiricism and who believed that the only form of rationality is that of connecting symbolic logic to bare experience, whatever this might mean. But let's move on; attaching this or that label to something is seldom productive. In response to the gist of your question, then, I would like to point at a number of questions that have not been asked, at least in Anglo-Saxon philosophy of science. For example: How do we differentiate between the different sciences and between the different scientific disciplines? What are the criteria of identity for each science and for each scientific discipline? In what ways is physics different from chemistry? Why do we say that a given theory, concept or problem belongs in biochemistry and not, say, in chemistry or in biology? No one has really raised such questions, except, perhaps, in more or less sociological terms.

Things look different in the French epistemological tradition of the 1960s and the 1970s. A lot of significant work was done on such issues at that time because the main concern of those who worked within the context of that period was, or at least so I claim, to pin down the exact epistemological status of the so-called social and human sciences. To mention two prominent examples, the main aim of the work of Althusser was to *demonstrate philosophically*—in the full sense of the phrase—that historical materialism constitutes what he calls a "scientific continent," while at least one of Lacan's central aims was to identify the epistemological status of psychoanalysis as a means for "stabilizing" the kind of knowledge that psychoanalysis provides. For my part, I can admit, if you like, that I do see myself as somehow belonging to this school of thought. This also permits me to make clearer my answer to your first question: the aim of my detour through physics is to equip myself with effective tools for tackling the general form of the question of what a science or a scientific discipline amounts to. My work on psychoanalysis can perhaps be better understood if regarded through this lens.

Given this, I also need to say, however, that I do not believe that the tradition of Bachelard, Koyré, and Althusser crystallizes in Kuhn's work. Despite the fact that there exist deep affinities between the two kinds of approach (for example, both emphasize the existence of decisive discontinuities in the evolution of science), despite the fact that Kuhn, on his own admission, was directly influenced by Koyré, the fact remains that Kuhn's main concepts, as well as his entire problematic, are very different from those shared by Bachelard and Althusser. Kuhn's work is certainly very important, but I think he does not avoid some pitfalls that characterize the Anglo-Saxon tradition in philosophy of science almost in its entirety. In Kuhn's case, I claim, it is what prevented him from raising the kind of questions I have just raised. More specifically, I believe that "paradigm" or "disciplinary matrix" remain ambiguous concepts because they confuse the category "science" or "scientific discipline" with the category "theory within a science or a scientific discipline." Popper shares the same confusion when he claims that psychoanalysis is not a science because it is not falsifiable, for the category "falsifiable" cannot apply to endeavors contending for the title of science as wholes but only to particular theories within such endeavors. For example, whereas it is absurd to wonder whether physics is "falsifiable" as a whole, it is not absurd when we refer the category—and again with important qualifications—to Newton's or to Einstein's theory. It is equally absurd to claim that psychoanalysis as a whole is or is not falsifiable, while, say, a theory of neuroses within psychoanalysis can very well be falsifiable.

Réginald Blanchet: What would your then say in connection to Popper, who writes, "*Traumdeutung* is a first-class contribution. But this contribution belongs more to pre-Democritian atomism than to a science that can be tested. . . . It constitutes rather a research program for a scientific psychology similar to that of atomism, materialism, the electromagnetic theory of matter or even Faraday's theory of the field, theories that have been all in their time research programs for physics. But it is a fundamental mistake for one to believe that Freudian interpretation, since it is continuously 'confirmed,' constitutes a science based on experience."[3]

Aristides Baltas: This passage confirms perfectly, I think, the point I just made. To explain what I mean, I would say that if Popper had tried to go deeper into what history of science actually teaches us (or, along another dimension, on what experience really amounts to), his views on the issue would have been very different. For one thing, according to his student Imre Lakatos, no isolated theories are ever encountered in science; science is composed only of "research programs." And for him the "hard core" of such programs is not falsifiable by definition. What happens is that the successive theories composing such a program are continuously undergoing tests in relation to their object. As a result of such tests, theories became amended, corrected, transformed, while retaining the same unfalsifiable "hard core" and thus continuing to be part of the same research program. Thus, research programs are not falsifiable in themselves and the distinction Popper makes in the passage in question cannot hold water. Research programs can progress or degenerate in accordance to how the theories composing them fare. We can say, if you like, that a particular theory within such a program is the result of the "falsification" of the one preceding it; however, such a conception of the term is too diluted to have much to do with Popper's synonymous criterion. And for what concerns us here, we can readily ascertain, I believe, that, at least on this level, psychoanalysis is not different from natural science: the individual theories that make up Freud's "research program" are subject to the corrections, emendations, modifications, in short, the changes demanded by their object. I would also add here that Adolf Grünbaum criticizes Popper's conception of psychoanalysis and shows, along lines not related to Lakatos, that psychoanalytic theories are indeed falsifiable. He then goes on to develop his own criticism of Freud, which, I believe, misses the mark.[4]

I think that the main problem with Popper, Grünbaum, and many others who have criticized psychoanalysis is that they do not have the correct picture of its object, of the status enjoyed by its universal "laws," and of the ways it treats singularity. Popper, for instance, believes that psychoanalysis is not falsifiable because, if, say, a child shouts "help" because it is drowning, there are psychical reasons explaining why someone dove into the water to save the child as well as why somebody else showed a total indifference. Therefore, he would argue, psychoanalysis has no predictive power and no event in the world can falsify it. But, as I have already said, psychoanalysis is the science of human subjectivity and all the phenomena that belong to its object are singular. The aim of psychoanalysis is to explain both the very particular psychical reasons that led one person to risk his life to save the child as well as the very particular psychical reasons that made the other person—or even the same person at another moment—ignore the cry for help. Under the condition, of course, that the persons involved enter the corresponding psychoanalytic sessions. It is the workings of such psychical reasons that form the object of psychoanalysis. It is not the ambition of psychoanalysis to investigate altruism in general so as to be able to make the relevant predictions, nor is it interested in the conditions under which people are willing to risk their lives to save children.

Réginald Blanchet: Popper simply says that the claims of psychoanalysis are not scientific theorems. Although psychoanalytic knowledge is worthy of respect, if falsifiability is the mark of a scientific theory, then psychoanalysis fails the test. For example, within the context of psychoanalytic theory, the question as to whether a dream could be anything else than the fulfillment of a wish, receives a categorically negative answer. Consequently, since it does not accept the logical possibility of something that could challenge its claims, psychoanalysis is not falsifiable. Hence it has no place in science.

Aristides Baltas: I don't think that this is how things stand, and I believe this for a number of reasons. First, if we take the qualification "logical" strictly and if we define "falsifiability" very loosely, it is, of course, *logically* possible that any theory can be falsified. For example, in the loose sense of "falsifiability," Einstein's theory obliged us to accept that Newton's theory was false and hence that it has been falsified. In the same vein, even the staunchest Freudian should accept that it is certainly *logically* possible that a new theory might compel us to accept that dreams are not the fulfillment of a wish or even that they have nothing to do with wishes. However, the advent of such a theory is no simple matter, for it should simultaneously provide reasons as to why the old theory was so successful while being that wrong. This is exactly what Einstein's theory does in respect to Newton's, and this exactly what the supposed new theory of dreams should do in respect to Freud's theory. At this abstract level of "logical possibility," I don't see how psychoanalysis can be different from physics. However, this sense of "falsifiability" has admittedly not much to do with Popper's use of the term.

Second, if we focus on Popper's use, we can argue that, by his criterion, practically no theory in the whole history of science should have ever been retained, for they all encountered very early on phenomena that "falsified" them. On Popper's view, these phenomena should have immediately led to the rejection of the theories in question. Some of these phenomena may well have been later explained by a proper modification of the corresponding theory but others like, say, the movement of Mercury's perihelion, remained fully unaccountable until a radically novel theory came along—

the general theory of relativity in this example—that managed to explain them. In either case however, the strict application of Popper's criterion should have led scientists to jettison even the most successful of our theories long before this happened historically.

It is mainly for this reason that Lakatos tried to forge a "sophisticated falsificationism." He wanted to save falsifiability from arguments like the above while making it conform to what history of science can actually teach us. His "methodology of scientific research programs" is a response to Popper along these lines. Nevertheless, the "sophisticated falsificationism" of Lakatos is too broad: it fails to provide any sharp criterion for when a theory or a research program is "falsified" or for when it can be responsibly called scientific. This led Paul Feyerabend to observe that, for Lakatos too as for himself, everything goes: his methodology does not provide the required criterion and hence it is no better than Feyerabend's own anarchistic or dadaistic "methodology." The debate went on. But what finally came out of it was not only that Popper's criterion is not a criterion at all but also that perhaps no such criterion can possibly exist. The title of a later essay by Larry Laudan is characteristic: "The demise of the demarcation problem."[5]

Third, even if we ignore such objections and manage to circumvent history of science altogether, there are deep structural reasons compelling us to maintain that no serious theory *can ever be* falsifiable in Popper's sense and hence no theory *can ever be* scientific in that sense. The work of Sneed, Stegmüller, and their co-workers or, along different lines, the work of Glymour shows this convincingly. For the case of classical mechanics, say, Newton's second law—force equals mass times acceleration—is not falsifiable per se: no single phenomenon and no experimental transaction that can be subsumed under the conceptual system of classical mechanics can possibly falsify this law because all phenomena and all experiments that this conceptual system allows *presuppose its validity*. Here, too, psychoanalysis is no different from physics and the work of Glymour that I just mentioned draws the analogy.[6]

To sum up, I think it is philosophically irresponsible to isolate Popper's "criterion" from this entire debate for the sole purpose of turning it against psychoanalysis. If the criterion does not work for physics—the science par excellence—why should it work for psychoanalysis?

Réginald Blanchet: But what about someone like Kuhn, who does not propose an absolute criterion and yet does not believe that psychoanalysis is a science?

Aristides Baltas: This is true, and it would be useful to take a closer look at why Kuhn adopts this position. To be able to say whether psycho-analysis is or is not a science, we should possess a clear picture of how a science becomes constituted, of how it is delimited, of how it is internally articulated, of how it functions. Let me try to explain by bringing in Spinoza. Spinoza tells us that, to be able to talk about truth, we must *already possess* a true idea. The *fact* that we possess this true idea amounts to our possessing the norm against which truth in general can and should be "measured." Following exactly this line of thought, I start from physics. I *already know* that physics is a science, I *already possess* a true idea about science, hence I have no need to wonder whether and in what sense phys-ics is or is not a science. To proceed further, I need a definition that could allow me to use the category "science" more generally. This can only be a kind of definition inspired by Spinoza's nominalism, a *minimal* definition that does not seal off the field of science keeping only physics and natural science inside, a definition broad enough to cover both natural science and cognitive endeavors radically different from it. This is the definition I tried to lay out earlier. It should be clear, however, that the formulation of this definition has not come out of the blue. Its guiding inspiration derives, again, from *a fact*, the fact that psychoanalysis is a cognitive endeavor that *works*, and that it works on its own, without needing to appeal to an exter-nal authority, philosophical or otherwise, that would legitimize it. It is this second fact that allows me to look at physics retrospectively and assess that it is constitutively incapable of covering the whole of reality under its purview, that it can constitute only one science among others, only a par-ticular form of rationality.

Kuhn refuses to ask what a science or a scientific discipline can amount to, following, I take it, more or less, the following line of thought: the entire discussion on an express criterion of what is scientific has been com-pletely unproductive while we have more or less come to know what we refer to when we are speaking about science. Hence there is no need for even a minimal definition, and we can go on with our business, examining this or that aspect of science and this or that aspect of scientific change. Such a line of thought, however, can have in view, even if only unawares, no more than the natural sciences and hence it cannot but block the field from the examination of other forms of rationality that can satisfy the minimal definition we are talking about while remaining radically different from physics and the other natural sciences.

To go one step farther, I would maintain that this particular form of blindness goes hand in hand with Kuhn's introduction of the category of "paradigm" or of "disciplinary matrix." For this category fails to include in its scope what I was saying before about sciences and scientific disciplines. For example, why physics, although characterized by the radical paradigm shifts that Kuhn describes, maintains the kind of unity that allows us to say that these shifts are precisely a matter *of physics* and not of chemistry, of biology or of natural science in general? In other words, the unity of physics *as physics*, of chemistry *as chemistry*, and so on, is invisible to Kuhn. Among other reasons, this blindness makes the category of "paradigm" highly ambiguous: sometimes it refers to an entire science, sometimes to a "big" theory within a science, sometimes to "small" theories therein, sometimes to the entire class of the natural sciences. This ambiguity has been criticized by a number of authors. Yet such criticism has never come from the direction I am trying to delineate here, namely that we need to pinpoint what gives each science and each scientific discipline its particular unity, its proper identity. This is the issue I am trying to discuss in an essay still in progress: "Physics as Self-Historiography *in Actu*: Identity Conditions for the Discipline."

Réginald Blanchet: In the end, would you say that Kuhn's position on psychoanalysis couldn't be justified?

Aristides Baltas: Yes, despite Kuhn's respect for psychoanalysis, I believe his position cannot be justified philosophically. In the discussion we had with him in 1997, he expressly states such respect.[7] However, he remains more or less in the grips of an ultimately Cartesian conception of science, according to which science can be of extension only. This means that, in the last analysis, only natural science, with its particular ways of delimiting the corresponding objects, of forming predictions, of carrying out the appropriate experimental tests and so forth can be real science. Kuhn was unable (and unwilling) to unyoke the category "science" from natural science. The cost for his otherwise extremely important work was that that this category could not be opened up to include radically different cognitive endeavors and hence radically different forms of rationality.

The Suspended Step of Louis Althusser

Réginald Blanchet: The assertion of Louis Althusser that Freud did not have the means to develop his discovery does not seem very different from what you say about Kuhn's position. Althusser seemed even more pessimistic toward the end of his life and included Lacan in this failure by maintaining that, at least in its present state of its theoretical development, psychoanalysis cannot claim to be scientific.[8] How do you comment on this?

Aristides Baltas: I think that, while in very different terms, Althusser's thought remains to a large extent captive of the "self-evident" identification of the general category "science" with natural science. I perceive him as somehow subjugated under an unsuspected and unacknowledged ideological awe in respect to physics and the other natural sciences from which, despite his sustained efforts, he never managed to become fully liberated. Although Althusser and many other thinkers of his generation were very critical of Cartesianism, such awe in respect to the supposedly only possible science in the full sense of the term lingers and can be traced in their work. It seems to me that these thinkers were in some sense afraid of posing directly the question as to what science amounts to and of trying answering it straightforwardly. This is remarkable also because Althusser's entire work not only revolves around this question, but also sets up the terms for an adequate answer.

What I mean is the following. To the direct question, "Why, dear Mr. Althusser, is historical materialism a science?" he does not answer simply and once and for all, "Because it satisfies the minimal definition; which is to say that, first, it possesses its own conceptual system which is precisely a system; second, it possesses its own distinct object that provides meaning for the concepts of this system while being delimited by it; and third, it possesses its proper experimental transactions that are defined exclusively by this system and that object and which test the claims formulated by the former in respect to the latter." To the further question, "What exactly are the experimental transactions proper to historical materialism?," a perfectly natural question given the hegemony of physics and the identification of the category "experiment" with "experiment in the natural sciences," he does not respond simply by stating that "these experimental transactions are constituted by communist political practice, as it evolves in the vast laboratory of class struggle." For it is through this practice, as performed in that laboratory, that the gaps, the deficiencies and the errors of the corresponding theory can come to the surface. For example, it was in this laboratory and through that practice that Marx was proved wrong in predicting that the revolution would take place in Germany. And again it was in this laboratory and through that practice that locating this error was inseparable from the Leninist theory of the "imperialist chain" and its "weakest link." The fact that Althusser does not refer to communist political practice as the experimental transactions proper to historical materialism is intriguing, given that both his work and his own political practice point unmistakably in this direction.[9]

Nasia Linardou: But there are experiments that cannot be repeated. They enjoy a singular status.

Aristides Baltas: Precisely. When I claim that psychoanalysis or historical materialism deal with singular phenomena, this is exactly what I mean. A singular phenomenon means precisely a phenomenon that is not repeated, that cannot be repeated, that it is unique. The difficulty we encounter in trying to relate the universal laws required by any endeavor aspiring to be scientific with phenomena that are strictly singular is indissolubly linked with the difficulty of conceiving what would amount to an experimental transaction in such a case. For obviously in such a case experiments cannot be repeated. What I mean is that as long as we stick to the self-evident idea that genuine experiments are by definition repeatable—since they are repeatable in natural science—remaining blissfully blind to the possibility of things being otherwise, then we cannot help upholding that, since psychoanalysis or historical materialism cannot support repeatable experiments, they cannot be scientific. This is exactly the pattern of thought I am trying to break by, among other things, expanding the category of experiment to include both repeatable and nonrepeatable experiments. To do this, I keep what I take to be the sine qua non characteristics of any experimental transaction and define "experiment" simply as a procedure for testing the hypotheses of a theory in respect to its object, a procedure that is being simultaneously bound both by the conceptual system and the object of that theory. At least this is the philosophical hypothesis I am working on. I am not saying that it is necessarily right; but I do believe that it might prove fruitful.

Réginald Blanchet: Would you say that even Althusser fell victim to this awe toward the natural sciences?

Aristides Baltas: If I were pushed for a sharp yes or no answer, I would be obliged to say yes, at the risk of oversimplifying the issue. I remember vividly the first time I read Althusser's essay "Sur la dialectique matérialiste" in his *Pour Marx*. While I found particularly stimulating his trying to read historical materialism on the model of science, I admit I was surprised that the category "experiment" was totally missing while being surreptitiously replaced by the category "method." I believe this shift is not innocent; it can have dire consequences for Althusser's whole project. And this for more reasons than one. Let me try to explain.

First, the category "method" can be also applied to endeavors that are not scientific; hence the distinction of historical materialism from such other endeavors becomes diluted and the demonstration that historical materialism constitutes a "scientific continent" becomes undermined.

Second and perhaps more importantly, the same shift lets the Cartesian tradition in through the back door. We know that, for this tradition, method is the cornerstone of science while the only proper science is that of extension, that is, natural science. Consequently, Althusser's position, by remaining thus indebted to the Cartesian conception, tends, even if only unawares, to retain natural science at the hegemonic position it presently finds itself in and thus wavers while the arguments supporting the scientific status of historical materialism tend correspondingly to lose their force. For reasons that would be worth examining in detail, Althusser never said that it is communist political practice that makes up the experimental transactions proper to historical materialism. I am saying all this because, for me at least, the title of science cannot be conferred to endeavors that do not contain procedures that can acknowledge failures and deficiencies and thus lead to the corresponding corrections or even to the overthrow of previously established theories. In the essay I just mentioned, I try to show that the structure of communist political practice, as conceived and performed mainly by Lenin and Mao, does not concern only political effectiveness. It also concerns directly the cognitive dimension of historical materialism. In fact, while I was writing the essay I was impressed by how well the political and the cognitive functions fit together once communist political practice is conceived as the experimental procedures proper to historical materialism. I would like to add that the communist political practice I am referring to has very little to do with what goes under the same name in Stalinist and post Stalinist regimes. But discussing this in the detail it merits would require too big a detour.

Réginald Blanchet: Althusser's definition of science seems to make him the philosopher with whom your views have the greatest affinity. Althusser's three dimensions of science bring to mind Aristotle. Jean-Claude Milner, on the other hand, follows an approach that breaks with Aristotelian epistemology. What are your views on Milner?

Aristides Baltas: Your reference here to Aristotle forms a vast and extremely interesting topic. But I confess I am not familiar with Milner's work.

Réginald Blanchet: There is a noticeable change in Lacan's views on the scientific character of psychoanalytic knowledge. Initially he held that psychoanalysis, as he was conceiving it starting from the subject of speech and language, could claim for itself a scientific status. He then held that psychoanalysis forms an idiosyncratic discourse which should align itself with the discourse of science, but of a science whose concept needed to overthrown. Finally, he accepted, together with Popper, that psychoanalytic enunciation belongs to the domain of the unfalsifiable and hence to that of pseudoscience. What are your comments on these reversals of Lacan's views?

Aristides Baltas: I have not followed Lacan's work that closely. However, speaking very schematically and from a distance, I believe that what I said earlier applies to Lacan as well. Lacan, at least during his early work, insisted that psychoanalysis is a science by following Freud, but also distancing himself from Freud in a number of very constructive ways. Althusser does something analogous with Marx and historical materialism, and he does this in a way that makes these two formally similar endeavors inspire each other and give food for thought to each other. Yet it seems that a sense of the immense and undeniable differences between physics and natural science, on the one hand, and historical materialism and psychoanalysis, on the other, makes both of them lose their courage and backtrack. What are these differences? None other than the ones we have already singled out: that physics relies on the certainty of mathematics, that it puts forward universal laws, that it can predict future outcomes and test its hypotheses, that experiments in natural science are repeatable, and so on. These are characteristics we cannot find in either historical materialism or psychoanalysis. I believe that Lacan and Althusser backtracked because they ignored royally the work on the epistemological status of physics and of natural science in general that was under way during the same period across the Channel. They ignored, that is, that the epistemological status of physics and of natural science generally had ceremoniously been stripped of the armor of logical inescapability that logical empiricism, at least in the initial stages of its development, as well as Popper throughout his work, had conferred to it. Most significantly, it was the experts themselves, the people who had worked almost exclusively in philosophy and history of natural science, that had exposed the weaknesses of such a conception, those who, in some cases, had even thrown the baby out with the bathwater by claiming that natural science has nothing to do with truth or certainty and hence—I am extrapolating—could be no better than psychoanalysis or historical materialism.

This entire debate, which tore apart logical empiricism, cast catalytic doubts on Popper's views and turned the spotlight on Kuhn's approach—this entire discourse, which sprang forth during the same period in the Anglo-Saxon world, was almost unknown in France, and, I believe, for reasons that were more sociological than theoretical. Recall, for instance, how long it took for Popper to be translated. Gossip has it that it was Raymond

Aron who stood in the way of Popper's translation because he wanted to conserve the monopoly of his ideas. Recall also the loneliness of Jacques Bouveresse and of the few people who thought that Anglo-Saxon philosophy is not just a collection of naïve trivialities and tried to introduce France to this tradition. As you understand, I am talking about the distinction between Anglo-Saxon and "Continental" philosophy, a distinction that is losing ground by the day and proves more and more untenable. I am also talking about the notorious French provincialism. I think that both Lacan and Althusser would be much relieved to know that things in natural science—or in mathematics, for that matter—are not that stable and not that certain, that they are not beyond doubt in the way they imagined.[10] Yet the prestige of physics, the absence of a philosophical education in the natural sciences, the Nobel Prize and its aura, the achievements of technology, and so forth have a cumulative effect on everyday ideas and tend to sustain and to reproduce such awe toward natural science.

The Stake of Psychoanalysis in the "Science Wars"

Réginald Blanchet: One of the important consequences of your attempt to give to the rationality of psychoanalytic knowledge the status it deserves and thereby bring out its scientific character is the attention you draw to the hegemonic position of natural science in respect to knowledge in general. Can we diagnose here a political intervention in the context of the "science wars" that have recently flared up again in, for instance, the Sokal affair?

Aristides Baltas: I have already written on the Sokal affair.[11] As for the rest, I agree with your formulation and I am glad that you bring up the issue. The political dimension, if you will, that my work tries to promote is, roughly, the following: I believe that that we stand to gain a lot if we broaden the field of science, if we make it more democratic, by allowing both psychoanalysis and historical materialism to be a part of it along, of course, with physics and the natural sciences that we ought to continue to respect fully. And this does not refer only to cognitive and philosophical gains. If peace prevails in these perfectly futile "science wars," if psychoanalysis starts to become respected as a full-fledged science, then some of the pharmaceutical companies, along with others that thrive on human suffering, will lose some of their own gains. In addition, if the scientific status of psychoanalysis becomes acknowledged, then the entire program of cognitive science that I mentioned before will be transformed drastically. The research programs investigating knowledge will no longer regard artificial intelligence as something of a philosopher's stone, and the whole project will become somehow detached from computers and from the companies that promote computers beyond all measure. I despise demagogy and sensationalism, especially when it touches on issues such as these, but I think we should not ignore these dimensions either.

Nasia Linardou: Do you mean that psychoanalysis might have something to do with what you call cognitive science?

Aristides Baltas: Absolutely. For the central question of cognitive science is what knowledge is and how it is acquired. This is to say that, since knowledge is something acquired by human subjects, to understand what knowledge is, we need to know what human subjectivity is. Accordingly, if psychoanalysis is the science whose object is precisely human subjectivity, as I claim to be the case, then psychoanalysis cannot but be a vital component of all cognitive science programs. As I have said earlier, cognitive science has already started taking seriously the fact that knowledge is always emotionally laden, the fact that knowledge is embodied, the fact that the living human body is by itself a knowing body, and so on. In other words, cognitive science has already started to examine, however timidly, a number of non-Cartesian options that do not separate the body from the mind, the spirit, or the soul. This is already a step in the direction of psychoanalysis for which the sharp divide in question has never meant much.

Nasia Linardou: Do we need psychoanalysis for all this, or is psychology sufficient?

Aristides Baltas: Again yes, absolutely. The relation between psychoanalysis and psychology is a very complex issue but, speaking extremely schematically, I would hazard the claim that psychology has more to do with a set of techniques—some of which may be particularly effective in practice while providing fractional knowledge of various sorts—than with a fully fledged science. For me, the science of human subjectivity is psychoanalysis. In its theory and in its practice, psychoanalysis deals effectively at both the cognitive and the therapeutic levels with most of the aspects of human subjectivity I have just spoken of. And if psychoanalysis is indeed the science of human subjectivity, then it is psychoanalysis than can be decisive in our efforts to understand human knowledge.

Nasia Linardou: In a word, are you saying that psychoanalysis would win if we endow it with the status of a science?

Aristides Baltas: To begin with, it is not we—whoever we might be—who can or will endow it with this or that status. Psychoanalysis does what it does regardless, and it has no need of this or that label to continue with its work. My claim is that if the work of *philosophers*—not necessarily of psychoanalysts—manages to broaden the field of science to include psychoanalysis, psychoanalysis will earn unavoidably the general respect it deserves. And this will be a significant gain not only for psychoanalysis but also for the entire intellectual landscape of our societies.

Nasia Linardou: In the end, do you think that this is the problem of psychoanalysis? Today, as psychoanalysis finds itself under siege from pharmacology, the criterion is not at all whether it is or it is not scientific; the criterion is whether it is effective.

Aristides Baltas: I am not sure I understand what you mean by "the problem of psychoanalysis." What I think is that the assault of pharmacology is made ideologically legitimate, at least in the last instance, because psychoanalysis is not considered to be a science.

Nasia Linardou: No, it is the fact that psychoanalysis is not considered effective.

Aristides Baltas: But how do you define "effective"? I don't think that "effective" can work, as a category, independently of theoretical context. The effectiveness gauge that you seem to suggest is completely untrustworthy because, independently of its various other decisive disadvantages, it is modeled on natural science without taking at all into account singularity and all the other genuine characteristics of human subjectivity. Therefore, we are back to our starting point: psychoanalysis is not considered effective because it is not considered to be a science.

Nasia Linardou: You are aware, however, that drugs don't claim for themselves a strict scientific status either. Pharmacological treatment is an empirical procedure and we often don't now how a certain drug works. But the criterion is simple: the drug is or is not effective. What do you think is at stake in the struggle of psychoanalysis to gain the title of science? How is the survival of psychoanalysis related to that specific struggle?

Aristides Baltas: As long as this struggle is not sustained, we remain under the hegemony of physics and natural science in general with the consequence that psychoanalysis remains open to the attacks of pharmacology—a discipline belonging both de facto and de jure to natural science. To explain myself better, let me say that, in respect to the domain that is properly its own, pharmacology is a perfectly legitimate scientific endeavor. Moreover, I am not opposed to drugs in principle, for many drugs can be effective and thus very useful. This is also to say that it may become sooner or later possible to show in the proper scientific manner, to discover through pharmacology, physiology, neurophysiology and so on, the exact way a drug works and why taking it is effective. However, I also do believe—and I think I could prove it—that today pharmacology is attacking psychoanalysis for narrowly ideological reasons with no scientific warrant whatsoever while there exist important vested interests behind this attack. This is an attack carried out under the banner of the one and only "real" science, natural science. As long as the ideological positions behind this attack remain unquestioned, those who practice psychoanalysis remain vulnerable to the accusation that, at least in the final analysis, they are charlatans. As long as psychoanalysis keeps its drawbridge up and encloses itself within its own practice and theory, without claiming for itself the title of science in the open market of ideas, it remains vulnerable to such attacks. The title of science is much in demand these days because, within the present ideological conjuncture, it may legitimize almost anything. On the other hand and speaking more generally, the name and title of an endeavor are always very important matters. The refusal of psychoanalysis to claim for itself the title of science in the only right way, through philosophy and by the means of philosophy, is a form of capitulation that reduces its scope and weakens it dangerously.

Réginald Blanchet: But you speak as if psychoanalysis has only one identity. Does it?

Aristides Baltas: Your observation is extremely important, because it has to do with a further fundamental characteristic of psychoanalysis but also of historical materialism. Althusser called both of them "schismatic sciences," by which he meant that, for deep structural reasons, these are endeavors that spontaneously generate multiple and often antagonistic versions of what constitutes them. I have in mind the various "revisionisms" in the history of both historical materialism and psychoanalysis. We don't encounter this characteristic in physics, in the other natural sciences or in mathematics. Of course, antagonistic theories arise within these disciplines from time to time, but, sooner or later, one theory predominates for reasons, I claim, that are epistemological rather than social. In respect to natural science, theory change, theory competition, theory choice, and so on, are topics that have been discussed at length within Anglo-Saxon philosophy of science and we have learned a lot from the corresponding debates. Regarding psychoanalysis, I would maintain that to understand its schismatic character, we should start from the fact that the subjectivity of the analyst, that is, of the person *who formulates and develops the theory of psychoanalysis*, is involved *within the very object* of the same theory. Permit me to refer to *Louis Althusser and the End of Classical Marxism*, in which this is discussed in more detail, but in respect to historical materialism, where the situation is analogous.[12] Generally speaking, a philosophy of psychoanalysis, if it is to be at all adequate, ought to confront the issue headlong. And confront it with all the seriousness required by trying, among other things, to determine the *epistemological reasons* that allow—or compel—psychoanalysts, namely those who actually practice and develop psychoanalytic theory, to "choose" one version of psychoanalysis over another, as well as the epistemological grounds that can justify why and in what sense one version is more adequate than another.

Réginald Blanchet: Yet your own approach leads you to believe that Lacan's version is more scientific than Freud's or of that called "ego psychology"?

Aristides Baltas: From the little I know or believe to have understood, I would say the following: Ego psychology may have therapeutic effects and hence can be useful in that respect, but I think that it is more concerned with adaptation in the corresponding social environment than with genuine knowledge of the subjectivities involved. Thus, it fails to satisfy the "definition" of psychoanalysis as the science of human subjectivity. On the other hand, the kind of return to Freud that Lacan proclaims detaches psychoanalysis further from the model of natural science, a model to which Freud remained to an extent indebted. I see this detachment as constituting a second rung of the "epistemological break" performed by Freud's work. In this sense, this "return to Freud" is particularly fertile without necessarily being the last important word that psychoanalysis will ever pronounce. One of the things that make it fertile is that it sheds light retroactively on the entire history of psychoanalysis from Freud to the present, thereby fleshing out more fully its scientific status. What I mean is that, as Bachelard has taught us, exactly the same pattern is witnessed in the case of physics: a novel theory within a scientific discipline sanctions, in the properly disciplined way, some parts of the old theory while discarding some other parts. The saved parts form the *histoire sanctionnée* of the discipline, while the discarded parts make up the *histoire périmée* of the same discipline. Hence and in one word, if Freud is the Galileo of psychoanalysis, Lacan is its Newton.

Toward a Research Program Rooted More Deeply in Philosophy

Réginald Blanchet: Your research program is heading toward a new conception of knowledge that will include psychoanalytic knowledge securing thereby its status as a form of rationality. I think that you rely for this on the contrast (Politzer's?) between "first person knowledge" and "third person knowledge." Are there affinities here with Lacan, who includes the analyst in the very category of psychoanalytic knowledge? Would it then be true to say, along with Lacan (in the first pages of Seminar XI, *The Four Fundamental Concepts of Psychoanalysis*, 1964), that psychoanalysis is closer to alchemy than to chemistry, since the effectiveness of alchemy depends on the purity of the experimenter's soul? Would you go further in that direction or do you disagree with this idea? What can we say then about the epistemological status of, say, magic, religion or delirium, which include the subject as a key element of their discourse without, for that matter, rejecting the principle of an active cause that they try to investigate? Does this also count as "first-person knowledge"?

Aristides Baltas: This is once more a very interesting remark. Let me begin by explaining how I use the theme of the different "persons" of knowledge. The distinction between the first-person and the third-person perspective is widely discussed in philosophy of mind and in cognitive science, although significantly different viewpoints on what the distinction precisely amounts to and on how it should be fleshed out are being developed in both of these fields. In one of its common versions in the philosophy of mind, first person knowledge is, for example, knowledge of the *qualia* of my emotions, that is, items that I can rarely communicate, if at all, to others. These include, say, the feeling I am experiencing while looking at a sunset, the exact emotion accompanying some of my dreams, etc. In this context, the distinction relies on the idea that there is more happening "inwardly"—the first person—than can be expressed "outwardly"— the third person. In a more extreme formulation, none of the things I feel or think are available to others in exactly the way they are available to me. This is one of the basic ideas behind the distinction, although there does exist a great variety of approaches, depending on whether the emphasis is epistemological, metaphysical or linguistic. I would add that, for a number of philosophers and cognitive scientists, third-person knowledge is the kind of knowledge that can be put in propositional form; this is knowledge that can be articulated, communicated and tested through propositions. Scientific knowledge and a great deal of trivial knowledge is third-person knowledge.

This leads us to another distinction, namely that between "knowing what" and "knowing how." This is a distinction based on the fact there are many things that I know how to do with my body but that I cannot describe and communicate in propositional form. These are related to the fact that I possess a certain set of abilities. For instance, I know how to ride a bicycle, but I cannot teach this knowledge exclusively through propositions. I cannot communicate through a class of finite propositions what exactly it is that I know when I extend my hand as much as I need to lift this glass, or exactly what it is that I know when I cross a street without being hit by a car. This distinction became very useful in cognitive science when it was understood that a computer can be "trained" only through propositions and so cannot simulate human intelligence, even of the simplest everyday sort. It became clear that the living human body is knowledge bearing, that it acquires knowledge in its own nonpropositional ways, and so on. In a word, knowledge is an intrinsic dimension of the human body because knowledge is embodied.

I bring these distinctions to psychoanalysis only to claim that, while in cognitive science or in the philosophy of mind, first-person and third-person knowledge, as well as "knowing what" and "knowing how," seem very different, and hence the question of how they are connected becomes inevitable and pressing, psychoanalysis has already solved the question in practice and for its own practice. During the psychoanalytic session, third-person knowledge (that is, knowledge inscribed in psychoanalytic theory) and first-person knowledge (that is, knowledge including all the things that the analyst and the analysand know of their emotions, of their relationship, of their subjectivity in general) operate in unison more or less unproblematically. At the same time, the body is considered from the very start as a knowing body: psychosomatic symptoms imply exactly that. If Anglo-Saxon philosophy of mind and cognitive science pose a question on how these forms of knowledge can possibly work together, psychoanalysis offers in practice, *à l'état pratique*, an answer.

Réginald Blanchet: And what is this answer?

Aristides Baltas: You can't seriously expect me to come up with such an answer here! But let me say that an answer must perhaps begin from exactly what you have said, namely that the analyst is included in the concept of psychoanalytic knowledge. And I would like to add that I find the comparison with alchemy, insofar as "the purity of the soul of the experimenter" is concerned, very fruitful and this for a number of reasons. First, it seems to me that such "purity" refers directly to the nonnegotiable ethics of psychoanalysis. If this is correct, then, second, the attainment of the corresponding ethical stance, the attainment of such "purity of the soul," refers directly to the training the psychoanalyst should undergo in order to be in a position to practice psychoanalysis. Third, the reference to alchemy brings to the scene the times before the Scientific Revolution, when the world was still "enchanted." What I mean is that the Scientific

Revolution, by constituting physics, by making the science of extension the only possible science, elevated the third-person perspective to the rank of the only possible scientific perspective. The first person was expelled from the province of scientific knowledge; the world became "disenchanted" and made impersonal. Psychoanalysis, by bringing the first person back into the game, by demanding that we understand its role and function on its own proper terms, by compelling us to acknowledge its singularity and its fundamental historical dimension, marks a kind of return to the Middle Ages. But this is a return that does not belittle the achievements of the Scientific Revolution and the Enlightenment, and does not deny physics, chemistry, biology, and the other natural sciences their genuine scientific titles. From this point of view, the change in the category "scientific knowledge" to which the existence of psychoanalysis pushes us may indeed be radical.

As a side remark and lest I become misunderstood, let me clarify that, in talking about the first and third person, I am not at all ignoring the importance of the second person in the theory and practice of psychoanalysis. The analytic session is a dyadic relation. My reference to the first and third persons was simply an attempt to connect the issues in cognitive science and in the philosophy of mind to the *problématique* of psychoanalysis.

Réginald Blanchet: Isn't this distinction connected to the views of Politzer?

Aristides Baltas: I need to think more about the connection with Politzer.

Réginald Blanchet: What are the next stages of your research program?

Aristides Baltas: What interests me most at present are the epistemological, the broader philosophical, presuppositions of what I have been trying to work on. Some time ago I happened to read *Mind and World* by John McDowell. Much as all his work has been highly respected in the entire Anglo-Saxon philosophical community, this is a book, I believe, that is truly important. Discreetly inspired by Wittgenstein, it carves out a novel path toward the solution—or the dissolution—of the constitutive problem of philosophy, namely the relation between these two realms. I admit that reading this book worked as a kind of revelation for me, despite the fact that McDowell's work has nothing to do with Marx or Freud and very little to do with either science or its philosophy. I mean that it offered me invaluable insights for starting to think on the general philosophical foundations of my own work. We held a seminar on the book in which my students and I discussed it as comprehensively as we could, while a number of PhD students are writing on issues that are directly connected to the ideas it expresses. *Mind and World* also reinvigorated my interest in Wittgenstein. In a later seminar we read *Tractatus Logico-Philosophicus* line by line. Through this reading, a number of very interesting connections started to emerge between Wittgenstein's early philosophy and the philosophy of Spinoza. In any case, it is becoming more and more clear to me that philosophy of science reaches very quickly its limits if it does not connect with "great" philosophy, with philosophy tout court. It is as if someone were to try to walk on one leg. This is more or less my answer to your question.

Réginald Blanchet: Thank you very much.

Aristides Baltas: It is I who thank you.

MODELING FREUD AND FUNDAMENTALISM
Andrew Parker

1. Sigmund Freud, *The Future of an Illusion*, trans. James Strachey (New York: Norton, 1989), 43.

2. See Robert Jay Lifton, *Destroying the World to Save It: Aum Shinrikyo, Apocalyptic Violence, and the New Global Terrorism* (New York: Henry Holt, 2000), and *Superpower Syndrome: America's Apocalyptic Confrontation with the World* (New York: Nation Books, 2003). In *Dark Continents: Psychoanalysis and Colonialism* (Durham, N.C.: Duke University Press, 2003), Ranjana Khanna suggests that psychoanalytic efforts to understand "fundamentalist" acts of violence depoliticize these acts by definition (2).

3. Michael Hardt and Antonio Negri, *Empire* (Cambridge, Mass.: Harvard University Press, 2001), 146–47.

4. Slavoj Žižek, *On Belief* (New York: Routledge, 2001), 68–69. See also his "A Lacanian Plea for Fundamentalism," a lecture delivered at the University of Pennsylvania on September 18, 2000: http://www.english.upenn.edu/~wh/theorizing/archives.html.

5. Slavoj Žižek, *Welcome to the Desert of the Real* (New York: Verso, 2002), 52. In *The Sublime Object of Ideology* (London and New York: Verso, 1989), Žižek argues (following Lacan) that it was Marx who "invented" the symptom.

6. See Sigmund Freud, *New Introductory Lectures on Psycho-Analysis*, trans. James Strachey (New York: Norton, 1965), 158: "sociology . . . cannot be anything but applied psychology. Strictly speaking there are only two sciences: psychology, pure and applied, and natural science."

7. Matthew Sharpe, "The Sociopolitical Limits of Fantasy: September 11 and Žižek's Theory of Ideology," *Cultural Logic* 5 (2002), §8.

8. See Céline Surprenant, *Freud's Mass Psychology: Questions of Scale* (Basingstoke: Palgrave Macmillan, 2003). Surprenant concludes that, from *Totem and Taboo* onward, Freud's frequent appeal to the analogy between individuals and groups is matched by his equally frequent warning concerning the limits of analogical thinking: "The first phase of the perception of identity between two domains is invariably mitigated by the gradual discovery of the

dissimilarity up to the point where the analogy breaks down and must be abandoned" (69–70).

9. Sigmund Freud, *Group Psychology and the Analysis of the Ego*, trans. James Strachey (New York: Norton, 1959), 3.

10. See Mladen Dolar, "Freud and the Political," *Theory & Event* 12, no. 3 (2009): "One may say that for psychoanalysis there is no such thing as an individual, the individual only makes sense as a knot of social ties, a network of relations to the others, to the always already social Other, the Other being ultimately but a shorthand for the social instance as such. Subjectivity cannot make sense without this inherent relation to the Other, so that sociality has been there from the outset, say in the form of that minimal script presented by Oedipus, a social structure in a nutshell. Thus the reflections on the social which Freud increasingly undertook in his later life are not an addition, an application of psychoanalysis to a new field of research, but rather the unfolding of what has been there from the start. One can see the two terms of the title, group psychology and the analysis of the ego, as standing in relation of mutual implication: group psychology relies on a certain structure of the ego and is made possible by it, and the analysis of the ego implies, always already, a group structure. So Freud tries to present this as a seamless transition, a mere deduction, or a magnification and a multiplication of what was present on the small scale. The individual, the ego, the subject are inconceivable without a theory of a social tie."

11. Freud, *Group Psychology*, 4.

12. Sigmund Freud, *Civilization and Its Discontents*, trans. James Strachey (New York: Norton, 1961), 91.

13. Ruth Stein, *For Love of the Father: A Psychoanalytic Study of Religious Terrorism* (Stanford: Stanford University Press, 2009), 18–19. Despite this, Stein analyzes Atta's suicide letter, providing her readers with what seems a diagnosis in all but name.

14. Sigmund Freud, *Moses and Monotheism*, in *The Standard Edition of the Complete Psychological Works*, ed. and trans. James Strachey (New York: Norton, 1963), 23:188.

15. Ibid., 23:99–100.

16. A question posed most brilliantly by Gilles Deleuze and Félix Guattari: "The father, the mother, and the self are at grips with, and directly coupled to, the elements of the political and historical situation—the soldier, the cop, the occupier, the collaborator, the radical, the resister, the boss, the boss's wife—who constantly break all triangulations, and who prevent the entire situation from falling back on the familial complex and becoming internalized in it. In a word, the family is never a microcosm in the sense of an autonomous figure, even when inscribed in a larger circle that it is said to mediate and

express. The family is by nature eccentric, decentered. We are told of fusional, divisive, tubular, and foreclosing families. But what produces the hiatuses (*coupures*) and their distribution that indeed keep the family from being an 'interior'? There is always an uncle from America; a brother who went bad; an aunt who took off with a military man; a cousin out of work, bankrupt, or a victim of the Crash; an anarchist grandfather; a grandmother in the hospital, crazy or senile. The family does not engender its own ruptures. Families are filled with gaps and transected by breaks that are not familial: the Commune, the Dreyfus Affair, religion and atheism, the Spanish Civil War, the rise of fascism, Stalinism, the Vietnam war, May '68—all these things form complexes of the unconscious, more effective than everlasting Oedipus. . . . [W]hat is invested by the libido throughout the disjoined elements of Oedipus—especially given the fact that these elements never form a mental structure that is autonomous and expressive—are these extrafamilial, subfamilial gaps and breaks (*coupures*), these forms of social production in conjunction with desiring-production" (*Anti-Oedipus: Capitalism and Schizophrenia*, trans. Robert Hurley, Mark Seem, and Helen R. Lane [New York: Viking, 1977], 97–98).

17. Jean Laplanche, *Essays on Otherness* (New York: Routledge, 1999), 189.

18. Robert M. Young, "Psychoanalysis, Terrorism and Fundamentalism," http://human-nature.com/rmyoung/papers/pap139h.html.

19. Stein, *For Love of the Father*, 52. Stein's one break from Freudian orthodoxy is her insistence that Islamic terrorism is exclusively religious in nature, rather than political or even religio-political. Freud saw the Father in both God and Leader. See in this connection Philippe Lacoue-Labarthe and Jean-Luc Nancy, "La panique politique," in *Retreating the Political*, ed. Simon Sparks (New York: Routledge, 1997), 1–31.

20. Eric L. Santner, *On the Psychotheology of Everyday Life: Reflections on Freud and Rosenzweig* (Chicago: University of Chicago Press, 2001), 8.

21. Žižek, *On Belief*, 2–3.

22. The quotations here are from Freud, *The Future of an Illusion*, at 31, 47, and 54–55.

23. Joel Whitebook, *Perversion and Utopia: A Study in Psychoanalysis and Critical Theory* (Cambridge, Mass.: MIT Press, 1995), 98. See also Jacques Derrida, "Faith and Knowledge: The Two Sources of 'Religion' at the Limits of Reason Alone," trans. Samuel Weber, in *Acts of Religion*, ed. Gil Anidjar (New York: Routledge, 2001), 43: "Knowledge and faith . . . will always have made common cause, bound to one another by the band of their opposition."

24. J.-B. Pontalis cited in Laplanche, *Essays on Otherness*, 193. Pontalis puns on two senses of the German verb *glauben*.

25. Santner, *Psychotheology*, 9. See also Jacquy Chemouni, *Freud et le sionisme: Terre psychanalytique, terre promise* (Paris: Solin, 1988).

26. See Jacques Derrida, "Above All, No Journalists!" in *Religion and Media*, ed. Hent de Vries and Samuel Weber (Stanford: Stanford University Press, 2001), 74: "I don't know if there is a word for 'religion' in Arabic, but it is certainly not an adequate translation of 'religion.' Is Judaism a 'religion'? Buddhism is certainly not a religion. . . . All these religions are doubtless religions with a universal vocation, but only Christianity has a concept of universality that has been elaborated into the form in which it today dominates both philosophy and international law."

27. Jacques Derrida, "Geopsychoanalysis: '. . . and the rest of the world,'" in *The Psychoanalysis of Race*, ed. Christopher Lane (New York: Columbia University Press, 1998), 87, 69.

28. Special thanks to my linguistic informants Jamal Elias, Suvir Kaul, Alan Keenan, and Ania Loomba, and, for much more, to Stathis Gourgouris.

MYTH AND DOGMA IN 1920: THE FUNDAMENTALIST-MODERNIST
CONTROVERSY AND FREUD'S "DEATH DRIVE"
David Adams

1. Hagee's sermons are broadcast on Christian television stations nationwide. This series of sermons on political issues played repeatedly on WTLW TV44 (Lima, Ohio) in the weeks leading up to the 2004 presidential election. I completed revisions of this essay in December 2004. .

2. George M. Marsden writes, "A fundamentalist is an evangelical who is angry about something. That seems simple and is fairly accurate. Jerry Falwell has even adopted it as a quick definition of fundamentalism that reporters are likely to quote. A more precise statement of the same point is that an American fundamentalist is an evangelical who is militant in opposition to liberal theology in the churches or to changes in cultural values or mores, such as those associated with 'secular humanism'" (Marsden, *Understanding Fundamentalism and Evangelicalism* [Grand Rapids, Mich.: Eerdmans, 1991], 1). Marsden and Falwell are echoing the observation of Harry Emerson Fosdick, a prominent liberal pastor and favorite target of the fundamentalists in the 1920s, that fundamentalists are "mad evangelicals" (quoted in R. Scott Appleby, "Fundamentalism," *Encyclopedia of Politics and Religion*, ed. Robert Wuthnow [Washington, D.C.: Congressional Quarterly Press, 1998], 282).

3. John Hagee, "Iraq: The Final War," *JHMagazine* 15, no. 4 (May–June 2003): 4–6. Apparently this essay is excerpted or adapted from a sermon, for it is accompanied by an advertisement for a recording of a sermon series with the same title.

4. For a sampling of work analyzing the political effects of Christian eschatology under George W. Bush, see Paul S. Boyer, "When U.S. Foreign Policy Meets Biblical Prophecy," Alternet, February 20, 2003; David Domke, *God*

Willing? Political Fundamentalism in the White House, the "War on Terror," and the Echoing Press (Ann Arbor, Mich.: Pluto, 2004); and Robert Jay Lifton, *Superpower Syndrome: America's Apocalyptic Confrontation with the World* (New York: Thunder's Mouth Press, 2003).

5. Consciousness of an interdenominational conservative movement based on the fundamentals was evident by the spring of 1919, when the World Conference on Christian Fundamentals took place in Philadelphia. Similarly, the concept of the death drive might be dated to the spring of 1919, when Freud drafted the text that would become *Beyond the Pleasure Principle* (although the editors of the Standard Edition observe that no record survives of Freud using the term before February 1920, the month his daughter Sophie died, when he mentions it in a letter, and he spent months revising the text in 1920 before finally publishing it in December). In both cases, the new terms were introduced to the public, consolidating certain responses to the war, in 1920.

6. Curtis Lee Laws, "Convention Side Lights," *The Watchman-Examiner* 8 (July 1, 1920), 834.

7. *The Fundamentals: A Testimony to the Truth* (Chicago: Testimony Publishing, [1910–15]), 1:4.

8. David S. Katz, *God's Last Words: Reading the English Bible from the Reformation to Fundamentalism* (New Haven: Yale University Press, 2004).

9. Ernest R. Sandeen, *The Roots of Fundamentalism: British and American Millenarianism, 1800–1930* (Chicago: University of Chicago Press, 1970), 273–77.

10. Eldred C. Vanderlaan, ed., *Fundamentalism Versus Modernism* (New York: Wilson, 1925), 21.

11. George M. Marsden, *Fundamentalism and American Culture: The Shaping of Twentieth-Century Evangelicalism: 1870–1925* (Oxford: Oxford University Press, 1980).

12. William B. Riley, "The Great Divide, or Christ and the Present Crisis," *God Hath Spoken: Twenty-five Addresses Delivered at the World Conference on Christian Fundamentals* (Philadelphia: Bible Conference Committee, 1919), 44.

13. Karen Armstrong, *The Battle for God* (New York: Knopf, 2001), 139.

14. Hans Blumenberg, *Work on Myth* (Cambridge, Mass.: MIT Press, 1985).

15. Sigmund Freud, *Standard Edition*, 21:54.

16. Ibid., 22:158.

17. Ibid., 22:182.

18. Ibid., 21:54.

19. Ibid., 18:38. For Freud's "*Trieb*," I have silently emended the translations to read "drive" rather than "instinct." Emphases are in the original.

20. Ibid., 19:46.

21. On this issue, compare Judith Roof's recent reading of "indifference" and sameness in fundamentalism and *Beyond the Pleasure Principle*. Roof, "Indifference," *UMBR(a): A Journal of the Unconscious* (2002): 97–113.

22. Freud, *Standard Edition*, 18:64.

23. Ibid., 18:59.

24. Ibid., 18:39.

TREES, PAIN, AND BEYOND: FREUD ON MASOCHISM
Branka Arsić

1. Sigmund Freud, *Civilization and Its Discontents*, trans. James Strachey (New York: Norton, 1989), 25.

2. Sigmund Freud, *Three Essays on The Theory of Sexuality*, trans. James Strachey (New York: Basic Books, 1962), 23–24.

3. See Richard von Krafft-Ebing, *Psychopathia Sexualis*, trans. Franklin S. Klaf (New York: Arcade, 1998), 90, on "ideal masochism."

4. Freud, *Civilization and Its Discontents*, 26.

5. Ibid., 27.

6. Ibid.

7. Interestingly, after offering a short analysis of the beneficiary effects of cocaine on the troubled body and after comparing the mental condition of the cocaine user to that caused by mania, Freud introduces the idea of something that, for want of a better word, might be called "pharmaceutical thought": "Besides this [the pathological state of mania] our normal mental life exhibits oscillations between a comparatively easy liberation of pleasure and a comparatively difficult one, parallel with which there goes a diminished or an increased receptivity to unpleasure. It is greatly to be regretted that this toxic side of mental processes has so far escaped scientific examination" (29). According to this scenario—developed within the space of two short manic paragraphs—thoughts are "intoxicating" or, better still, chemical ingredients of our bodies. Some of them increase pleasure, others pain. Some of them put our bodies—chemically—into a manic state some of them into nirvana, otherwise artificially induced by nonchemical yoga practices. The whole difference among our thoughts would thus correspond to the difference among opium, cocaine, heroin, LSD, and ecstasy, and one would or would not think certain thoughts depending on what kind of a junkie one was.

8. Freud, *Three Essays*, 24.

9. Ibid.

10. Ibid.

11. Ibid., 30.

12. Ibid., 31.

13. Ibid., 32.

14. Ibid., 34.

15. Ibid.

16. Ibid.

17. Ibid., 32.

18. Ibid.

19. Ibid., 16.

20. Sigmund Freud, *Group Psychology and the Analysis of the Ego*, trans. James Strachey (New York: Norton, 1989), 58.

21. Ibid., 42.

22. Ibid., 43.

23. Sigmund Freud, "On Narcissism: An Introduction," in *On Metapsychology: The Theory of Psychoanalysis*, trans. James Strachey, ed. Angela Richards (London: Penguin Books, 1991), 68.

24. I will not analyze various types of object-cathexis, which transcends the scope of this essay. For a sound analysis of it, especially of the attachment type of love, see Mikkel Borch-Jacobsen, *The Freudian Subject*, trans. Catherine Porter (Stanford: Stanford University Press, 1988), 103–6.

25. Ibid., 99.

26. Ibid., 100.

27. Freud, "On Narcissism," 78.

28. Ibid., 81–82.

29. Ibid.

30. Ibid., 83.

31. Borch-Jacobsen, *The Freudian Subject*, 108. For a reading that suggests that such a domination in the attachment type of love cannot take place "prior to any sexual characterization" see Judith Butler, *The Psychic Life of Power* (Stanford: Stanford University Press, 1997), 132–50.

32. Sigmund Freud, "Beyond the Pleasure Principle," in *On Metapsychology*, 326.

33. Ibid., 317.

34. For the idiosyncratic use of sources in Freud's essays, see John Kerr, "Freud, Jung, and Sabina Spielrein," in *Freud: Appraisals and Reappraisals— Contribution to Freud Studies*, ed. Paul E. Stepansky (Hillsdale, N.J.: The Analytic Press, 1988), 10–12.

35. Freud, "Beyond the Pleasure Principle," 317–18.

36. Ibid., 318.

37. Ibid., 328.

38. Ibid.

39. Ibid.

40. Sabina Spielrein, "Destruction as a Cause of Coming into Being," *Journal of Analytical Psychology* 39, no. 2 (1994): 155–86. Hereafter abbreviated D.

41. Ibid., 170. Spielrein refers to Nietzsche not only when she defines her crucial terms (destruction, coming into being, overcoming, etc.), but also when she elaborates her theory of love and creativity, loss of the self, becoming another (which in her argument is related to the potentially creative aspect of masochism). Critics, however, tend to overlook this profoundly Nietzschean aspect of her theory, probably because of her Freudian/Jungian vocabulary and because of her private relations with Jung (analyst, lover) and Freud (teacher, analyst). Scholarship on Spielrein's philosophy is not extensive (and unfortunately is always tied to her private story with Jung). Perhaps most influential is John Kerr's study *A Most Dangerous Method: The Story of Jung Freud and Sabina Spielrein* (New York: Random House, 1994). See also Aldo Carotenuto, *A Secret Symmetry: Sabina Spielrein Between Jung and Freud* (New York: Pantheon, 1982), and *Sabina Spielrein: Forgotten Pioneer of Psychoanalysis*, ed. Coline Covington and Barbara Wharton (New York: Routledge, 2003). Elizabeth Marton directed a documentary film on Spielrein, *My Name Was Sabina Spielrein.*

42. Kerr, "Freud, Jung, and Sabina Spielrein," 22.

43. Ibid., 26.

44. Ibid.

45. Ibid., 32–33.

46. Ibid., 32.

47. Ibid., 33.

48. Sigmund Freud, "A Child Is Being Beaten," in *Sexuality and the Psychology of Love* (New York: Simon & Schuster, 1997), 118.

49. Kerr, "Freud, Jung, and Sabina Spielrein," 10.

50. Friedrich Nietzsche, *Ecce Homo*, trans. Walter Kaufman (New York: Vintage Books, 1989), 296.

51. Gilles Deleuze, *Masochism, Coldness and Cruelty*, trans. Jean McNeil (New York: Zone Books, 1991), 9–10.

OF RATS AND NAMES
Gil Anidjar

1. Partially retrofitted for the purpose of this volume, this essay was first published as "Of Rats and Names (Reflections on Hate)" in *Historein: A Review of the Past and Other Stories* 8 (2008): 29–40. It is part of a longer project entitled *Against Anti-Semitism*, which I am in the process of completing. The reading I offer here of Freud's "Notes on a Case of Obsessional Neurosis," better known as *Rat Man*, is provisional and dependent on the larger frame structuring what is now called "anti-Semitism," a term operating in popular and political discourse in France, the United States, and Germany. This implies much that I cannot possibly reproduce or even summarize here at the

risk of creating more obscurity than usual. I have used Philip Rieff's edition
(Sigmund Freud, *Three Case Stories: The 'Wolf Man,' the 'Rat Man' and the
Psychotic Doctor Schreber* [New York: Collier Books, 1993]) and, for the
German, *Gesammelte Werke*, vol. 7, *Werke aus den Jahren 1906–1909*
(Frankfurt am Main: Fischer Taschenbuch Verlag, 1999).

2. On Rat Man's Jewishness, the rising Jewish population of Vienna
between the nineteenth and early twentieth century, the climate of anti-
Semitism within which both Rat Man and Freud found themselves at the time,
and the identifications at work between analyst and analysand, transference
and countertransference, see Patrick J. Mahony, *Freud and the Rat Man* (New
Haven: Yale University Press, 1986). Pointing out some of the Yiddish expres-
sions used during the analysis but cleaned up by Freud in the final version of
the case study, Mahony refers his readers to the complete notes made by Freud
during the treatment, notes that he had consulted in manuscript form but
which had been published in a bilingual edition (French and German) by Elza
Ribeiro Hawelka (S. Freud, *L'homme aux rats. Journal d'une analyse*, ed. E. R.
Hawelka [Paris: Presses Universitaires de France, 1974], hereafter, *Journal*).
In what follows, I will refer to Freud's patient, Ernst Lanzer, as Rat Man.
Incidentally, Mahony also discovered that Rat Man's Jewish middle name was
the same as that of Freud's own father, Jacob. Whether Freud knew this or
not is unclear. Throughout his study, Mahony also underscores the link
between obsessional neurosis and religion in Freud's work.

3. As I try to argue elsewhere, this question traverses the entirety of
Jacques Derrida's work and it informs my reading here as well. Gil Anidjar,
"Traité de Tous les Noms (What Is Called Naming)," *Epoché: A Journal for the
History of Philosophy* 10, no. 2 (Spring 2006): 287–301.

4. For a related discussion, see Alain Badiou, "Uses of the Word 'Jew,'" in
Polemics (London: Verso, 2006), 157–254.

5. I was going to add: "and vice versa." But this too would take much
longer to explain.

6. Freud, *Rat Man*, 52. As much as I hate to grant them originality, the
Nazis may have been the first to compare Jews to rats, which would begin to
explain the lack of explicit references in *Rat Man* and in discussions thereof.
As identifications such as rats and money ("Jeder Gulden—eine Ratte"), and
rats and syphilis (a well-known "Jewish" disease) demonstrate, the association
is nonetheless operative in Freud's text ("*So treffen in Ratten, Geld und Syphilis
zusammen*," Freud, *Journal*, 166–68). Rat Man retrospectively attributes
syphilis to his father and tells numerous stories about rats. And cats. One of
them is even made gruesomely "kosher" (174).

7. Freud, *Rat Man*, 20/G400.

8. Immanuel Kant had already associated the Jews, "those Palestinians
living among us," with that particular undecidability, locating them in the

space between blessing and curse (for a discussion of that passage in Kant's *Anthropology*, see Avital Ronell, *Stupidity* [Urbana: University of Illinois Press, 2002], esp. 302–3).

9. As Freud reports, Rat Man's father never wanted to be baptized himself, "but he much regretted that his ancestors did not spare him this unpleasant affair [*aber sehr bedauert dass seine Ahnen ihm nicht diess unangenehme Geschäft abgenommen*]." As to his son, Heinrich Lanzer often said that he would not oppose his conversion to Christianity (Freud, *Journal*, 204). One can only wonder about Heinrich's sentiments vis-à-vis his in-laws, the Saborskys, who were themselves observant Jews. It is during the same session of December 27, 1907, and in the process of detailing this religious matter, that Rat Man recalls expecting the return of his father's ghost at night, working and masturbating, devoted and defiant, wishing him ill and well. Heinrich is later, and somehow obscurely, said to have put "the Jews" to work to clear up the snow blocking the arrival of the trains. The Jews—but why the Jews?—were exceptionally allowed entry on the marketplace in order to work, a place from which they were usually barred (212). The episode leads to an unpleasant exchange with an officer whose gesture of gratitude and recognition for a job well done appears to the father as highly hypocritical. Complex circuits of anti-Semitism are here difficult to ignore.

10. Sigmund Freud, *Rat Man*, 19. And later: "This crazy conduct becomes intelligible if we suppose that he was acting as though he expected a visit from his father at the hour when ghosts are abroad. He had on the whole been idle at his work during his father's lifetime, and this had often been the cause of annoyance to his father. And now that he was returning as a ghost, he was to be delighted at finding his son hard at work. But it was impossible that his father should be delighted at the other part of his behavior; in this therefore he must be defying him" (45). A final discussion of the father's ghost occurs on page 59. Freud mentions and quotes Shakespeare on page 24 (*Julius Caesar*) and quotes *Hamlet* in particular toward the end of the case history (75 n. 15). Avital Ronell attributes to Patrick Lacoste the pointing out of the "father complexes shared by both heroes," namely, Hamlet and Rat Man. Ronell underscores the concern with rats that they also share ("Hamlet, when he kills Polonius, rather convulsively screams 'a rat, a rat'") and points to "the famous acknowledgment of the doctor in Vienna to whom Hamlet futurally appeals." Avital Ronell, "The *Sujet Suppositaire*: Freud, And/Or, the Obsessional Neurotic Style (Maybe)," in *Finitude's Score: Essays for the End of the Millennium* (Lincoln: University of Nebraska Press, 1994), 116.

11. Freud, *Rat Man*, 9. And later: "And thereupon the idea had come to him that she [namely, the little girl the patient had been fond of at the time] would be kind to him if some misfortune were to befall him; and as an instance

of such a misfortune his father's death had forced itself upon his mind. He had at once rejected the idea with energy. And even now he could not admit the possibility that what had arisen in this way could have been a 'wish'" (23). Finally, "Several years after his father's death, the first time he experienced the pleasurable sensations of copulation, an idea sprang into his mind: 'This is glorious! One might murder one's father for this!'" (43).

12. Ronell, "The *Sujet Suppositaire*," 113.

13. Avital Ronell, *The Telephone Book: Technology, Schizophrenia, Electric Speech* (Lincoln: University of Nebraska Press, 1989). The question of the call runs through all of Ronell's work, and more recently in *Stupidity* (Urbana: University of Illinois Press, 2002). For a critical review of the literature on interpellation, see Judith Butler's work as given in note 26.

14. Louis Althusser, "Ideology and Ideological State Apparatuses," trans. Ben Brewster in *Lenin and Philosophy and Other Essays* (New York: Monthly Review Press, 1971), 178.

15. Althusser, "Ideology," 174–75.

16. In the original notes, Rat Man had said that the scene, which he could not remember, had been repeatedly reported to him by his father ("*die man ihm sehr oft berichtet hat, der Vater selbst*"), not by his mother (Freud, *Journal*, 106).

17. Jean-François Lyotard, *Le différend* (Paris: Minuit, 1982).

18. Focusing on postal figures and offices, Ronell engages the problems of address in the case of Rat Man, pointing out that it neatly "inserts itself into the idiom of the Derridean text (*The Post Card*) concerned with the technology of the courier" (117; and see also 119ff.). Mahony and others have remarked that Freud had conducted himself unprofessionally with Rat Man when the latter had sent him, on one occasion, a postcard.

19. "Paul" is Freud's substitute for Rat Man's name, namely, Ernst. According to the nurse's awkward report, the father had asked "*Sind Sie der Ernst?*" (Freud, *Journal*, 64).

20. As Ronell puts it, "plain assertions of the sheerly constative sort, when deposited into Rat Man, spontaneously acquire the authority of commands" (121).

21. Freud, *Journal*, 46.

22. Ibid., 136.

23. Ibid., 177 n. 360.

24. Ibid., 176.

25. In the space of this question, Ronell and Derrida insert Abraham (the biblical Abraham and Kafka's Abraham), and his famous answer: "Here I am."

26. Judith Butler, *The Psychic Life of Power: Theories in Subjection* (Stanford: Stanford University Press, 1997), 95; on the issue of insults and hate speech as

interpellation, Butler pursues her reflections in *Excitable Speech: A Politics of the Performative* (New York: Routledge, 1997), especially in her introduction, "On Linguistic Vulnerability."

27. On the productive and proliferating dimension of interpellative and other powers, see Butler, *Psychic Life*, 58ff.

28. Jacques Derrida, *Limited Inc.* (Evanston, Ill.: Northwestern University Press, 1988).

MAD COUNTRY, MAD PSYCHIATRISTS:
PSYCHOANALYSIS AND THE BALKAN GENOCIDE
Dušan I. Bjelić

I thank Rosemary Miller for her generous help in producing this essay.

1. As tension grew between Serbia and Croatia at the beginning of the 1990s, Rašković became an increasing obstacle to the pragmatic and aggressive politics of the Milosevic government. His politics of spiritual awakening were replaced with direct military engagement with the Croatian government. And, instead of getting help from the collective unconscious, the Serbs were receiving military help from the Yugoslavian Peoples' Army run by Serb generals, among them Ratko Mladić. Rašković disapproved of these developments, and retired to Belgrade. The fire he set could not have been controlled by a psychiatrist, but became very useful in the hands of Serbian generals. On January 24, 1992, the Zagreb newspaper *Vjesnik* carried an interview with Rašković, which is testimony to his failed project: "I feel responsible because I made the preparations for this war, even if not the military preparations. If I hadn't created this emotional strain in the Serbian people, nothing would have happened. My party lit the fuse of Serbian nationalism, not only in Croatia but everywhere else in Bosnia and Herzegovina. It's impossible to imagine an SDS in Bosnia and Herzegovina or a Dr. Karadžić in power without our influence. We have driven this people and we have given it an identity. I have repeated again and again to this people that it comes from heaven, not earth." (Quoted in Steven M. Weine, *When History Is a Nightmare: Lives and Memories of Ethnic Cleansing in Bosnia-Herzegovina"* [New Brunswick, N.J.: Rutgers University Press 1999], 91.) One may read Rašković's confession as one more example, perhaps the final one, of his professional delusion. The resurgence of the Serb collective identity and the genocide that followed were surely, as he acknowledges, his responsibility.

2. To my knowledge, only Steven M. Weine has written extensively on that topic (*When History is a Nightmare*), and one can find the occasional article in the Scientology press on that topic. One such is Patricia Forestier, "Genocide! How the Barbarities of 'Ethnic Cleansing' Were Spawned by a Psychiatrist," *Freedom*, May 1993, 11.

3. Larry Wolff, *Inventing Eastern Europe: The Map of Civilization on the Mind of the Enlightenment* (Stanford: Stanford University Press, 1994); Maria Todorova, *Imagining the Balkans* (Oxford: Oxford University Press, 1997).

4. See Iver B. Neumann, *Uses of the Other: "The East" in European Identity Formation* (Minneapolis: University of Minnesota Press, 1999).

5. See Milica Bakić-Hayden, "Nesting *Orientalisms:* The Case of Former Yugoslavia," *Slavic Review* 54, no. 4 (Winter 1995): 917–31.

6. See Celia Brickman, *Aboriginal Populations in the Mind: Race and Primitivity in Psychoanalysis* (New York: Columbia University Press, 2003).

7. On the issue of psychoanalysis and colonialism, see Christiane Hartneck, *Psychoanalysis in Colonial India* (New Delhi: Oxford University Press, 2001).

8. Quoted in Slavoj Žižek, *For They Know Not What They Do: Enjoyment as a Political Factor* (London: Verso, 1996], 8.

9. Sigmund Freud, *The Standard Edition of the Complete Psychological Works of Sigmund Freud*, translated by James Strachey (London: Hogarth Press, 1968), 10:215.

10. Ibid., 12:187–203.

11. Ibid., 3:292.

12. Peter Swales, "Freud, Death and Sexual Pleasures: On the Psychical Mechanism of Dr. Sigmund Freud," *Arc de Cercle: International Journal of Mind Sciences* 1, no. 1 (January 2003): 62.

13. Freud, *Standard Edition*, 4:207.

14. Ernest Jones, "Freud's Early Travels," *The International Journal of Psycho-analysis* 35, part 2 (1954): 81.

15. *The Freud/Jung Letters: The Correspondence Between Sigmund Freud and C.G. Jung*, edited by William McGuire, translated by Ralph Manheim and R. F. C. Hull (Princeton: Princeton University Press, 1995), 225.

16. Ibid., 226.

17. Sandor Ferenczi, *The Clinical Diary of Sandor Ferenczi*, edited by Judith Dupont, translated by Michael Balint and Nicola Zarday Jackson (Cambridge, Mass.: Harvard University Press, 1988), 93.

18. In a letter to Spielrein's mother, Jung writes: "Therefore I would suggest that if you wish me to adhere strictly to my role as doctor, you should pay me a fee as suitable recompense for my trouble. In that way you may be *absolutely certain* that I will respect my duty as a doctor under all *circumstances*. As a friend of your daughter, on the other hand, one would have to leave matters to Fate. For no one can prevent two friends from doing as they wish. . . . My fee is 10 francs per consultation." In Bruno Bettelheim, *Freud's Vienna and Other Essays* (New York: Alfred A. Knopf, 1990), 71.

19. *Freud-Jung Letters*, 90.

20. For Jung's Russian stereotypes, see James L. Rice, "Russian Stereotypes in the Freud-Jung Correspondence," *Slavic Review* 41 (1983): 19–34.

21. Alexander Etkind, *Eros of the Impossible: The History of Psychoanalysis in Russia*, translated by Noah and Maria Rubins (Boulder: Westview Press, 1997), 33.

22. Ibid., 34.

23. Ibid., 32.

24. John Kerr, *A Most Dangerous Method: The Story of Jung, Freud, & Sabina Spielrein* (New York: Vintage Books, 1993), 416.

25. Etkind, *Eros of the Impossible*, 158.

26. Ibid.

27. Quoted in Martine Gallard, "Jung's Attitude During the Second World War in the Light of the Historical and Professional Context," *Journal of Analytical Psychology* 39 (1994): 211.

28. Slavoj Žižek, *For They Know Not What They Do: Enjoyment as a Political Factor* (New York: Verso, 1996), 55n.

29. Ibid., 9.

30. Rastko Močnik, "The Balkans as an Element in Ideological Mechanisms," in *Balkan as Metaphor: Between Globalization and Fragmentation*, edited by Dušan I. Bjelić and Obrad Savić (Cambridge, Mass.: MIT Press, 2002), 95.

31. Slavoj Žižek, *The Metastases of Enjoyment: Six Essays on Woman and Causality* (New York: Verso, 1994), 205.

32. Ibid., 121.

33. Ibid.

34. Even if one agrees with Žižek that sexual perversion is a universal, inbuilt psychological structure linked to the Name-of-the-Father and, as such, is essential to the well-being of a nation, the fact remains that mass rapes were instrumental in carrying out the policy of "ethnic cleansing" in the ex-Yugoslavia. As Julie Mostov demonstrates, the perception of a woman's body as an extension of nation and national space served to rationalize mass rape as conquest of *de facto* enemy territory. (Julie Mostov, " 'Our Women'/'Their Women': Symbolic Boundaries, Territorial Markers, and Violence in the Balkans," in *Peace a Chance* 20, no. 4 (October 1995): 515–29.)

35. Žižek, *Metastases*, 75.

36. Mladen Dolar, "Freud in Yugoslavia" (unpublished manuscript).

37. Žižek was not alone in finding perversion in the Bosnian unconscious. Serbian academic Nada Todorova characterizes the Bosnian Muslims' unconscious as perverse because they read *1001 Arabian Nights*: "It is certain that they (Muslims) read them carefully during puberty; their effect on their personality is clearly evident. In committing atrocities (rapes) in Bosnia-Herzegovina, (their) conscious, sub-conscious, and unconscious levels or

personality have been at work." (Quoted in Norman Cigar, *Genocide in Bosnia. The Policy of "Ethnic Cleansing"* [College Station: Texas A&M University Press, 1995), 70.

38. Julia Kristeva, *Intimate Revolt: The Powers and Limits of Psychoanalysis*, translated by Jeanine Herman (New York: Columbia University Press, 2002), 245.

39. Ibid., 177.

40. Julia Kristeva, *Nations Without Nationalism*, translated by Leon S. Roudiez (New York: Columbia University Press, 1993), 54.

41. Julia Kristeva, *Revolt She Said*, translated by Brian O'Keeffe (Los Angeles: Semiotext(e), 2002), 106.

42. Ibid.

43. Ibid., 46.

44. Tzvetan Todorov, *Morals of History*, translated by Alyson Waters (Minneapolis: University of Minnesota Press, 1995).

45. There is an excellent example of this self-orientalizing mechanism in Michael Ignatieff's book *The Warrior's Honor*. Ignatieff recounts his interview with a Serb soldier who has been fighting his Croat neighbors for two years. The conversation takes place in eastern Croatia in the village of Mirkovci ("place of peace"). Attempting to engage the soldier in a multicultural debate, Ignatieff asks him how he is different from a Croat. To the author's evident satisfaction, the answer corroborates Freud's theory of the "narcissism of small differences," and Ignatieff's own view that this is, in fact, the moving force behind the Balkan fratricide. The soldier lists many irreconcilable differences between Serbs and Croats and accuses foreigners of not understanding why they are so different, even though they look alike. Then, obviously becoming irritated by the inquiry and wanting to end it, he suddenly reverses his position, saying, "Look, here's how it is. Those Croats, they think they're better than us. They want to be gentlemen. They think they're fancy Europeans. I'll tell you something. We're all just Balkan shit." When pressed to declare who he is by the Western journalist educated in psychoanalysis, the Serb soldier spontaneously assumes the position of abject and self-identifies with the Balkans' anal character. Michael Ignatieff, *The Warrior's Honor: Ethnic War and the Modern Conscience* (New York: Henry Holt and Company, 1998), 36.

46. Jovan Rašković, *Luda Zemlja (Mad Country)* (Belgrade: Akvarijus, 1990). *Luda Zemlja* less analytical and clinical than his previous publications, opens with details of the author's life growing up as a Serb in Krajina, a region in Croatia populated by the Serbs since the sixteenth century, with the Croatian genocide and postwar communism. The book closes with his psychoanalytic observation of the political scene in the post-Titoist Yugoslavia, and

with an appendix consisting of transcriptions of interviews, conversations, and news coverage of his activities as a Serb political leader. We learn that as a young psychiatrist in the Croatian port city, Sibenik, he had encountered in clinical practice many instances of devastating psychic trauma to his Serb patients caused by the Croatian genocide in World War II and postwar communism. This experience has aroused his concern for the well-being of his ethnic group and has pushed him into the political arena at the end of the eighties and the beginning of the nineties on behalf oh his Serb minority. Dobrica Ćosić, the spiritual father of Serb nationalism and at one point a president of the remaining part of Yugoslavia during the regime of Slobodan Milosevic, has in the foreword to *Luda Zemlja* described the author as an anti-political politician, a man not interested in politics but who, as a Freudian, relates to Serbs on the ontological level, speaking directly to their unconscious and which unconscious has drawn him into the politics. According to Ćosić and his own account, Rašković's conversion to politics seems to be the result of what Frantz Fanon has characterized as an "unconscious effect" upon those not interested in politics which causes them to get involved during troubled times. Rašković's *Luda Zemlja* has never been published in any language other than Serbian and thus has remained relatively unknown outside of the ex-Yugoslavia.

47. Rašković, *Luda Zemlja*, 128.

48. Ibid., 204.

49. Ibid., 30–31.

50. Ibid. 127–29.

51. Ibid. 132–33.

52. Ibid. 72.

53. Ibid., 85–86.

54. Ibid., 124.

55. A paradoxical aspect of Rašković's work is that, despite his use of orthodox clinical practices such as electro-shock, he also belonged, in the 1970s, to a small circle of Yugoslav psychiatrists who studied, lectured, and published on antipsychiatry. The notion of psychiatry as an institution of oppressive power, and madness as a product of institutional psychiatry which acts on behalf of oppressive social authority, that true madness is a special or even blessed state of self-inquiry——all of these antipsychiatric postulates were known to him, and, in a perverse way, informed his political action. His quest, he has claimed, was to liberate the authentic, healthy, and true Serb madness from oppression by rationalism. Regarding clinical madness as a product of institutional psychiatry, his project was to take "madness" out of the psychiatric ward and into the streets to face its social cause and find its "authentic" form.

56. Sabina Spielrein, "Destruction as the Cause of Coming Into Being," *Journal of Analytical Psychology* 39 (1994): 155–86.

57. Sigmund Freud, *Collected Papers*, 18:65.

58. See Etkind, *Eros of the Impossible*, 110. One may challenge this ethnic connection to death by saying that before the Russians became aware of it as their "unique" ethnic feature, the Vienna of the second half of the nineteenth century was obsessed with sex and destruction (Bruno Bettelheim, *Freud's Vienna* [New York: Knopf, 1990], 10–11). Spielrein's will in which she offers her body to the local school, bears out Rice's argument: "After my death I will permit only my head to be dissected, if it is not too dreadful to look at. No young person is to be present at the dissection. Only the very keenest student may observe. I bequeath my skull to our school. It is to be placed in a glass container, decorated with everlasting flowers. The following is to be inscribed on the container in Russian: And let young life play at the entrance of the tomb and let indifferent nature shine with eternal splendour. My brain I give to you. Just place it, as it is, in a beautiful vessel, also decorated, and write the same words on it. My body is to be cremated. But no one is to be present for this. Divide the ashes into three parts. Place one part in an urn and send it home. Scatter the second part on the ground over biggest field. Plant there an oak tree and write on it: 'I too was once a human being. My name was Sabina Spielrein.' My brother will tell you what is to be done with the third part." (Victor Ovcharenko, "Love, Psychoanalysis and Destruction," *Journal of Analytical Psychology* 44, no. 3 (July 1999): 3.)

59. Bruno Bettelheim, *A Secret Symmetry* (New York: Knopf, 1988), xxxviii.

60. Kerr, *A Most Dangerous Method*, 313.

61. Judith Butler, *Bodies That Matter: On the Discursive Limits of "Sex"* (New York: Routledge, 1993), 79.

62. Quoted in Forestier, "Genocide!" 11.

63. Quoted in Jay Surdukowski, "Is Poetry a War Crime? Reckoning for Radovan Karadžić the Poet-Warrior," *Michigan Journal of International Law* 26, no. 673 (Winter 2005): 673.

64. Radovan Karadžić, "Da li je ovo bio rat?" ("Was this a war?") in Ljiljana Bulatović, *Zavet Majke Radovana Karadžića* (The Covenant of Radovan Karadžić's Mother) (Belgrade: Neofarmis & IKP Nikola Pašić, 2005), 119–21. It is illuminating to compare Karadžić's eroticization of death with Žižek's construction of a psychology of the "radical intellectual" out of Hegel's philosophy of the negative. This "radical intellectual" should not be immersed in a life of multicultural tolerance, but, fully committed to negation, should become as intimate with death as the Zen master who begins the day as if already dead or the Japanese soldier who performs his own funeral rites before leaving for the front. Žižek insists, "Instead of dismissing this feature as part

of fascist militarism, one should assert it as also constitutive of a radical revolutionary position." *In Defense of Lost Causes* (London: Verso, 2008), 170.

65. Branka Arsić, "On the Dark Side of Twilight," *Social Identities* 7, no. 4 (2002): 551–71.

66. Ibid., 565–66.

67. Laurence A. Rickels, *Nazi Psychoanalysis* (Minneapolis: University of Minnesota Press, 2002), 1:28.

68. Radman Šelmić, "Infrastructure Against Nationalism: The Case of Dr. Dabić," unpublished manuscript presented at the Association for the Study of Nationalities annual meeting, Columbia University, April 2009.

69. Slavoj Žižek, *The Abyss of Freedom* (Ann Arbor: University of Michigan Press, 2004), 9.

70. Sherry Turkle, *Psychoanalytic Politics: Freud's French Revolution* (New York: Basic Books, 1978), 238.

71. Slavoj Žižek, *Interrogating the Real* (London: Continuum, 2006), 241.

72. Slavoj Žižek, "The Military-Poetic Complex," *London Review of Books*, 14 August 2008, 17.

73. Slavoj Žižek, *The Sublime Object of Ideology* (London: Verso, 1997), 82.

74. Cited in Geoffrey Cocks, *Psychotherapy in the Third Reich: The Göring Institute* (New York: Oxford University Press, 1985), 51.

EVERYTHING YOU ALWAYS WANTED TO KNOW ABOUT DAVID LYNCH,
BUT SHOULD BE AFRAID TO ASK SLAVOJ ŽIŽEK
Kriss Ravetto-Biagioli

1. William David Hart, "Can a Judgment Be Read? A Response to Slavoj Žižek," *Neplanta* 4, no. 4 (1992): 192.

2. Slavoj Žižek, *The Metastases of Enjoyment: Six Essays on Woman and Causality* (New York: Verso, 1994), 175. He writes, "I resort to these examples above all in order to avoid pseudo-Lacanian jargon, and to achieve the greatest possible clarity not only for my readers but also for myself—the idiot from whom I endeavour to formulate a theoretical point as clearly as possible is ultimately myself." Yet, this gesture is also placed in the tradition of Lacan, who as Žižek writes "is the idiot" who writes against his own previous writings, who overcomes himself. (This is also repeated in his book *Organs Without Bodies* [New York, Routledge, 2004], 49). But rather than suggest that he (Žižek) is going to risk interpreting texts, Žižek splits himself as both idiot and a reader of "Lacan contre Lacan" (the Kantian Judge) as suggested by Jacques-Alain Miller in his seminar by the same name. Oddly, Žižek claims to be both the idiot who works through desire and the analyst who is external to that desire.

3. Ibid.

4. Gilles Deleuze and Felix Guattari, *What Is Philosophy?* (New York: Columbia University Press, 1994), 61–63.

5. On a more personal level the spectre of Lacan is linked to the Master-signifier, the master Imposter, the idiotic Master, the monstrous Imposter, etc. In a footnote to *Enjoy Your Symptom* (New York: Routledge, 1992), Žižek likens the Lacanian analyst to "Hannibal Lecter, the sadist/mastermind psychiatrist from Thomas Harris's serial-killer novels (*The Red Dragon, Silence of the Lambs*)," when he writes that this "is the closest mass culture can get to the figure of the Lacanian analyst." However, later in the text (45–47), Žižek likens, through the analogy of suicidal acts, Lacan's act of dissolution of the Ecole Freudienne de Paris in 1979 to Tito's rejection of Stalin in 1948—marking what Žižek has called the start of the fall of communism—to de Gaulle's "no" to Pétain and to French capitulation in 1940, and finally to Antigone's "no" to Creon, and "to state power." All of which he reads as feminine acts, as opposed to the masculine act (Lacan's) of founding the *Ecole de la Cause*. Hence, Lacan transforms from monster back to heroine, and then hero.

6. In *Metastases of Enjoyment* (173) Žižek proposes to "read Lacan contre Lacan," which is the title, as he points out, of the 1993–94 Jacques-Alain Miller seminar, suggesting that Žižek is closer to Miller's readings or writings for Lacan than others. Yet, his approach (relation) to Lacan is itself by no means consistent: while in his early texts like, *The Sublime Object of Desire* and *Looking Awry*, Žižek often quotes Lacan, his later work sometimes uses quotations without any reference or paraphrases Lacan. But, even in *Looking Awry* he admits that sometimes he misquotes Lacan to serve his own purposes, as, for example, when he writes: "the quotation is, of course, slightly changed to suit our purposes" (175 n. 9). Here it is not clear with whom he is speaking. That is, whom does he want to make complicit in his misquotation of the text?

7. In *Looking Awry* (136) Žižek explains the relation of reality to "irreality." First, he argues: "existence in the sense of a 'judgment of existence,' by which we symbolically affirm the existence of an entity; existence is here synonymous with symbolization, integration into the symbolic order—only what is symbolized fully 'exists.' Lacan uses existence in this sense when maintaining that 'Woman does not exist' or that 'there is no sexual relation.' Neither woman nor the sexual relationship possess a signifier of their own, neither can be inscribed into the signifying network, they resist symbolization." Second, he writes: "existence in the opposite sense, as ex-sistence, as the impossible-real kernel resisting symbolization. . . . It is this ex-sistence of the real, of the Thing embodying impossible enjoyment, that is excluded by the very advent of the symbolic order."

8. Žižek, *Organs Without Bodies*, 151–52.

9. Žižek, *Metastases of Enjoyment*, 122.

10. Žižek, *Tarrying With the Negative*, 187.

11. Žižek, *Metastases of Enjoyment*, 122.

12. Jacques-Alain Miller, "Des semblants dans la relation entre les sexes," *La Cause Freudienne* 36 (1997): 7–15, quoted in Slavoj Žižek's *The Art of the Ridiculous Sublime: On David Lynch's Lost Highway* (Seattle: University of Washington Press, 2000), 8.

13. Žižek, *The Art of the Ridiculous Sublime*, 9.

14. *The Art of the Ridiculous Sublime*, p. 6.

15. Ibid., 15.

16. Žižek has admittedly borrowed the reading of Frank Booth as a paternal figure from Michel Chion's *David Lynch* (London: BFI, 1995), 95–97.

17. Žižek, *The Art of the Ridiculous Sublime*, 18–19.

18. Ibid., 35.

19. Ibid., 15.

20. Ibid., 16.

21. Ibid., 17–18.

22. Žižek, *Metastases of Enjoyment*, 119.

23. Michel Foucault, *Language, Counter-Memory, Practice*, trans. Donald F. Bouchard and Sherry Simon (Ithaca, N.Y.: Cornell University Press, 1987), 155.

24. Slavoj Žižek, *Invisible Remainder* (London: Verso, 1996), 95.

25. See Žižek, *The Metastasis of Enjoyment*, 90–95, and Chion's *David Lynch*, 95–96, where they talk about Dorothy as "collapsing, slipping into the void of a terminal depression." Chion also treats Frank as a father figure to Jeffrey, not just in the "Oedipal scene" where Jeffery watches as Frank rapes Dorothy, but also, as Chion argues, Frank loves Jeffrey, providing him some parental stability, so that Jeffrey can then kill him off and make his own Oedipal dynamic.

26. Žižek *Metastases of Enjoyment*, 122.

27. Ibid., 114–15.

28. Ibid., 119.

29. Ibid., 121.

30. Jacques Lacan, *Ecrits*, trans. Alan Sheridan (New York: Norton, 1997), 321.

31. Žižek, *Metastases of Enjoyment*, 78. See also his *The Plague of Fantasies* (London: Verso, 1997), where he argues: "When attention is draw to the fact that women often *do* fantasize about being handled brutally and raped, the standard answer is either that this is a male fantasy about women or that women do it in so far as they have 'internalized' the patriarchal libidinal economy and endorsed their victimization—the underlying idea being that the

moment we recognize this fact of daydreaming about rape, we open the door to male-chauvinist platitudes about how, in being raped, women only get what they secretly wanted: their shock and fear only express the fact that they were not honest enough to acknowledge this. To this commonplace, one should answer that (some) women may actually daydream about being raped, but this fact not only in no way legitimizes actual rape—it makes it even more violent" (188). Oddly, he offers no reading of why these fantasies occur, especially since in other places he argues that women merely mimic male fantasies, nor does he present them as symptom of some larger problem. If indeed these fantasies are part of some larger problem — the internalization of the patriarchal libidinal economy—then it would suggest that Žižek would consider that depression is not primal but and effect of such an economy.

32. Žižek, *Plague of Fantasies*, 185–86.

33. Ibid., 186.

FICTIONS OF POSSESSION: PSYCHOANALYSIS AND THE OCCULT
Lecia Rosenthal

1. For Jones's resistance to Freud's "conversion," see Ernest Jones, *Sigmund Freud: The Life and Work* (London: Hogarth Press, 1953–57), 3:422. Strachey's comments are from the "Editor's Note" to the *New Introductory Lectures, The Standard Edition of the Complete Psychological Works of Sigmund Freud*, trans. James Strachey (London: Vintage Books, 2001), 22:4. Hereafter, *SE*.

2. Several recent studies have brought renewed attention to Freud's writings on the occult, and indeed to the occlusions of those writings within the history of psychoanalysis. See in particular Nicholas Royle, *Telepathy and Literature: Essays on The Reading Mind* (Oxford: Basil Blackwell, 1990); John Forrester, "Psychoanalysis: Gossip, Telepathy and/or Science?" in *The Seductions of Psychoanalysis: Freud, Lacan and Derrida* (Cambridge: Cambridge University Press, 1992); Pamela Thurschwell, *Literature, Technology and Magical Thinking 1880–1920* (Cambridge: Cambridge University Press, 2001); Roger Luckhurst, *The Invention of Telepathy 1870–1901* (Oxford: Oxford University Press, 2002). Each of these has contributed to my thinking about the status and proliferation of the occult within Freud's writings. As I hope to show, there is more that remains to be read in Freud's inscription of the occult as a figure for psychoanalysis and its particular mode of (dis)belief. Taking up what Thurschwell calls the "occult's incompletely excavated place in the history of psychoanalysis" (151), I want to read the occlusion of the occult, or the ways in which the (unsuccessful) burial of the occult haunts Freud's theorizations of the psychoanalytic unconscious as well as of psychoanalysis "itself"—a psychoanalysis that would stand apart from the occult claims it diagnoses, surpasses, puts to rest.

3. For the "explosive" element of such a connection, see Freud's warning to Ferenczi (1925) against advertising his own "experiments" in telepathic communication, in which he analogizes the effects of any such discussion as "throwing a bomb into the psychoanalytical house which would be certain to explode" (Jones, 393–94).

4. Freud, "Psycho-analysis and Telepathy," *SE* 18:178.

5. As is well known, "Dreams and Telepathy," though written as a lecture, was never delivered as such. For the publication history of the essay, including the note in the original manuscript indicating that it was a "lecture given before the Vienna Psycho-Analytical Society," see Strachey's introduction, *SE* 18:196. On the phrase "fake lectures," see Derrida, "Telepathy," trans. Nicholas Royle, *Oxford Literary Review* 10 (1988): 18.

6. Freud, "Dreams and Telepathy," 197.

7. Avital Ronell, *The Telephone Book: Technology, Schizophrenia, Electric Speech* (Lincoln: University of Nebraska Press, 1989), 387. For Freud's figuration of both telepathy and the tele-work of psychoanalysis in terms of the telephone, see, respectively, "Dreams and Occultism," 55, and "Recommendations on Technique," *SE* 12:115–16.

8. Freud, "Dreams and Telepathy," 220.

9. Derrida, "Telepathy," 21.

10. Freud comments on the "private" nature of his "prejudice toward telepathy" in a letter to Jones (Jones, *Sigmund Freud*, 395). Of course, the very notion of the "private" is threatened by the possibility of telepathy, a power that would endanger the promise of keeping thoughts to, for and even from oneself.

11. It is this possibility, or more precisely this possibility in its seeming unthinkability, that Derrida's "Telepathy" takes on, playing with the rhetoric of receiving, overhearing, corresponding with Freud. In a similar vein, Nicholas Royle has addressed the relationships between telepathy and literature, linking the two through their mutual rhetoric of access to a "character's" thoughts. See Royle, *Telepathy and Literature*, as well as "The 'Telepathy Effect': Notes toward a Reconsideration of Narrative Fiction," in *Acts of Narrative*, ed. Carol Jacobs and Henry Sussman (Stanford: Stanford University Press, 2003), 93–109.

12. Jones, *Sigmund Freud*, 375, 376. For an historical treatment of the complex relationship between the modern and the occult, see Gauri Viswanathan, "The Ordinary Business of Occultism," *Critical Inquiry* 27 (Autumn 2000): 1–20. Reading the occult "revival" within the colonial context, Viswanathan argues that the colonial appropriation and routinization of occult practices in late-nineteenth- and early-twentieth-century India served both to bolster and challenge the hegemony of colonial power and the security of "secularism" as an achieved threshold.

13. Jones, *Sigmund Freud*, 377–79.

14. Strachey, "Editor's Note," 4.

15. For a definition of occultism that emphasizes initiation as its most salient feature, see Leon Surette, *The Birth of Modernism: Ezra Pound, T.S. Eliot, W.B. Yeats and the Occult* (Montreal: McGill–Queen's University Press, 1993), 13.

16. It is just such a structure of discrete processing that Maria Torok calls attention to in her reading of telepathy as "the name Freud unwittingly gave to a foreign body within the corpus of psychoanalysis, a foreign body that retains its own individuality, walls, partitions." Torok, "Afterword: What Is Occult in Occultism?" in *The Wolf Man's Magic Word: A Cryptonymy*, trans. Nicholas Rand (Minneapolis: University of Minnesota Press), 86. Thus telepathy, and along with it the occult, become a kind of "crypt" within psychoanalysis (and for Torok within Freud himself), or "a place *comprehended* within another but rigorously separate from it, isolated from general space by partitions, an enclosure, an enclave." Jacques Derrida, "Foreword: *Fors:* The Anglish Words of Nicolas Abraham and Maria Torok," trans. Barbara Johnson, ibid., xiv.

17. Within Freud's writings on the occult, the moments that most clearly resemble such a discrete structure of acknowledgment and dismissal are those that deal with telepathic dreams. Repeatedly, Freud takes up the possibility of telepathic dreams only to conclude that even were such a possibility to be proved, it would in no way "alter" the psychoanalytic approach to dreams; as far as the dream-work is concerned, a telepathic message would be merely one "stimulus," real or imagined, among others ("Dreams and Telepathy," 197, 207; for similar claims, see "The Occult Significance of Dreams," in "Some Additional Notes on Dream-Interpretation as a Whole," *SE* 19:136). Subordinating telepathy to the fundamental "laws" of psychoanalysis, Freud draws a speculative conclusion, one that demonstrates the in/significance of telepathy to Freud's theorization of the unconscious: "If the phenomenon of telepathy is only an activity of the unconscious mind, then, of course, no fresh problem lies before us. The laws of unconscious mental life may then be taken for granted as applying to telepathy" ("Dreams and Telepathy," 220).

18. Theodor Adorno, "Theses Against Occultism," *Minima Moralia*, trans. E. F. N. Jephcott (London: Verso, 1974), 238–43. For historical accounts of the ties between fascism and occultism, see Laurence A. Rickels, *Nazi Psychoanalysis*, 3 vols. (Minneapolis: University of Minnesota Press, 2002), as well as Surette, *The Birth of Modernism*, and James Webb, *The Occult Establishment* (La Salle, Ill.: Open Court, 1976).

19. Adorno, "Theses Against Occultism," 241, 240.

20. In the introduction to "Psycho-analysis and Telepathy," Freud historicizes the "trend" to return to occultism, finding in its resurgence as an

"expression of the loss of value by which everything has been affected since
the world catastrophe of the Great War . . . it is also an attempt at compensation, at making up in another, a supermundane, sphere for the attractions
which have been lost by life on this earth" (177). For an account of the resurgence of spiritualism in the context of the Great War, see Jay Winter, *Sites of
Memory, Sites of Mourning* (Cambridge: Cambridge University Press, 1995).

21. Freud, "Psychoanalysis and Telepathy," 178; "Dreams and
Occultism," *SE* 22:31.

22. "Psycho-analysis and Telepathy," 178. "Dreams and Occultism" uses
similar language towards an oblique definition of occultism, which, Freud
argues, "asserts that there are in fact 'more things in heaven and earth than
are dreamt of in our philosophy'" (31).

23. Freud, "Dreams and Occultism," 36.

24. Freud, "Psycho-analysis and Telepathy," 184; "Psychoanalyse und
Telepathie," *Gesammelte Werke* (London: Imago, 1941), 17:35.

25. Freud, "Dreams and Occultism," 39. In "The Occult Significance of
Dreams," Freud puts forth a similar emphasis on the transference of a "mental
process," defining telepathy as "the reception of a mental process by one
person to another by means other than sensory perception" (136).

26. Freud, "Transference," *SE* 16:444. For a discussion of Freud's attempts
to differentiate the "physical" and phylogenetically residual bases for thought-
transference from the "psychical" domain of transference, see Thurschwell,
"Freud, Ferenczi and psychoanalysis's telepathic transferences," in *Literature,
Technology and Magical Thinking*, 115–50. See also Luckhurst's reading of the
"telepathic aura around transferential relations" and his hypothesis that "the
central psychoanalytic concept of 'transference' would be inconceivable
without the prior theorization of telepathy" (*The Invention of Telepathy*, 275).
Yet if telepathy is the "prior" site of theorization, that priority is neither
historical—Freud discusses transference long before he figuratively lends his
ear to the always irrecoverable silent scene of the telepathic transfer—nor is it
conceptual, for to privilege telepathy as the meta-concept that binds together
all Freud's work on transference is to miss the ways in which Freud writes
telepathy as an event of vanishing, an imagined possibility that figuratively
enacts the limitations of any giving "voice" to the mind, not to say the unconscious, of the other.

27. Freud, "Analytic Therapy," *SE* 16:449.

28. Freud, "Dreams and Occultism," 55; "Traum und Okkultismus,"
Gesammelte Werke (London: Imago, 1940), 15:59. I include the German so as
to highlight a thread in which *Phantasie* variously takes on a positive or
negative value for Freud. For the central significance of *Phantasie* in Freud's
work, see Cornelius Castoriadis, *World in Fragments: Writings on Politics,*

Society, Psychoanalysis, and the Imagination, trans. David Ames Curtis (Stanford: Stanford University Press, 1997), 247–72.

29. In his discussion of telepathy's "critical potential," Marc Redfield theorizes the implications of telepathy in terms similar to those that I am trying to outline. "Telepathy," he argues, "communicates a fantasy of unmediated communication, and at the same time records, in its very name, an irreducible distance within self-presence." Redfield, "The Fictions of Telepathy," *Surfaces* 2, no. 27 (1992): 5.

30. As part of this capacity for resistance to dominant media and official institutions of knowledge, telepathy, and mediumship more broadly, is often gendered, invoking longstanding notions of "feminine" sensitivity and receptivity. For a discussion of the feminization of telepathy, see Luckhurst, "The Woman Sensitive," in *The Invention of Telepathy*, 214–51. For two recent literary instances in which telepathy is figured as enabling a critique of official, masculine-dominated institutions, see Doris Lessing, *The Four-Gated City* (New York: Knopf, 1969), and Angela Carter, "The Bloody Chamber," *The Bloody Chamber and Other Stories* (New York: Penguin, 1979).

31. Jacques Derrida, *Of Grammatology*, trans. Gayatri Chakravorty Spivak (Baltimore: Johns Hopkins University Press, 1974), 145.

32. Freud, "The Dynamics of Transference," *SE* 12:104.

33. For Freud's elaboration of this "fundamental rule," which involves a suspension of resistance on the part of both physician and patient, see "Recommendations on Technique," 115–16.

34. Freud, "Psycho-analysis and Telepathy," 184–85.

35. Ibid., 178, 180.

36. For Myers's definition, which is used by the *OED* in its definition, see Royle, *Telepathy and Literature*, 2; for an extensive discussion of Myers and the Society for Psychical Research, see Luckhurst.

37. Freud, "Dreams and Occultism," 34; "Traum und Okkultismus," 35.

38. Freud, "Dreams and Occultism," 36.

39. Freud, "The Occult Significance of Dreams," 136.

40. Freud, "Dreams and Telepathy," 217–18.

41. Ibid., 217.

42. Jacques Derrida, *Resistances of Psychoanalysis*, trans. Peggy Kamuf (Stanford: Stanford University Press, 1998), 19–20.

43. Freud, "Transference," 435.

RELIGION AND THE FUTURE OF PSYCHOANALYSIS
Jacob Taubes

1. Two recent explorations of this theme have helped to suggest the setting and context of the present essay: Benjamin Nelson, "The Future of Illusions,"

Psychoanalysis, II. 4 (Summer 1954), pp. 16–37, reprinted in slightly revised form in *Man in Contemporary Society*, ed. by the Contemporary Civilization Staff of Columbia College (New York: Columbia University Press, 1956), II, pp. 958–79; Herbert Marcuse, *Eros and Civilization* (Boston: Beacon Press, 1956).

2. [Ed.: Taubes published his essay "Religion and the Future of Psychoanalysis" in 1957. It appeared in a special issue of the journal *Psychoanalysis* devoted to the psychoanalysis of the future.]

3. *Moses and Monotheism* (New York: Alfred A. Knopf, 1939), p. 130.

4. *Civilization and Its Discontents* (London: Hogarth, 1930), p. 128.

5. Ibid., pp. 121–22.

6. *Moses and Monotheism*, p. 136.

7. Ibid., p. 137.

8. Ibid., p. 139.

9. Ibid., p. 214.

10. Nietzsche, *The Will to Power*, par. 1052.

11. See Karl Löwith, *Meaning in History* (Chicago: University of Chicago Press, 1949), in Epilogue.

THE CONTRIBUTION OF PSYCHOANALYSIS TO UNDERSTANDING
THE GENESIS OF SOCIETY
Cornelius Castoriadis

1. [Trans.: This lecture was delivered in Greek on February 23, 1993, at L'Institut Français of Thessaloniki, in the context of a series of seminars under the general title "From Psychoanalytic Theory to Psychiatric Practices" (February–June 1993). It was subsequently published in a collection of Castoriadis's Greek writings, *Anthropologia, Politiké, Philosophia* (Athens: Ypsilon, 1993), 33–58.]

2. [Trans.: In Cornelius Castoriadis, *World in Fragments: Writings on Politics, Society, Psychoanalysis, and the Imagination*, trans. David Ames Curtis (Stanford University Press, 1997), 137–71.]

THE HERMENEUTICS OF SUSPICION RECONSIDERED
Joel Whitebook

1. See Hubert Dreyfus, "Foreword to the California Edition," in *Michel Foucault: Mental Illness and Psychology*, trans. Alan Sheridan (Berkeley: University of California Press, 1972), xxviii.

2. See Paul Ricoeur, "Technique and Non-Technique in Interpretation," *The Conflict of Interpretations*," ed. Don Ihde (Evanston, Ill.: Northwestern University Press, 1974), 177–95.

3. Richard Rorty, "Habermas and Lyotard on Postmodernity," ed. Richard J. Bernstein (Cambridge, Mass.: MIT Press, 1985), 161.

4. See Jean-Francois Lyotard, *The Postmodern Condition: A Report on Knowledge*, trans. Geoffrey Bennington and Brian Massumi (Minneapolis: University of Minnesota Press, 1984), xxiv–xxv.

5. The demotion of science to one language game among many helped pave the way for the recent religious turn in postmodern philosophy. If science is on the same level as religion, there is no argument against embracing religion as the privileged discourse.

6. See Brian Leiter, "The Hermeneutics of Suspicion: Recovering Marx, Nietzsche, and Freud," University of Texas School of Law: Public Law and Legal Theory Working Paper No. 72, March 2005, 152.

7. See, for example, David Allison, ed., *The New Nietzsche: Contemporary Styles of Interpretation* (Cambridge, Mass.: MIT Press, 1985).

8. See Albrecht Wellmer, "The Dialectic of Modernism and Postmodernism: The Critique of Reason Since Adorno," in *The Persistence of Modernity: Essays on Aesthetics, Ethics and Postmodernism*, trans. David Midgley (Cambridge: Polity Press, 1991), 57–84.

9. Fenichel makes the following observation about the psychological origins of the urge for metaphysics. Needless to say, this observation has no bearing on the truth or falsity of any metaphysical theory: "The eternal longing for the limitless, the unbounded, the all-powerful . . . a longing for the absolute, for the primal beginning, whence we have arisen. . . . It was so once before (within the mind of the infant. But not in reality—only in the psyche which was not yet able to grasp reality. . . . The development of the mind began with the All. Metaphysical intuition wants to return to this starting point. . . . Metaphysics mistakes endopsychic ontogeny for real phylogeny." Otto Fenichel, "Psychoanalysis and Metaphysics," in *Collected Papers of Otto Fenichel: First Series*, (New York: Norton, 1953), 25.

10. See John McDowell, *Mind and World* (Cambridge, Mass.: Harvard University Press, 1996), 13.

11. Ibid., 11.

12. See W. V. Quine, "Two Dogmas of Empiricism," in *From a Logical Point of View*, (Cambridge, Mass.: Harvard University Press, 1961), 41.

13. Ibid., 18. Today, even a linguistic idealist and proponent of the consensus theory of truth like Habermas feels compelled to make a defense of scientific realism after the linguistic turn. See Jürgen Habermas, "Introduction: Realism After the Linguistic Turn," in *Truth and Justification*, trans. Barbara Fultner (Cambridge, Mass.: MIT Press, 2005), 1–49.

14. Theodor W. Adorno, *Negative Dialectics*, trans. E. B. Ashton (London: Routledge & Kegan Paul, 1973), 185.

15. Cornelius Castoriadis makes the following observation: "That a philosophy was able to affirm that it could furnish the conditions of possibility

for experience by looking uniquely at the subject—claiming, therefore, that what it says would and does have validity *in any world whatsoever*—is one of the most astonishing absurdities ever registered in the history of great thought. It is this absurdity that is at the foundation of *The Critique of Pure Reason*—which, in a paradox familiar within the history of philosophy, does not prevent the *Critique* from remaining an inexhaustible source for reflection." Castoriadis, "The Ontological Import of the History of Science," in *World in Fragments* (Stanford University Press 1997), 346.

16. Ibid., 181.

17. Ibid., 184.

18. See T. W. Adorno, *Kant's Critique of Pure Reason*, ed. Rolf Tiedemann, trans. Rodney Livingston (Stanford: Stanford University Press, 2001), chapter 18.

19. Ibid., 183 ff.

20. Ibid., 185.

21. Ibid.

22. Ibid., 181.

23. See Cornelius Castoriadis, "The Logic of Magmas and the Question of Autonomy" in *The Castoriadis Reader*, ed. David Ames Curtis (Oxford: Blackwell, 1997), 293.

24. Herbert Schnädelbach, "The Face in the Sand: Foucault and the Anthropological Slumber," in *Philosophical Interventions in the Unfinished Business of Enlightenment*, ed. Axel Honneth et al. (Cambridge, Mass.: MIT Press, 1992), 334. See also Joel Whitebook, "Against Interiority: Foucault's Struggle with Psychoanalysis," in *The Cambridge Companion to Foucault*, rev. ed. (New York: Cambridge University Press, 2005), 312–347.

25. Adorno, *Negative Dialectics*, 185.

26. Ibid., 185.

27. See Adorno, *Lectures on Kant's Critique of Pure Reason*, 167.

28. Ibid., 215.

29. Ibid., 214.

30. The assertion that a given philosophy—Kant's Copernican Revolution or Marx's materialism, for example—constitutes an unsurpassable theoretical horizon that cannot be violated has always struck me as philosophically naïve. To assert the unsurpassable condition of any position is to deny the historicity and openness of philosophy. However compelling—indeed, even necessary—a particular position may seem at a given moment, philosophy is a fallible enterprise, and we cannot predict what may happen in the future.

31. See Yirmiyahu Yovel, *Spinoza and Other Heretics* (Princeton: Princeton University Press, 1989), 2 vols., passim.

32. I would like to mention that an aspect of the concept of naturalism I wish to defend is related to the philosophical anthropology of Feuerbach and

the young Marx. It takes the sensuous—I might even say suffering—human being as its point of departure.

33. McDowell, *Mind and World*, and "Two Types of Naturalism."

34. See Michel Foucault, "Nietzsche, Genealogy, History," in *Language, Counter-Memory, Practice: Selected Essays and Interviews by Michel Foucault*, ed. Donald F. Bouchard, trans. Donald F. Bouchard and Sherry Simon (Ithaca, N.Y.: Cornell University Press, 1977), 139–64. For the argument that Foucault misrepresented Nietzsche, see Raymond Geuss, "Nietzsche and Genealogy," in *Morality, Culture and History: Essays in German Philosophy* (Cambridge: Cambridge University Press, 1999), 1–28.

35. Friedrich Nietzsche, *Daybreak* (1983).

36. See Geuss, "Nietzsche and Genealogy," and Bernard Williams, *Truth and Truthfulness* (Princeton: Princeton University Press, 2002), Chapter 2. Geuss uses the notion of "pedigree" to explicate the meaning of legitimizing critique. According to this notion, a person's or a thing's value in the present must be traced back through a number of intermediary states to an original person or thing that possesses intrinsic value. Moreover, this chain of transmission must be relatively unbroken and each intermediary state must itself possesses value. Guess cites the *Iliad* as an example. In Book II, the pedigree of Agamemnon's scepter, from whence he derives his authority, is traced back to the original authority of Hephaistos and Zeus. While the idea of pedigree does indeed provide an example of legitimizing genealogy, for our purposes, it suffers from one serious limitation. It is, by definition, conservative. A person or thing deserves to be valorized insofar as its genesis can be traced back to the value-bestowing acts of the ancestral past. What we need is a nonconservative form of legitimizing genealogy.

37. See Castoriadis, *The Imaginary Institution of Society* (Cambridge, Mass.: MIT Press 1987).

38. In his work on Leonardo, Freud argues, against the vulgar pathographers, that even if all biographical material of Leonardo's childhood were available to him, it would still be impossible to deduce the form that the artist's mature personality assumed. "We must recognize here," he writes, "a degree of freedom which cannot be resolved any further by psycho-analytic means." Sigmund Freud, "Leonardo Da Vinci and a Memory from His Childhood," *SE* 11:135.

39. See Adam Philips, *Darwin's Worms* (New York: Basic Books, 1999).

40. See Heinz Hartmann, *Ego Psychology and the Problem of Adaptation* (New York: International Universities Press, 1958).

41. See Jean Laplanche, *New Foundations for Psychoanalysis*, trans. David Macey (Cambridge: Basil Blackwell, 1989), 17–28.

42. Paul Ricoeur, "Image and Language in Psychoanalysis," in *Psychoanalysis and Language*, ed. Joseph H. Smith, M.D. (New Haven: Yale University Press, 1978), 293–324.

43. Jean Laplanche and J.-P. Pontalis, *The Language of Psychoanalysis*, trans. Donald-Nicholson-Smith (New York: Norton, 1974), 433. See also Castoriadis, *The Imaginary Institution of Society*, and Joel Whitebook, *Perversion and Utopia: A Study in Psychoanalysis and Critical Theory* (Cambridge, Mass.: MIT Press, 1995), Chapter 5.

44. McDowell, *Mind and World*, 84ff., and "Two Types of Naturalism," 181–82.

45. See Joel Whitebook, "Weighty Objects: On Adorno's Kant-Freud Critique," *The Cambridge Companion to Adorno* (New York: Cambridge University Press, 2004).

46. Freud, "Leonardo Da Vinci and a Memory from His Childhood," *SE* 11:63.

47. Ibid., 130.

48. See D. W. Winnicott, *Maturational Processes and the Facilitating Environment: Studies in the Theory of Emotional Development* (London: Karnac Books, 1996).

49. See G. W. F. Hegel, *The Philosophy of Right*, trans. T. M. Knox (Oxford: Clarendon Press, 1952), 110–25.

50. See, for example, Cornelius Castoriadis, "Reflections on Racism," in *World in Fragments: Writings on Politics, Society, Psychoanalysis and the Imagination*, ed. and trans. David Ames Curtis (Stanford: Stanford University Press, 1997), 30–31.

ON THE EPISTEMOLOGICAL STATUS OF PSYCHOANALYSIS
Aristides Baltas

1. Aristides Baltas, "Do Mathematics Constitute a Scientific Continent?" *Neusis* 3 (1995) (in Greek).

2. See Aristides Baltas, "On the Grammatical Aspects of Radical Scientific Discovery," *Philosophia Scientiae* 8, no. 1 (2004): 169–201.

3. Karl Popper, "Realism and Science," postscript to *The Logic of Scientific Discovery* (London: Routledge, 1992).

4. See Adolf Grünbaum, *The Foundations of Psychoanalysis* (Berkeley: University of California Press, 1984).

5. Larry Laudan, "The Demise of the Demarcation Problem," in *Physics, Philosophy and Psychoanalysis: Essays in Honor of Adolf Grünbaum*, ed. R. S. Cohen and L. Laudan (Dordrecht: Kluwer, 1992). I note that "demarcation" is the technical term referring in this context to the distinction between science and other endeavors that aspire to be scientific.

6. Clark N. Glymour, *Theory and Evidence* (Princeton: Princeton University Press, 1980)

7. Published in Thomas Kuhn, James Conant, and John Haugeland, eds., *The Road Since Structure: Philosophical Essays 1970–93* (Chicago: University of Chicago Press, 2000).

8. See Louis Althusser, "The Discovery of Dr. Freud," in *Writings on Psychoanalysis* (New York: Columbia University Press, 1999).

9. This is an issue I try to discuss in my essay "La confutabilità del materialismo storico e la strutura della pratica politica," *Nuova Civiltà delle Machine* 3, no. 4 (1986).

10. For example, Morris Klein has written a very interesting book on this issue with a very suggestive title: *Mathematics: The Loss of Certainty* (New York: Oxford University Press, 1980).

11. Aristides Baltas, "The Sokal Affair: Context and Conjuncture," *Synchrona Themata*, February 1997 (in Greek).

12. See Aristides Baltas and George Fourtounis, *Louis Althusser and the End of Classical Marxism* (Athens: O Politis, 1994), esp. 85–90 (in Greek).

DAVID ADAMS is associate professor of English at Ohio State University, where he teaches twentieth-century literature and culture on the Lima campus. He is the author of *Colonial Odysseys: Empire and Epic in the Modernist Novel* (Cornell University Press, 2003), and of various articles.

GIL ANIDJAR teaches in the Department of Middle East, South Asian, and African Studies and in the Department of Religion at Columbia University. He is the author of *Our Place in al-Andalus* (Stanford University Press, 2002), *The Jew, the Arab: A History of the Enemy* (Stanford University Press, 2003), and *Semites* (Stanford University Press, 2007).

BRANKA ARSIĆ is associate professor of English at the University at Albany. She is the author of *The Passive Eye: Gaze and Subjectivity in Berkeley (via Beckett)* (Stanford University Press, 2003), *Passive Contributions or 7½ Times Bartleby* (Stanford University Press, 2007), and *On Leaving: A Reading in Emerson* (Harvard University Press, 2010). She has also co-edited (with Cary Wolfe) a collection of essays on Emerson, entitled *The Other Emerson: New Approaches, Divergent Paths* (University of Minnesota Press, forthcoming 2010). She is currently working on a book on Henry David Thoreau called *Grief*, exploring Thoreau's theory of perpetual mourning without melancholy, and a volume on the feminine spirituality of the early Americas called *Of Stones and Loving*, which will discuss how a variety of thought experiences—from contemplation to possession—affects the identity of persons.

ARISTIDES BALTAS is professor of philosophy of science at the National Technical University of Athens. He has coedited, with Peter Machamer and Marcello Pera, *Scientific Controversies* (Oxford University Press, 2000) and, with Dionysios Anapolitanos and Stavroula Tsinorema, *Philosophy and the Many Faces of Science* (Rowman & Littlefield, 1998). In Greek, he has written numerous books on the thought of Althusser, Derrida, and Freud. His *Objects and Aspects of Self* was awarded the National Prize for Nonfiction for 2002. His new book (in English) is on Spinoza and Wittgenstein.

DUŠAN BJELIĆ is a professor in the Department of Criminology at the University of Southern Maine at Portland. He is coeditor, with Obrad Savić, of *Balkan as Metaphor: Between Globalization and Fragmentation* (MIT Press, 2002) and the author of *Galileo's Pendulum: Science, Sexuality, and the Body-Instrument Link* (SUNY Press, 2003). He is currently working on a manuscript provisionally titled *Freud on the Balkans: Psychoanalysis and Europe's Subaltern*.

CORNELIUS CASTORIADIS was born in Constantinople (1922) and died in Paris (1997). A philosopher, economist, psychoanalyst, and all-around political actor, he is arguably one of richest and most radical minds of postwar European thought. Along with Claude Lefort, he was the leading figure of *Socialisme ou Barbarie* (1949–66), one of the key sources of the radical imagination expressed in the events of May 1968. Subsequently, he worked as an analyst and taught a series of seminars at the Ecole des Hautes Etudes en Sciences Sociales on an enormous project he called *The Human Creation*. The projected publication of these seminars is well under way, the most recent one being *La cité et les lois* (Seuil, 2008). In English, his magnum opus *The Imaginary Institution of Society* was published in 1997, and more recently *Figures of the Thinkable* (Fordham University Press, 2007) and *A Society Adrift* (Fordham University Press, 2009).

STATHIS GOURGOURIS is professor of classics, English, and comparative literature and director of the Institute for Comparative Literature and Society at Columbia University. He is the author of *Dream Nation* (Stanford University Press, 1996) and *Does Literature Think?* (Stanford University Press, 2003) and is currently at work on two volumes of lessons in secular criticism.

ANDREW PARKER is professor of English at Amherst College, where he has taught since 1982. His recent work includes the translation of Jacques Rancière's *The Philosopher and His Poor* and an expanded version of *After Sex? Writing since Queer Theory* (edited with Janet Halley). A new book, *The Theorist's Mother*, is nearing completion.

KRISS RAVETTO-BIAGIOLI is senior lecturer in film studies at the University of Edinburgh. She is the author of *The Unmaking of Fascist Aesthetics* (University of Minnesota Press, 2001) and of numerous articles on film theory, Italian and Eastern European cinema, Pasolini, and performance and installation art.

LECIA ROSENTHAL is assistant professor of English at Tufts University. She is the author of *Mourning Modernism: Literature, Catastrophe, and the Politics of Consolation* (Fordham University Press, forthcoming), as well as numerous essays on literary theory and modernist literature.

JACOB TAUBES was born in Vienna in 1923 and died in Berlin in 1987. He was a distinguished thinker—a philosopher, a sociologist of religion, and a scholar of Judaism. Although he published little in his lifetime, his thought is now recognized to have been enormously influential. After 1965, he held the Chair of Hermeneutics at Frei Universität in Berlin. Before that, he taught for a time as Professor of Religion at Harvard and Columbia. His first work to be translated in English was *The Political Theology of Paul* (Stanford University Press, 2004), which has been followed by the publication of *Occidental Eschatology* (Stanford University Press, 2009) and a collection of essays *From Cult to Culture: Fragments Toward a Critique of Historical Reason* (Stanford University Press, 2009).

JOEL WHITEBOOK is a trained philosopher and a practicing psychoanalyst, as well as director of the Columbia University Psychoanalytic Studies Program. He is the author of *Perversion and Utopia* (MIT Press, 1995), as well as numerous articles on psychoanalysis, philosophy, and critical theory. He is currently writing an intellectual biography of Freud commissioned by Cambridge University Press.

INDEX

Boldface page numbers signify material written by the individual, as opposed to references to the individual's name.